ALSO BY RAY TAKEYH

The Receding Shadow of the Prophet:
The Rise and Fall of Radical Political Islam
(with Nikolas K. Gvosdev)

The Origins of the Eisenhower Doctrine:
The United States, Britain and Nasser's Egypt, 1953–1957

HIDDEN IRAN

HIDDEN IRAN

PARADOX AND POWER
IN THE ISLAMIC REPUBLIC

RAY TAKEYH

A COUNCIL ON FOREIGN RELATIONS BOOK

TIMES BOOKS
Henry Holt and Company   New York

Times Books
Henry Holt and Company, LLC
Publishers since 1866
175 Fifth Avenue
New York, New York 10010
www.henryholt.com

Henry Holt® is a registered trademark of
Henry Holt and Company, LLC.

Distributed in Canada by H. B. Fenn and Company Ltd.

Library of Congress Cataloging-in-Publication Data

Takeyh, Ray, date.
    Hidden Iran : paradox and power in the Islamic Republic / Ray Takeyh.
        p. cm.
    Includes bibliographical references and index.
    ISBN-13: 978-0-8050-7976-0
    ISBN-10: 0-8050-7976-9
    1. Iran—Politics and goverment—1979–1997.   2. Iran—Politics and government—1997–
3. Iran—Foreign relations—1979–1997.   4. Iran—Foreign relations—1997–   I. Title.
DS318.825.T355 2006
327.55—dc22   2006043981

Henry Holt books are available for special promotions and
premiums. For details contact: Director, Special Markets.

First Edition 2006

Designed by Kelly Too

Printed in the United States of America
1 3 5 7 9 10 8 6 4 2

To Alex:

With the hope that he will read this book one day, and be proud.

CONTENTS

HIDDEN IRAN

INTRODUCTION:
GETTING IRAN WRONG

In his State of the Union address on January 31, 2006, President George W. Bush turned his attention to Iran, describing it as a "nation now held hostage by a small clerical elite that is isolating and repressing its people." The president went on to stress that the "Iranian government is defying the world with its nuclear ambitions, and the nations of the world must not permit the Iranian regime to gain nuclear weapons."[1] The reaction from Tehran was predictably swift and uncompromising; President Mahmoud Ahmadinejad denounced Bush as the one "whose arms are smeared up to the elbow in the blood of other nations" and pledged that "God willing, we shall drag you to trial in the near future at the courts set up by nations."[2] For a quarter-century, such undiplomatic discourse has defined U.S.–Iranian relations, but this particular exchange of epithets hints at the real root of the estrangement—a profound and frequently mutual misunderstanding of the enemy. Indeed, getting Iran wrong is the single thread that has linked American administrations of all political persuasion. From the original 1979 revolution that launched the Islamic Republic to the more recent confrontation over Iran's nuclear intentions, the United States has persistently misjudged Iran's clerical oligarchs.

Contrary to President Bush's assertions, and his previous depiction of Iran as a member of an "axis of evil," an unsavory state on a par with the totalitarian regimes of Saddam Hussein in Iraq and Kim Jong Il in North Korea, Iran differs dramatically from its Arab neighbors, much less the hermetic North Korean regime. Iran's institutions, elections, and political factions matter and wield considerable impact over the government's course of action. Debates rage within the parliament and the presidential office, in the seminaries and on the street, among the media and in the halls of academia. Far from being a stagnant author-itarian state, Iran's elaborate and Orwellian bureaucracy, its fiercely competitive political culture, and its singular personalities perennially jockey for influence and power. It is the interplay of all these institu-tions and actors that ultimately determines Iran's policies.

After more than a quarter-century in power, the Islamic Republic is at a crossroads as a new generation of stern conservatives has assumed power with a determination to return to the "roots of the revolution." However, the conflict gripping Iran stems not from a straightforward resurgence of reactionary politics, but from a contradiction deeply embedded in its governing structure. From its inception, the Islamic Republic was a state divided between competing centers of power and profoundly differing conceptions of political authority. The origi-nal constitution pledged that the foremost purpose of the state was to "create conditions under which may be nurtured the noble and univer-sal values of Islam."[3] To achieve this mission, unelected institutions, such as the Supreme Leader and the Guardian Council, were created and empowered with the ultimate authority over national affairs. Yet the structure of the Islamic Republic differed significantly from that of a typical totalitarian state since it sanctioned the populace to elect the president, parliament, and municipal councils. Such perplexing duality reflects the legacy of a revolution that saw a diverse coalition of secularists, liberals, and fundamentalists uneasily cooperating in the overthrow of the monarchy. Since then, disagreements and tensions have persisted between those seeking to establish a divine order and those advocating a more representative polity. Despite its absolutist pretensions, the clerical estate has never managed to exercise undisputed dominance over public affairs. Throughout its tenure, popular will, however circumscribed by theological fiat, remained an important arbiter of the Iranian state's legitimacy and thus its very survival.

Iran today is a nation in search of an identity, a state that oscillates between promises of democratic modernity and retrogressive tradition. Despite all the sensational setbacks of Muhammad Khatami's reform movement, the one enduring legacy of its electoral triumphs in 1997 and 2001 has been to make it impossible for Iran to become a rigid authoritarian state. The call for representation and the rule of law, for accountability and equality, have transformed the average Iranian from a passive observer of clerical politics into an active agent of change. The resilience of the forces of progress stems from their diversity. Clerical reformers, disillusioned youth, a burdened middle class, women seeking emancipation, and intellectuals yearning for freedom of thought have come together in their demand for a government responsive to its citizenry. Despite the apparent consolidation of conservative power and the election to the presidency in 2005 of an unreconstructed ideologue, Iran will change. In the long run, Iran's sophisticated and youthful populace can be neither appeased by cosmetic concessions nor silenced by threats of coercion.

However, Iran's democratic transition must come on its own terms, and at its own pace. An American president castigating Iran as part of an "axis of evil," or denigrating its political process by proclaiming its elections a fraud even before they take place, only provides ammunition to hard-liners decrying Iran's democrats as unwitting agents of Western machinations. Contrary to Washington's depictions, the struggle in Iran is not a simple conflict between the people and the mullahs. Iran's factional politics, ideological divisions, and political rivalries are much more complex and nuanced. The dissident clerics within the seminaries, the young functionaries waging a turf war in the government, the student organizations defying the authorities, and the women who persistently challenge the prevailing religious strictures are all part of the same movement seeking to liberalize the parameters of the state. The stark distinction between the people and the regime quickly fades when one considers how decentralized and flexible Iran's Islamic order has become in the intervening three decades. Before stepping into the convoluted fray of Iranian politics, Washington would be wise to have a better appreciation of Iran's complexities and contradictions.

In a similar manner, America's continued denunciation of Iran as a militant state determined to subvert its neighbors and impose its Islamic template on an unwilling Middle East is exaggerated and flawed. The best way to understand Iran's foreign policy is to imagine a matrix with three competing elements—Islamic ideology, national interests, and factional politics—all constantly at battle. As such, Iran's policy has always been characterized by a degree of inconsistency and wild oscillation between pragmatism and dogma. It is this central paradox that has perplexed both critics and supporters of Iran's regime.

Throughout the tenure of the Islamic Republic, there have been occasions when ideology has displaced moderation, when national interests have been sacrificed at the altar of Islamist militancy. The 1980s represent the high point of revolutionary activism, as the war with Iraq and conflict with America defined the pillars of Iran's international relations. The first decade of the revolution was indeed a heady time, for the founder of the world's first modern theocracy, Ayatollah Ruhollah Khomeini, did not see himself as simply a head of state but the leader of the entire community of believers. This was to be a "revolution without borders," seeking to emancipate the Islamic *ummah* from the transgressions of American imperialism and Israeli Zionism. Khomeini's Iran thrashed about the Middle East looking for dragons to slay, seeking to undermine established authority in the name of Islamic authenticity. This was the stage of the revolution without the compromises and concessions that states normally adopt.

Khomeini's more subdued successors gradually came to appreciate that his divisive diplomacy had not only isolated Iran in the region but paved the way for a more robust American presence in their neighborhood. In the 1990s, a fundamental shift occurred in Iran's international orientation, enshrining national interest calculations as the defining factor in its approach to the world. By cultivating favorable relations with key global powers such as China and Russia, Tehran sought to craft its own "coalition of the willing," and to prevent the United States from enlisting allies in its coercive approach to Iran. Under the auspices of the Supreme Leader Ayatollah Ali Khamenei, a loose coalition of reformers and conservatives emerged around the notion that Iran cannot remain isolated from the global order.

Such realistic moderation is today experiencing its most sustained challenge, as disciples of Khomeini seem determined to assert revolutionary convictions as the basis of their rule. As the revolution matures and those politicians who were present at the creation of the Islamic Republic recede from the scene, a more austere, dogmatic generation is beginning to take the reins of power. In response to Iran's manifold problems, Ahmadinejad and his cabinet frequently criticize their elders' passivity in imposing Islamic ordinances and for the rampant corruption that has engulfed the state. On the foreign policy front, Iran's hard-line president has dispensed with Khatami's "dialogue of civilizations" rhetoric and displays not just a marked hostility to reestablishment of ties with America but also indifference to European opinion.

However, despite the emergence of the "New Right," it is hard to see how Ahmadinejad and his allies can turn the clock back to the early days of the revolution. The transformations that Iran has undergone during the intervening decades, the persistence of its factional politics, and the continued power of the elders of the revolution such as Ali Khamenei and Akbar Hashemi Rafsanjani impose serious checks on Ahmadinejad's enterprising designs. Iran's reactionary president may share Khomeini's strident ideological pretensions, but he has neither the authority nor the stature to impose such a vision on his country's competing centers of power. In the end, despite the injection of a new, strident voice in Iran's foreign policy deliberations, the same be-wildering mixture of realism and ideology, pragmatism and militancy is likely to continue to guide the Islamic Republic.

As with its internal politics, Iran's foreign policy offers it own set of paradoxes and contradictions. In essence, Iran has not undergone the typical experience of a revolutionary state—namely, relinquishing its radical patrimony for more mundane temptations. The perennial con-flict between ideological determinations and practical considerations continues to plague the Islamic Republic. On the one hand, Iran is no longer a radical state seeking to upend the regional order in the name of Islamic legitimacy. Yet Tehran's penchant toward terrorism, its ap-proach to the Arab-Israeli conflict, and its relations with America are still derived from a self-defeating calculus comprised in equal parts of domestic political considerations and ideological imperatives. As such, Iran today poses a particular problem for the United States that cannot be addressed by facile calls for regime change or simple name calling. In dealing with such a perplexing quandary, the United States would be wise to employ the full range of its diplomatic, economic, and political tools.

Thus at this point we must return to our original question: Why have so many gotten Iran so wrong? In a sense, such persistent failure is easy to understand, as Iran has often confounded our expectations. The notion of a theocracy coming to power in the late twentieth cen-tury contravened the conventional wisdom about progress, which presumed that modernizing societies necessarily discard their tradi-tions. Today, yet another consensus is emerging in American political circles, stressing that the fragile revolutionary regime may easily col-lapse if only America would exert greater pressure and sharpen its co-ercive policy. It is likely that the Islamic Republic's durability will once more defy the latest Washington truism. The American func-tionaries who failed to predict the original Iranian revolution are once more failing in their forecast of its demise.

As Iran's nuclear program crosses successive thresholds and as Tehran emerges as an influential power broker in Iraq, America may no longer have the luxury of misunderstanding the Islamic Republic, its motives, and its ambitions. From the proliferation of weapons of mass destruction to terrorism, from human rights to democratization, Iran cuts across a wide range of American concerns. And all of this is taking place at a time of the most intense U.S.–Iranian confrontation since the hostage crisis. The American leaders routinely characterize Iran as a grave threat while often musing about the eventual necessity of using military force to destroy its nuclear infrastructure. To properly contemplate the Iranian conundrum, it is important to demystify the clerical regime and have a better understanding of its factions and debates, its power struggles and rivalries. It is only through deciphering the hidden Iran that we can address the true challenge that the Islamic Republic poses.

1

KHOMEINI'S
LEGACY

In June 2005, Iran held a momentous presidential election whose results stunned both the international community and many within Iran itself. The hard-line mayor of Tehran, Mahmoud Ahmadinejad, defied expectations and captured 62 percent of the vote in a runoff against the powerful former president Akbar Hashemi Rafsanjani. In the first round of the election, while Rafsanjani and all the other presidential candidates were running glossy ads promising greater cultural liberalization, political reform, and mending ties with the United States, Ahmadinejad talked of returning to the "roots of the revolution," pledging economic justice and political conformity. His rhetoric and appearance harkened back to an earlier age, when Islamic revolutionaries still insisted on the relevance of their mission. The fact that in 2005 Iran produced a presidential candidate like Ahmadinejad and that he triumphed in a competitive election reflects a society whose essential political identity is still conditioned by the legacy of Ayatollah Ruhollah

Khomeini. As the Islamic Republic charts its course, Khomeini remains the central actor in Iran's melodrama.

The endurance of Khomeini's message twenty-seven years after the Islamic revolution and nearly two decades after his death defies the popular depiction of him as a stern mullah professing a retrogressive ideology. More than his revolutionary brethren, Khomeini was an innovator, borrowing ideas from secular philosophies, even dispensing with Shiite traditions when they appeared inconvenient. The Imam, as his followers would call him, forged his own path and articulated a distinct set of ideas that cleverly integrated Islamic principles, populist slogans, Persian nationalist themes, and leftist concepts into a seamless narrative. Far from being a fundamentalist mullah, Khomeini successfully married the diverse strands of Iran's opposition movement into a cohesive national force. All this is not to suggest that he did not wage his revolution for Islamic empowerment, but to recognize his intellectual suppleness and tactical dexterity. Khomeini was the ultimate crafter of "coalitions of the willing," with all participants, knowingly or not, advancing his agenda.

Thus, Khomeini is no passing figure and his revolutionary template is not about to be displaced by contrasting ideologies. Khomeini's revolution lives on, through institutions that he created and politicians such as Ahmadinejad, whom he has molded. The current Iranian president was in his early twenties when Khomeini returned from his exile, yet in his rhetoric and outlook he carefully emulates the founder of the republic. Nor is Ahmadinejad alone as Iran's leaders across the political spectrum feel the compulsion to sanction their priorities by appropriating Khomeini's words and insisting on the compatibility of their policies with his vision. Given his centrality to Iran, it is appropriate to begin with a discussion of Khomeini's philosophy and of how an aging cleric managed to weave his ideology into Iran's social fabric.

THE IMAM'S PATH

Ayatollah Ruhollah Khomeini was born in 1902, and during his lifetime he witnessed the totality of Iran's modern struggles, from the tumultuous world wars that led to the occupation of the Middle East by the great powers to the changing fortunes of the Pahlavi dynasty and its struggle to modernize Iran. Toward the end of his life, Khomeini reemerged as the leader of a populist revolution and an Islamic Republic that pledged to remake the entire region into its image. Beyond doubt, the forbidding Iranian cleric remains one of the most significant figures in the contemporary Middle East.

Khomeini's success stemmed not just from his steely determination in the face of remarkable odds but from his intuitive understanding of a country he would lead through revolution and war. More than any other Iranian leader, Khomeini would continuously tailor his message to conform to Iran's core values and grandiose self-perceptions. Successive Persian monarchs and empires perceived Iran as the epicenter of the region, a country that by the dint of its history and civilization was ordained to lead the Arab states. Khomeini's message of spreading the revolution and establishing the Islamic Republic's preeminence fits this pattern of Persian expansionism and proved appealing to a significant segment of the public. This is not to suggest that Iranians were eager to suffer the consequences of Khomeini's dogmatic pursuit of the revolution, but at a certain level his message resonated with his constituents' historic aspirations.

In a similar vein, Khomeini's call for a state that reflects Islamic values attracted Iranians from across the political spectrum. Khomeini sensed that in the midst of tumultuous changes, Iranians were still searching for authenticity and meaning despite the monarchical conceit that a modernizing Iranian society was rapidly discarding its traditions. Again, the attachment to religious identity is different from a desire for a theocratic state, but Khomeini was imaginative and effective in manipulating such sentiments behind his revolutionary message. Not only was he innovative in his ideas but he was also successful at building coalitions across a contested political terrain, and ambiguous when such subtlety was politically expedient. Khomeini had a plan, a vision he had spent decades contemplating and developing—a plan that would serve as the blueprint of Iran's populist revolt.

As early as the 1940s, Khomeini came to articulate a distinct ideology with its own symbols and values. A careful reading of his speeches and writings reveals that the central tenet of his ideology was the notion of justice—a powerful concept in both Persian nationalism and Islamic jurisprudence. Khomeini's dissent was not just against monarchical absolutism in Iran but also in opposition to tyranny across the Islamic realm, appealing to his countrymen and to all Muslims oppressed by forces of despotism and imperialism. Under the banner of Islamic liberation, Khomeini saw his revolution as an inclusive statement of dissent against a multiplicity of forces, actors, and conspiracies, both real and imagined. In many ways, the clerical champion of tradition came to embrace an entire range of Third World grievances and then proceeded to sanctify them through the power of religious approbation.[1]

The prevailing traditions among the clerics in the first half of the twentieth century was to disdain politics for the more exalted mission of spiritual training. Nonetheless, Khomeini always exhibited an activist strain, arguing that the clerical class was obligated—indeed, commanded by God—to protect the masses from oppressive rulers and the inequities of the temporal order. The Grand Ayatollahs may have been satisfied with retreating into their seminaries and preoccupying themselves with esoteric theological disputations, but for Khomeini the world outside the mosque always seemed more relevant, even attractive.[2]

In many ways Khomeini had the misfortune of existing in a clerical establishment that was dominated by the quietist Shiite political tradition. Under the leadership of Ayatollah Muhammad Hussein Borujerdi, who had emerged by the mid-1940s as the sole *marjá-e taqlid*, the highest religious post in Shiite Islam, the clerical elite devoted itself to strengthening the seminaries and developing the religious sciences.[3] An aspiring ayatollah was to preoccupy himself with his studies and forgo the temptations of politics. Indeed, the revolution's historical revisionism notwithstanding, the clerical estate traditionally maintained amicable relations with Persian monarchs and was often employed by them against their secular leftist nemeses.[4]

The young Khomeini, however, chafed under such restrictions and perceived these traditions as alienating the clergy from the masses.[5] His 1942 book, *Kashf-e Asrar,* was at once a call for limitations of the monarchy's powers and an implicit criticism of its clerical allies. In a speech in 1944, Khomeini bitterly complained, "It is our selfishness and abandonment of an uprising for God that have led to our present dark days and subjected us to world domination."[6] Khomeini pointedly deprecated the notion that religion and politics should remain separate, noting, "Islam has provided government for about 1,500 years. Islam has a political agenda and provides for the administration of a country."[7]

During this time Khomeini's evolving thought process was characterized by a penchant to defy the norms of the clerical community and embrace alternative ideas. At a time when the path to promotion within the Shiite clerical hierarchy mandated concentration on jurisprudence, Khomeini studied philosophy and toyed with mysticism and poetry.[8] The clerical power barons demonstrated an instinctive hostility toward the secular leftists, yet Khomeini was attracted to their ideas on the inequities of the international system and the rapacious nature of capitalist states. Throughout his career, Khomeini would draw on leftist, even Marxist, discourse, as he often spoke about the oppressive essence of the West.[9]

Far more than his clerical brethren, Khomeini proved to be a man of his time, and he sensed that the changing politics of Iran offered a unique opportunity to propagate his Islamic ideology. The 1950s and 1960s were heady times in the Middle East, with anticolonial movements and a new generation of leaders stepping forward to reclaim their societies and their traditions.[10] The clerical establishment's reluctance to join this struggle had led to its isolation from the emerging nationalist constituencies, particularly among the youth and the middle class. Khomeini anguished about the irrelevance of religion to this emerging struggle and called for reclaiming the young in the name of a progressive faith. "The irrational person has taken it for granted that religious people have trampled upon the rule of reason and have no regard for it. Is it not the religious people who have written all the books on philosophy and the principles of jurisprudence?" he pointedly asked.[11] For Islam to remain vital, he argued, it had to embrace a distinct political content and be part of the larger struggle sweeping the developing world.

In his social criticisms, Khomeini avoided the traditional clerics' acceptance of the existing economic arrangements and their instinctive embrace of private enterprise. He laced his pronouncements with the word *mostaz'afin,* the downtrodden, and insisted that the exploited classes were the victims of greedy capitalist forces. Khomeini denounced the Shah for wasting Iran's oil revenues, exacerbating the gap between the rich and the poor, failing to establish a viable industrial infrastructure, and massive corruption. (Ironically, decades later, these would be the same themes that Mahmoud Ahmadinejad would employ in his successful presidential campaign. The one difference was that the target of his accusations was not the Shah, but the clerical leaders who had seemingly abandoned Khomeini's values for the privileges of power.)

In this sense, Khomeini's rhetoric mirrored that of Ali Shariati, the famed intellectual who spent much of the 1960s seeking to infuse Islam with the Third-Worldist revolutionary spirit of thinkers such as Frantz Fanon and Jean-Paul Sartre. Shariati, a French-trained sociologist, was part of a new generation of Iranian intellectuals who were seeking a more authentic ideology consistent with their identity as both Muslims and modernists. Shariati saw the men of religion as a stagnant cohort preaching a fossilized retrogressive faith of submission to authority. This was hardly the Islam of the Prophet who had waged war, reconstructed his society, and revolutionized his epoch.[12] Khomeini noted the popularity and the acclaim that Shariati enjoyed among Iran's youth, as he emulated his rhetoric.

However, such flirtations with progressive concepts ought not to be confused with any inclination by Khomeini to accept a system of governance based on anything other then an unyielding interpretation of Islam. In his most influential book, *Hukumat-e Islami* (Islamic Government), Khomeini radically departed from prevailing Shiite traditions; his concept of *velayat-e faqih* (guardianship of the jurist) called for direct assumption of political power by the clergy. After all, he observed, the Prophet of Islam was not just a spiritual guide but an administrator, an executor of justice, and a political leader. "He cut off hands, chopped off limbs, stoned adulterers to death," Khomeini wrote approvingly.[13] Given the need to conform the social order to religious injunctions, the clergy must rule as they are most knowledgeable of divine law. Khomeini admonished those who stressed that the clergy should retreat to the mosque and leave politics to the professionals:

> Do not listen to those who are against the line of Islam and consider themselves enlightened persons and who oppose the government of the jurists. If there is no government of the jurists there will be *taghut* [illegitimate government].[14]

Khomeini's concept of Islamic government may have been for the people, but it certainly was not democratic. He exhibited a disdain for the collective will, stressing, "People are deficient and they need to be perfected." The manner of such perfection would be a clerical regime whereby the populace would submit to the superior authority of the clergy. In essence, Khomeini's concept of proper governance was one of religious autocracy that could not be reconciled with pluralistic imperatives. The Islamic Republic's persistent inability to liberalize itself can be partly attributed to this onerous legacy and its contempt for democratic accountability.

It would be a mistake to believe that Khomeini focused his ire purely against the Shah. A cursory examination of his writings reveals a sustained attack on the West, which in his view had always displayed a hostile attitude toward Islamic civilization.[15] Khomeini's work is marked by disdain toward external powers and the perception that

Iran's problems, ranging from the unaccountable monarchy to economic mismanagement, were in some form due to the influence of imperial powers. In a sense, Khomeini's suspicions were reinforced by a populace that was deeply averse to great power manipulation and a political culture that often perceived conspiracies as the root of its misfortunes. Khomeini was shaped by and, in turn, captured a national narrative that always mistrusted foreign elements.

It was this suspicion and contempt for foreign intervention that became the basis of Khomeini's foreign policy postulations. The Shah was not a mere tyrant but an agent of Western imperialism and Israeli Zionism. Iran and Islam were endangered by the same external forces and their monarchical accomplice. Such a message attracted both leftist intellectuals with their Third-Worldist hostility to America as well as traditional classes concerned about foreign encroachment of Islam's domain. The protection of Islam and the liberation of Iran were effortlessly conflated in Khomeini's conception. Decades later, the Islamic Republic's self-defeating hostility to America and Israel reflects an inability to transcend Khomeini's enduring antagonisms.

The first manifestation of Khomeini's enmity toward the West came during the crisis of 1963, when an uprising in the holy city of Qom developed in response to parliamentary legislation exempting U.S. military personnel from prosecution in Iran. The so-called capitulation laws invoked nationalistic hostility and anticolonial sentiment among the Iranian populace. The duality of Khomeini's evolving ideology was in full view, as he saw the accord as both a transgression against Islam and an assault on Iran's national integrity. Khomeini castigated the agreement, proclaiming, "They have sold our independence, reduced us to the level of a colony, and made the Muslim nation of Iran appear more backward than savages in the eyes of the world."[16] Yet at the same time he transcended traditionalist language and condemned the accord as an "enslavement of Iran." From the outset, he sought to unite the totality of Iranian opposition into a cohesive anti-Western bloc. America was not just a cultural affront, but a colonial power seeking to subjugate Third World countries.[17]

The 1963 crisis is often recalled as the occasion that finally caused Khomeini's expulsion from Iran. However, the significance of the event lies in the fact that it was the first attempt by Khomeini to reach out to Iran's growing intelligentsia and student activists. The only manner in which the traditional institutions could attract such forces was to represent their struggle in the language of modern dissent. The politically astute Khomeini clearly noted this view:

> They can no longer call us reactionary. The point is that we are fighting against America. All the world's freedom fighters will support us on this issue. We must use it as a weapon to attack the regime so that the whole nation will realize that the Shah is an American agent and this is an American plot.[18]

In the ensuing struggles, Khomeini perceived that the instrument of Iranian resistance to foreign influence (and its cat's-paw, the Shah) had to be Islam, not the passive, indifferent establishment Islam, but a revolutionary, politicized, uncompromising devotion of the sort that had launched the initial Islamic empire under the leadership of the Prophet. The united Muslim masses would once more redeem their faith from the transgressions of the West and the stagnation of the corrupt ruling class. By appropriating Islam's sacred symbols and by invoking the history of struggle against foreign infidels, Khomeini transformed Islam into an anti-Western ideology. Such a faith would galvanize the believers to once more defend their rights and reclaim their lost dignity.

Given such perceptions, for Khomeini the conflict with the United States was inevitable, as Iran could not abide the presence of a Western superpower seeking to dominate politics in the Islamic world. "We must settle our accounts with the great powers and show them that we can take on the whole world ideologically, despite all the potential problems that face us," he declared.[19] In the postrevolutionary period, sacrifice, conflict, resistance, and defiance would be the currency of Iran's international relations. Iran would not seek to balance the superpowers or transact alliances, but instead would reject the entire doctrine of international relations. When President Ahmadinejad in 2005 declared that Iran has no use for America, he was drawing on a rich revolutionary legacy and establishing his connection with the founder of the theocratic regime.

From the outset, Khomeini's vision transcended Iran. Iran's revolution would be the initial indispensable step toward establishing a virtuous regional order. "Islam is a sacred trust from God to ourselves and the Iranian nation must grow in power and resolution until it has vouchsafed Islam to the entire world," he said.[20] The viability of the revolution and the exalted divine mission mandated the export of Iran's Islamic template. At the core, Khomeini's ideological conception rejected the concept of the nation-state and an international system with its arbitrary territorial demarcations. As early as 1942, in *Kashf-e Asrar,* Khomeini decried the notion of the nation-state as the creation of "weak minds" who failed to appreciate the mandate from heaven.[21]

Beyond his objections to the Middle Eastern borders drawn by the Western powers, Khomeini also perceived unique opportunities for the export of his revolution. Though national revolutions have often sought to inspire similar movements in other countries, Khomeini was always careful to differentiate Iran's revolution from its French or Russian predecessors, stressing that Iran's revolt was predicated on a divine message while previous revolutions had been based on material considerations. For Khomeini, "only the law of God will always stay valid and immutable in the face of changing times."[22] Thus, the Islamic Republic he envisioned would be uniquely capable of ushering in a new age while previous revolutions ultimately stagnated and faded from the scene. Beyond such self-appreciation, Khomeini perceived that the bankruptcy of Soviet Marxism and Western capitalism had created an ideological vacuum that Iran should fill. Thus, once in power he confidently asserted, "We should set aside the thought that we do not export the revolution, because Islam does not regard various countries as different."[23] Such grandiose pronouncements may seem excessively ambitious for a leader of a developing country, but historically Iran's monarchs and mullahs have proved men of expansive vision and seldom adhered to the limits of their state.

These ambitions should not conceal the more parochial calculations behind the export of the revolution. Like most revolutionaries, Khomeini perceived that the best way to consolidate his regime at home was to pursue a confrontational policy abroad. Should the Islamic Republic remain inward-looking and focused on its internal developments, then it was bound to languish and eventually collapse. Once more, Khomeini was defiant, noting, "All the superpowers have risen to destroy us. If we remain an enclosed environment, we shall definitely be destroyed."[24] The contradiction between the export of the revolution and the preservation of Iran's practical interests was not evident to Khomeini.

Toward this end, Khomeini would strike out not only at the West but also at the regional powers who cooperated with the United States. He derisively condemned the Gulf states, Egypt, Saudi Arabia, and other American allies as mini-Satans who served to accommodate the transgressions of the "Great Satan." He had no compunction about calling on the local populace to emulate Iran's revolutionary model and would actively plot to overthrow the princes and the presidents that ruled sovereign states. "Cut off the roots of those who betray Islam and the Islamic countries," he implored.[25] The division of the region between the oppressed masses and the oppressive rulers serving as agents of American imperialism was the vision that would define Iran's international orientation. The ideological challenge to the ruling order would be complemented by an aggressive strategy of assisting opposition groups, militant forces, and a wide range of terrorist organizations.

Khomeini's revolution would thus be a curious mixture of dogmatic objectives and ideological flexibility, relentless determination and tactical retreats. A coalition that featured bearded mullahs, westernized intellectuals, defiant students, middle-class professionals, and traditional merchants would be held together by a cleric who came to personify Iran's struggles and tribulations. Khomeini offered something to everyone: he was a religious leader who would redeem the prophetic quest for construction of a pious order; a Third Worldist with a determination to emancipate his state from America's encroaching capitalist empire; a modernist with an appreciation of democratic ideals, a defender of women and the oppressed; and, always, a Persian nationalist seeking to restore Iran to its rightful place. Far from being a monolithic platform, Khomeini's message was an opportunistic one that concealed his essential objectives in order to broaden his coalition.

On that crisp February day in 1979 when Khomeini returned to Tehran on the heels of one of the most populist revolutions in history, he brought with him a set of beliefs that he was determined to imprint on Iran. The early period of the revolution would prove formative, as Khomeini sought to consolidate his rule, dispense with his allies of convenience, and ensure that clerical hegemony of power would persist long after he disappeared from the scene. The same dexterity and skill that had brought him to the pinnacle of power would now be used to ensure the institutionalization of his vision: the adroit use of foreign crises to generate a radical momentum sweeping away moderate forces; the gradual introduction of a constitutional order that made the clerical hijacking of power seem legal; and, of course, the use of terror and violence to intimidate the opposition were all legitimate strategies for an aging cleric determined to foster a new epoch.

CONSOLIDATION OF GOD'S WILL

At times in history there are watersheds, where a spectacular event alters existing norms, political perceptions, and fundamentals of state power. The year 1941 was the time America's foreign policy changed; in the aftermath of the Pearl Harbor bombings, the notion of splendid isolation was eclipsed by the imperative of international engagement. America became a global superpower that year, as successive Democratic and Republican administrations insisted that events abroad have an immeasurable impact on America's domestic security. The years 1979–81 were Iran's defining moment. During this pivotal period Khomeini and his cohort imposed changes on Iran's institutions and political culture that imprinted the notion of theocratic rule on Iran's national identity. The theocracy would change, redefine itself, at times becoming more reactionary and at times less intrusive, but a certain governing arrangement was implanted that is likely to endure. The American politicians who argue that economic sanctions, international ostracism, and threats can somehow dislodge the Islamic Republic ignore the deep roots that this most peculiar of regimes has cultivated.

Was it inevitable that Iran's revolution would degenerate into a theocratic autocracy, commanded by clerics in the name of a seventh-century faith? The revolution gave rise to a variety of political movements, ranging from reactionary to liberal, fundamentalist to secular, Marxist to capitalist. Khomeini was the leader, but by no means the only actor in one of the momentous revolutions in modern Middle Eastern history. The pathway to consolidation of clerical power came through the creation of a constitutional order that made secular and liberal inroads impossible. By creating nonelected institutions such as the Guardian Council that had the power to veto parliamentary legislation and presidential determinations, Khomeini ensured that the decisions of the elected branches of government would not effect the essential demarcations of power. Iran would always feature elections and plebiscites, but so long as nonelected clerics held the reins of power, the popular clamor for change would be contained, even negated.

The other aspect of Khomeini's ingenuity was his creation of a new political elite composed of both clerics and religiously devout laymen. The Islamic Republic is different from its revolutionary counterparts, as the ideology of the state is its religion. To be sure, this is a politicized and radicalized variation of Shiite Islam, but nonetheless religion is the official dogma. A dedicated core of supporters would remain loyal to this ideology, determined to perpetuate it long after Khomeini himself disappeared from the scene. Revolutionary regimes have usually collapsed when their once-ardent supporters grow disillusioned and abandon their faith. It is, after all, easy to be an ex-Marxist, as this is merely a sign of intellectual maturity. But how easy is it to be an ex-Shiite? In one case, renouncing the prevailing ideology is mere political defection; in the other case, it is apostasy. Although the Islamic Republic has grown extremely unpopular over the years, for a small but fervent segment of the population it is still an important experiment in realizing God's will on earth. And it is this sector of the society that continues to produce leaders such as Ahmadinejad, who are determined to return to the "roots of the revolution."

Despite the clerical determination to assume power, a look back at Iran in 1979 actually reveals the influence of the secular forces. The first postrevolution prime minister of Iran was Mehdi Bazargan, who despite his revolutionary disposition was a true democrat. The liberal movement led by the venerable National Front with its strong nationalist credentials commanded substantial support among the middle class and was strongly represented in the new provisional government. Even the radical Left still had a growing audience, particularly among the youth and industrial workers. The discursive message of the Mojahedin-e Khalq (MEK), with its mixture of Marxism and Islam, still lured many university students. The Fadayan-e Khalq could still mobilize hundreds of thousands for their demonstrations, and their newspaper enjoyed widespread circulation. Even the Communist Party, the Tudeh, with its long history of struggle against the monarchy and claims of economic justice, proved tantalizing to an intelligentsia attuned to the cause of Third World liberation.[26] The forces of secularism also garnered support from senior traditionalist clerics such as Ayatollah Kazem Shariatmadari, who were urging their fellow mullahs to retreat from the political sphere and concentrate on their priestly duties.

The original draft of the Islamic Republic's constitution was a further rebuke to Khomeini's vision of theocratic absolutism. Modeled along the lines of the French constitution, the Iranian document encompassed provisions for a strong presidency, an elected assembly, and individual rights. The notion of clerical monopoly of power and the subordination of the popular will to the dictates of a Supreme Leader were markedly absent. Despite vague assertions of Islam's importance to the nation, the document was not just progressive but reflected the influence of the secular parties and leftist forces.[27] The critical question remains: How did Khomeini and his disciples manage to silence such an impressive array of actors?

Unlike the divided secular opposition and the quietist ayatollahs, Khomeini and his supporters had long honed their organizational skills through decades of exile and oppositional activities. Through the effective use of mosques (Iran's only nationwide network), the creation of shadowy organizations with their own militias and effective manipulation of external crises, Khomeini gradually managed to displace his challengers. At every step of the way, he and his supporters proved more ardent in their faith, more manipulative in their conduct, and more merciless in their retaliations. The aged cleric who had waited decades to impose his mandate from heaven had limited inhibitions about abandoning erstwhile supporters and ignoring his pledges of an inclusive polity.

Soon after returning to Iran, Khomeini implored his allies to be vigilant and aggressive in their efforts to establish the theocratic order. "They want to make a Western country for you in which you will be free, you will be independent, but in which there is no God. This will lead to our destruction," he warned.[28] Through domination of the revolutionary committees overseeing local affairs, appropriation of the defunct regime's wealth, and mobilization of their zealous supporters, Khomeini and his allies fashioned a parallel regime with more authority than the tentative and moderate provisional government. While the government continued to issue orders, the secretive Council of the Revolution, manned by Khomeini loyalists such as Akbar Hashemi Rafsanjani, Ali Khamenei, and Muhammad Beheshti, was busy countermanding its decisions. However, to truly consolidate their power, the revolutionaries still needed a crisis that would effectively radicalize the population and discredit their foes. And the American embassy proved a tantalizing target.

On Sunday, November 4, 1979, a group of Iranian students took over the U.S. embassy in Tehran, beginning a crisis that would last 444 days. The ostensible purpose of the hostage taking was the students' alarm that the admission of the ailing Shah to the United States for medical treatment was an attempt by Washington to orchestrate a coup against Iran's nascent revolution. For a generation of Americans, the seizure of the embassy is seen as an egregious violation of international law by a contemptible regime. For Khomeini, it was the occasion where his vision of Islamic society would be transformed into a ruling ideology free from the constraint of coalition politics and democratic dissent. More than the pressing international issues or the entanglements of U.S.–Iranian relations, it would be the domestic political imperatives that would determine Tehran's approach to the American hostages.[29]

As the images of blindfolded Americans dominated the airwaves, a gratified Khomeini blessed the conduct of the students as ushering in the "second revolution," whose assault against the "Great Satan" made it an even nobler act than the original revolution.[30] Iran's media soon praised the event, proclaiming, "The true Iranian revolutionaries will remain in the U.S. embassy and they will not give up this fortress cheaply."[31] The hapless hostages proved to have remarkable utility for Iran's domestic politics, and Khomeini exploited them as a means of radicalizing the populace, claiming that the revolution was in danger from the manipulations of America and its internal accomplices. The issue, as framed by Khomeini, was now a contest between a rapacious, satanic United States and the sublime theocracy. The revision of the constitution and the demise of Bazargan's prime ministership were now sanctioned by the struggle against America. To be for pluralism and democratic rule was to support American aggression against Iran.

In the midst of the enveloping turmoil, Iran held elections for parliament and for the Assembly of Experts, which was to evaluate the draft constitution. In the atmosphere of fear and uncertainty, the clerical hard-liners and their political party, the Islamic Republican Party (IRP), came to dominate the new parliament, further buttressing their encroaching institutional dominance. In a similar vein, the Islamist forces captured the majority of seats in the Assembly of Experts, ensuring them a commanding voice in the revision of the constitution. Khomeini blessed the new assembly, insisting that the "constitution must be 100 percent Islamic."[32]

The Islamic state as envisioned by Khomeini during his prolonged exile was now gradually coming to the surface. The new constitution created the unprecedented theory of *velayat-e faqih* whereby a religious leader would oversee all national affairs. This office, designed for Khomeini himself, had virtually unlimited responsibilities and was empowered to command the armed forces and the newly created Revolutionary Guards, dismiss any elected official, countermand parliamentary legislation, and declare war and peace. The new office was subject neither to elections nor to the scrutiny of the elected institutions and the larger public. Islamic law was to displace the existing legal codes, circumscribing individual rights and prerogatives. A Guardian Council, composed mainly of clerics, was to vet all legislation, ensuring their conformity with Islamic strictures.[33] The constitutional arrangement guaranteed that Khomeini's reinterpretation of Shiism would remain the ideology of the state and that only those devoted to his vision would command critical institutions.

On December 3, 1979, the new constitution, with its antidemocratic provisions, was duly ratified by a frenzied public in a national referendum. The foundations of the theocratic regime were thus born on the heels of anti-Americanism and the notion of resisting foreign intervention. As the spiritual leader of the students, Muhammad Musavi-Khoeniha, recalled, "We reaped all the fruit of our undertaking—we defeated attempts by liberals to take control of the machinery of the state. We forced Bazargan's government to resign. The tree of the revolution has grown and garnered strength."[34] But for the tree to continue to prosper, the revolutionaries now had to dispense with the remaining secular and clerical competitors and complete their monopolization of power.

At this point, Iran still had an elected president, Abolhassan Bani-Sadr, as well as a critical intelligentsia, defiant student organizations, leftist paramilitary forces led by the MEK, and secular parties disinclined to accede to the emerging clerical despotism. At every step of the way, the clerical militants had exploited external crises to accelerate the pace of the revolution and purge the regime of undesirable elements. On September 22, 1980, yet another international conflict convulsed the republic and paved the way for the complete control of the state by Khomeini and his narrow collection of disciples—Iraq's invasion of Iran. The Iraqi invasion was intended to destroy the theocratic regime, but it ended up buttressing the revolution and subverting the remaining moderates within the republic. Saddam had miscalculated, not for the last time.

The war transformed the internal debates and the nature of the Iranian political landscape. "I am certain that there exists a relationship between Saddam, America, and the internal opposition," exclaimed Rafsanjani, then serving as the speaker of the parliament.[35] The Friday prayer leaders who routinely used the religious occasion to indoctrinate the masses now alluded to similar conspiracies. The state broadcasting service took up this theme, noting, "In order to solve his domestic problems, Saddam is ready to be subservient to the two superpowers, and he is directly strengthening internal counterrevolutionaries."[36] The issue was no longer freedom versus autocracy, but loyalty to the revolution, national sovereignty, and resistance to Iraq and its imperial benefactor, America. A bewildered nation looked to its spiritual leader to manage the turbulent waters of the enveloping conflict. For the fundamentalists the war turned out to be, as Khomeini noted, "a blessing."

The persistent emasculation of the office of president, the negation of Bani-Sadr's authority by the parliament and its chosen prime minister, and the orchestrated propaganda campaign accusing the president of being a client of the West finally culminated in a crisis in 1981. The parliament suddenly began impeachment proceedings, stressing the president's insubordination to revolutionary organs and poor management of the war. In a similar vein, 130 judges and prosecutors of the Islamic Republic wrote an open letter to Khomeini, asking him to deal with the president, as he was creating national disunity. Khomeini granted his approbation to these efforts, warning Bani-Sadr and his supporters to "go back to Europe, to the United States, or wherever else you want."[37] Seeing the writing on the wall, the Islamic Republic's first elected president went into hiding and subsequent exile to France.

The masters of the Republic of Virtue were not just contemptuous of their secular detractors, they were equally dismissive of senior clergy. Iran's most esteemed clerics such as Ayatollah Shariatmadari, Muhammad Reza Golpayegani, and Shahabeddin Mar'ashi-Najafi still embraced the quietist Shiite tradition and insisted on the importance of political disengagement. The tensions between the Supreme Leader and the senior clerics, which had been evident for decades, now burst to the surface. Khomeini, who was always contemptuous of the clergy who abjured politics, warned the "turbaned deceivers" who were "infiltrating the clergy and engaging in sabotage." In an even sterner rebuke, he declared, "I warn the clergy. I tell them all that I dislodge myself of my final responsibility to repulse all these mullahs."[38] One of the many paradoxes of the Islamic Republic is that theocracy has been far more effective at persecuting the religious class than all of its monarchical predecessors. A special court for the clergy was established, and hundreds of Iran's most learned and distinguished clerics were defrocked and imprisoned.

Having dismissed the elected president and silenced their clerical detractors, Khomeini and his followers unleashed a reign of terror that was to disenfranchise the remaining secular opposition forces—the old elite had to be forcefully removed before the new one could ensure its political hegemony. Mass arrests, brutal suppression of demonstrations, and summary executions were the order of the day. A cursory reading of newspapers of the time reveals the scope of the regime's brutality, as every issue proudly noted the tally of the previous day's executions. The liberal National Front politicians, the radical MEK supporters, landlords, writers, intellectuals, and journalists were dismissed, imprisoned, and on occasion executed. The vengeance of God was swift and categorical. The violence of this period gave rise to the so-called Second Republic, a regime that consolidated its power through terror. This was essentially the end of the revolutionary promise of a progressive, inclusive society that embraced pluralism while remaining loyal to its religious traditions.

This process of consolidation of the revolution soon moved beyond the political elites as Khomeini proclaimed his own cultural revolution. The universities were closed for two years as their curriculum was altered, television and news media bombarded the populace with crass Islamic propaganda, and the women who had made up such a critical part of the revolutionary coalition were forced to wear strict religious dress. Every aspect of public life had to conform to Islamic strictures, with loyalty tests and ideological standards determining admission to universities, the civil service, and the armed forces. Children were encouraged to inform on their parents, students on teachers, employees on each other. The new stalwarts of the revolution who had survived assassination campaigns, American coercion, and Saddam's invasion seemed confident that God was on their side and the perpetuation of their regime was a sign of divine approbation. Throughout the 1980s, war, martyrdom, sacrifice, and vengeance were the themes of Iranian politics and national discourse.

During his first two years in power, Khomeini's achievements were considerable. He implemented the Islamic ideology that he had spent decades developing and refining, and he created a new constitutional system with clear redlines and an elite loyal to his vision, which ensured that the Islamic Republic would survive his passing. Iran would now be guided by activist clerics and a strict interpretation of Shiite Islam. Alternative ideologies such as liberalism or secularism and politicians and clerics challenging the prerogatives of the *velayat-e faqih* were simply excluded from the councils of power. To be part of the ruling echelon one had to be committed to the Islamic Republic and its mission of salvation.

Despite his imagination and innovative skills, Khomeini's political acumen failed him in some important respects. The reality remains that the Islamic Republic never evolved into a pure totalitarian state such as Saddam Hussein's Iraq. As the revolution settled into a more predictable pattern of governance and as the regime's detractors were eliminated from the scene, the differences and divisions among Khomeini's disciples began to surface. Pragmatists stressing the need for a greater focus on the economy, hard-liners insisting that their mandate from God empowered them to disregard popular aspirations, and reformers stressing the need for a more tolerant theocracy began to battle one another for influence and power. After all, not all revolutionaries are alike. President Ahmadinejad and his immediate predecessor, Muhammad Khatami, are both part of the same elite, yet on critical issues such as the importance of civil society and individual sovereignty they differ radically. To be sure, Iran's factions may submerge their differences and defend the regime when it is challenged by student protests or American threats, but the core disagreements within the elite remain unabridged. The Islamic Republic may not be a big tent, but it is still a tent with diversity of views and opinions.

In a perverse sense, Khomeini's determination to impose Shiite Islam as the dogma of the state was partly undermined by the traditions of that very same Shiite faith. Shiism—with its history of decentralized power, independent-minded clerics, and seminaries that vehemently disagree with one another—never evolved into a hierarchical priestly class similar to the Catholic Church. The spirit of boisterous debate soon infiltrated the Islamic Republic, as the system stubbornly featured diverse and contenting factions. The simmering tensions between clerical leaders and the popular base of the regime and its constitutional pledges and republican mandates ensured divisions and rivalries. Even within its restrictive confines, the Islamic Republic would always feature robust and lively debate. In the end, Khomeini did succeed in ensuring the perpetuation of an Islamic Republic, yet one that is hopelessly and irrevocably divided against itself.

2

CONSERVATIVES, PRAGMATISTS, AND REFORMERS

On June 6, 1989, the founder of the Islamic Republic finally died. On that tumultuous day when the guardians of the revolution gathered to bid farewell to their departed leader an uneasy future lay ahead. The simmering conflicts that had been held in check by Khomeini's authority now became all too evident, and his disciples soon lapsed into an intense factional struggle as contending interpretations of Islam, differences over economic policy, and Iran's role in the international community dissolved the unity of the clerical elite. In essence, the tensions between the regime's revolutionary ideals and its practical requirements burst to the surface, bedeviling Iran's new rulers. Without Khomeini available to resolve these disputes, stalemate and deadlock became the new currency of Iranian politics.

Three political tendencies now emerged in the struggle for the leadership of the Islamic Republic, all led by very different clerical politicians. The hard-liners, united by their contempt for democratic pluralism and their determination to sustain Khomeini's divisive legacy, would ultimately settle on the stern and forbidding Ali Khamenei as their standard-bearer. The more moderate and pragmatic elements within the clerical hierarchy would coalesce around Iran's ultimate political insider, Akbar Hashemi Rafsanjani. These more tempered clerics believed that the perpetuation of Islamic rule mandated a greater attention to the economic deficiencies of the state and integration into the global economy. The pragmatists would press for a degree of cultural freedom and normalized relations with states that Khomeini had long castigated. Finally, the Islamic Republic featured a dynamic cadre of clerical and intellectual reformers who stressed that the legitimacy of the state was contingent on the vitality of its representative institutions. Also drawing on Khomeini's legacy, they emphasized the elected branches of the state and the importance of popular will in charting the national course. Muhammad Khatami would emerge as the most important, but by no means the only, representative of this cohort. These factions would now battle one another for influence and power, as the Islamic Republic's institutions were increasingly pitted against each other.

The intriguing aspect of Iran that tends to persistently puzzle Western observers is that these political factions never completely lose their influence despite their electoral performance. The fact remains that they all represent important constituencies and have a presence in the complicated web of informal and formal institutions that govern the Islamic Republic. For example, Rafsanjani's failed bid to capture the presidency in 2005 has not necessarily lessened his influence, as he is still in command of the powerful Expediency Council, which is responsible for mediating disputes between Iran's institutions. It is now fashionable to suggest that the reform movement is all but dead, given its recent string of electoral failures. But in the early 1990s the reformers were similarly excised from the ruling establishment, only to come back in force a few years later. Through the adroit use of their newspapers, intellectual circles, and supporters within the bureaucracy, the reformers managed to make an astonishing return to prominence under Khatami in 1997. The point remains that these three broad factions are likely to challenge one another for control of the Islamic Republic, and despite the ebbs and flows of their political fortunes they will determine Iran's future. Thus, it is important to have a better understanding of their ideological precepts, sources of support, successes, and failures if we are to better appreciate Iran's internal political dynamics.

KHAMENEI AND THE MILITANT RIGHT

The figure that has come to dominate the conservative bloc since the death of Khomeini is the Supreme Leader, Ayatollah Ali Khamenei. In many ways, the uncharismatic and uninspiring Khamenei was an unusual choice to succeed the founder of the Islamic Republic.[1] A loyal aide to Khomeini, Khamenei was not one of his favorite disciples. After the removal of Bani-Sadr from the presidency in 1981 and a wave of terrorism that decimated the top echelon of the Islamic Republic, Khamenei was elevated to the presidency, an office whose powers at that point were largely symbolic. After Khomeini's death, and once the more esteemed and learned Ayatollah Ali Hussein Montazeri proved politically unacceptable, Khamenei emerged as the consensus choice within the clerical estate to be the new Supreme Leader. Khamenei would spend much of his early tenure compensating for his lack of erudition by seeking the approbation of the reactionary clerics who invested such august powers in him.[2] The relationship between Khamenei and the clerical oligarchs would evolve into one of mutual dependence: they needed him to assert their influence and he relied on them to buttress his lackluster theological credentials.

Despite the skepticism, if not derision, that greeted Khamenei's appointment among the more traditional senior clergy, he would prove an adept political survivor. By temperament, Khamenei was cautious and conservative, uneasy about radical solutions and self-defeating crusades. Over the years, the new Leader would become more conservative, even reactionary, undergoing a subtle transformation into a harsh, uncompromising ideologue. At its core, Khamenei believes that the mission of the Islamic Republic is to uphold religious norms and resist popular attempts to alter the regime along democratic lines.

Over the past few decades, Khamenei and the militant conservatives essentially ensured their political hegemony by dominating Iran's powerful nonelected institutions. Through their control of the Supreme Leader's office, the Guardian Council, and the judiciary, they sought to ensure that the prerogatives of the elected institutions and the demands of the public could be effectively negated. Clerical stalwarts such as Ayatollah Ahmad Jannati and Ayatollah Mahmoud Hashemi Shahroudi headed these organizations and openly acclaimed the virtues of despotic rule. The hard-liners took full advantage of Khomeini's constitutional manipulations, which granted clerical watchdog organizations ample power to thwart popular aspirations. In the name of Islamic salvation, the reactionary elements of the state obstructed a range of initiatives that would have made the Islamic Republic a more tolerant and inclusive polity.

Beyond the formal institutions of the state, the hard-liners also came to dominate the coercive instruments of power, particularly the Revolutionary Guards. The 125,000-strong Revolutionary Guard force is commanded by reactionary ideologues who are committed to the values and philosophical outlook of the clerical militants. Throughout the 1990s, they called for suppression of the reform movement and denounced its attempts to expand the political rights of the citizenry. The Guards were unleashed to deal with student protests and often pressed the leadership to violently dispense with pro-democratic forces. As they gained stature and wealth, the Guards have increasingly emerged as an independent pillar of the state whose predilections and demands cannot be ignored by the ruling authorities. Today the Guards are not just enforcers of the regime's determinations but active participants on issues ranging from internal security to the nuclear program.[3]

In recent years, the demographic complexion of the militant Right is beginning to change, with a younger generation coming to assume important leadership positions. President Ahmadinejad and the parliamentarians organized in the new political party Abadgaran are the future of the conservative movement.[4] The younger rightists have been molded not by the revolution but by the prolonged war with Iraq in the 1980s, leading them to be suspicious of the international community and treaties as a means of preserving Iran's interests.[5] Although committed to the religious pedigree of the state, the callow reactionaries have at times been critical of their elders for their passivity in the imposition of Islamic cultural restrictions and the rampant corruption that has engulfed the state. As Iran's revolution matures and the politicians that were present at the creation of the Islamic Republic gradually recede from the scene, a more dogmatic generation is beginning to take hold of the reins of power.

Iran's conservatives, both young and old, are imbued with an ideology that views the essential purpose of the state as the realization of God's will on earth. Such an exalted task mandates the assumption of power by clerics or by laymen who are religiously devoted. They see themselves as a vanguard class that retains loyalty to Khomeini's revolutionary vision and best understands the intricacies of religious jurisprudence, and for that reason they hold that their authority should neither be infringed upon by representative bodies nor challenged by popular will. In a defiant tone, one of the champions of the Right, Hojjat-ol-Islam Moslemin Ghavarian, declared, "In my view a despotism which is rational must be accepted. Genuine despotism means obeying the divine decree."[6] True to Khomeini's example, his disciples reject the Shiite traditions, pressing the clergy to remain aloof from politics and preoccupy themselves with theological disquisitions.

Given such ideological inclinations, the hard-liners are utterly contemptuous of democratic accountability and pluralistic precepts. Khamenei has led the chorus in condemning liberal rule by insisting that the Islamic Republic is not "prepared to allow flawed and non-divine perspectives and ideas that are aimed at enhancing the power of the individual to dictate its social and political lives."[7] Ayatollah

Muhammad Mesbah Yazdi, the spiritual adviser to Ahmadinejad and many within the Revolutionary Guards, captures this totalitarian sentiment by claiming, "The Prophets of God did not believe in pluralism. They believed that only one idea was right."[8] Assured of their ideological verities and still in command of powerful institutions, the hard-liners are unconcerned about loss of popularity and widespread dissatisfaction with theocratic rule. After all, as Hamid Reza Tariqi of the Islamic Coalition Society noted, "The legitimacy of our Islamic establishment is derived from God. This legitimacy will not wash away even if people stop supporting it."[9]

The reactionary politics of the conservatives is complemented by a stringent view of cultural rights and the necessity of the imposing Islamic strictures on a reluctant populace. The conservatives spend much time anguishing about Western cultural influences and are puzzled why younger Iranians do not want to spend their time reading their ponderous theological tracts. The segregation of the sexes, the enforcement of female dress codes, and the control of the media and the film industry are still the preferred methods for preventing cultural decadence. After twenty-seven years of struggle, the attempt to control Iran's youth is a losing battle that the conservatives nonetheless insist on waging.

Following Khomeini, a degree of contempt characterizes the clerical militants' approach to their constituents. They believe that the nation's citizenry has to change, purify itself, adhere uncritically to their ideological exhortations, and obey their commands. Only then will Iranians be worthy subjects of the divine republic. Ayatollah Ahmad Azari-Qomi reflected this sentiment, stressing, "The Leader was analogous to the head of the family and has the right to interfere in the house where he has delegated the housework."[10] Similarly, the hard-liners dismiss the notions of individual sovereignty and an empowered citizenry as a means of forging a new political community.

The economic perspective of the Right is as flawed and retrogressive as its political platform. The conservatives' economic policies stem from competing demands of their constituents in the bazaar and their revolutionary pledge to uplift the downtrodden. The clerical hard-liners have acclaimed the sanctity of private property and routinely assert Islamic injunctions endorsing commerce and free enterprise. After all, they say, the Prophet of Islam was a trader and the mullahs themselves have proved shrewd businessmen. However, in practice the hard-liners' economic conception does not entail the creation of a modern economy with its calls for transparency, the rule of law, and accountability. To such traditionalists, private economy has implied allowing their merchant allies to operate with limited state scrutiny.

In a paradoxical sense, the hard-liners' celebration of commerce militates against fostering a modern industrial economy. Indeed, the creation of such an infrastructure is at times explicitly rejected in favor of the merchant class with its trade monopolies and unregulated practices. Muhammad Reza Bahonar, the deputy speaker of parliament, noted, "In the commercial sector, our country has a great potential for becoming an international merchant. I don't have high hopes that our industry or agriculture can meet the country's expenditures."[11] A modern economy with its rational bureaucracy, cohesive administrative institutions, and a viable banking system are dismissed in favor of the existing opaque arrangements with their traditional means of exchange.

However, the conservatives face a contradiction in their attempt to reconcile the mandates of the private economy and the inequalities it produces with their revolutionary pledge to lift up the dispossessed. The notion of economic justice and egalitarianism still has a powerful resonance for a segment of the Right that is offended by the persistence of class cleavages and the inequality in the distribution of wealth. These themes mobilized the lower classes on behalf of President Ahmadinejad in the 2005 election as his message of equality of sacrifice proved alluring to the foot soldiers of the revolution. The conservative response to this conundrum has been massive subsidies on critical commodities such as bread, fuel, and sugar. The results have been predictably disastrous, and subsidies today consume approximately 20 percent of the country's GDP. A viable structural reform package would entail dispensing with these onerous subsidies and reducing the size and scope of the bloated bureaucracy. However, such reforms may cause short-term disruptions that a regime with a limited popular base is unwilling to countenance. Given its ideological commitments and its fear of antagonizing its lower-class constituents, the Right has jealously guarded the existing stagnant state with all its pathologies and deficiencies.

Hovering over all this is the reality that the hard-liners today are one of the few segments of Iranian society that is actually benefiting from the current economic order. The mainstay of the right-wing power bloc remains the vast religious foundations, the *bonyads,* which have come to dominate the trade and manufacturing sectors. The *bonyads* began in the aftermath of the revolution as religious foundations that expropriated the assets of the defunct monarchy for philanthropic purposes. However, in the intervening quarter-century they have metamorphosed into huge holding companies that dominate key industries while evading competition and state regulation. These interests are inimical to a truly free market and dissuade their beneficiaries— mostly conservative clerics and other defenders of the current system—from implementing any serious structural reforms to Iran's economy.

Such corrupt practices are now being emulated by the Revolutionary Guards, who in recent years have steadily intruded into economic activities, establishing their own commercial firms with privileged access to contracts in key industries such as telecommunications and imported consumer goods. Through this network of companies, the Guards have enhanced their patronage power, allowing them to further cultivate their constituents. In an even more ominous manner, much of Iran's nuclear infrastructure is being procured by firms owned by members of the Guards, making compromise on this issue even more difficult. At any rate, the fundamentals of economic reform, including decentralization, free competition, and the rule of law cannot be instituted without endangering the conservatives' lucrative power base.

In a sense, the hard-liners are offering the populace their own social compact, whereby in exchange for spiritual salvation, the public will relinquish the right to dissent. In such an order—where the task at hand is to construct a society seeking continuous conformity with God's will as seen by an enlightened clerical corps—there is no room for disagreement. The populace should be grateful, the hard-liners assert, that it is provided with a leadership and a social arrangement leading to celestial rewards. To disagree with clerical fiats and the accumulation of power by a narrowly self-selected group of religious reactionaries is to engage in a provocative act of defiance that must necessarily be suppressed. Iran's Right seems to perceive that it has reached "the end of history," where an exalted order has been constructed that requires no further reform or alteration.

The inflexibility of the hard-liners' outlook stands in stark contrast to a dynamic and changing Iranian society. By the time of Khomeini's death, the prolonged war with Iraq and the struggles on behalf of the revolution had convinced many social sectors that citizens have rights and are not mere actors obeying clerical dictates. Iran is also a young country, with an estimated 70 percent of the population under the age of thirty. A new demographic cohort has been evolving under the structure of the Islamic Republic, with its own demands and imperatives. Two other political tendencies have emerged seeking to accommodate such popular aspirations and balance the mandates of the revolution with the desires of its constituents.

RAFSANJANI AND THE POLITICS OF PRAGMATISM

The pragmatic wing of the clerical elite is led by a politician who defies easy characterization. Akbar Hashemi Rafsanjani was a longtime disciple of Khomeini, one of the architects of the revolution, and a politician who has held nearly every important office in postrevolutionary Iran. Rafsanjani reached the apex of his career in 1989 when he assumed the office of the presidency for two successive terms. A mixture of realism and self-interest would perennially lead Rafsanjani to embrace economic and cultural policies that contravened established orthodoxies and even theological norms. For him, the legitimacy of the state and the prolongation of Islamic rule were contingent on its economic performance. As such, he would spend much of his presidency, indeed his entire career, seeking to build strong institutions, buttressed by a competent and expanding bureaucracy to realize his vision of change and reform.[12]

Soon after Khomeini's death, Rafsanjani and his technocratic protégés began to assert their identity and political platform. They had risen to critical positions in the professional associations, the modern business community, and state bureaucracies. By 1996, they went one step further and established their own political party, the Servants of Construction (Kargozaran-e Sazandegi), whose declared mission was "the use of experts and creation of a domestic environment where ideas flowed."[13] Using China as a model, they hoped to conceive a new order that would be economically efficient, culturally tolerant, and politically autocratic. It is important to note that the aim of the pragmatists was never the creation of a democratic polity, but rather a stable society that would meet the economic needs of its constituents.

Given their preoccupation with economic rejuvenation, Rafsanjani and his allies pressed for tempering the Islamic revolution in terms of how Iran defined its priorities and formulated its policies. The conservatives' opaque economic practices and their emphasis on social justice were seen as militating against judicious economic planning. A technocratic cadre would have to displace the revolutionary loyalists in key ministries and private economics would have to assume priority over the revolutionary pledge to lift up the dispossessed. For Rafsanjani, Iran could best preserve its revolution only "under the aegis of rational and logical policy."[14] The pragmatists would seek to transcend Khomeini's populist policies by emphasizing private initiatives and attracting foreign investments. This would entail borrowing from the

World Bank and agreeing to partial foreign ownership of domestic industries. The Islamic Republic would no longer seek to challenge the prevailing international norms but would participate in the global economy. Foreign Minister Ali Akbar Velayati noted these sentiments in 1991 by stressing that "economic considerations overshadow political priorities."[15] Once a modern industrial economy was created, then not only would the regime's legitimacy be enhanced but problems of economic inequality would be similarly alleviated.

Although their economic focus precluded tackling issues of representation and pluralism, the pragmatists did stand against the totalitarian Islam of the Right. In the interest of stability they thought it necessary to accommodate at least some of the populace's political aspirations and thereby strengthen the republican pillar of the state. It was important, they believed, to grant the public a stake in the political process and national planning through competitive politics with elections among diverse choices of candidates and platforms. In their conception, the Supreme Leader was not just the guardian of a restrictive view of Islam, but an important politician with the responsibility to tackle thorny issues such as population growth and institutional decay that had obstructed Iran's development. All this is not to suggest an emerging appreciation for the collective will—Rafsanjani and his allies were not beyond manipulating the electoral process to achieve their desired results. Nonetheless, unlike the reactionary Right the pragmatists saw a rigid political order as detracting from the essential task of rehabilitating the economy.

On cultural issues, the pragmatists sought to avoid the coercive imposition of Islamic ordinances on the country's restive youth. Their focus was not on creating a more liberal society but a stable one that would lessen tensions. Such stability was unlikely to be fostered with a sullen, alienated generation resentful of the persistent and onerous state intrusions into their lives. Given their devotion to the essential institutions of the Islamic Republic, such enterprising moves would have distinct limits, as notions of equality of the sexes and gender emancipation were still dismissed on religious grounds. Despite such inhibitions, the pragmatists acknowledged that the relaxation of cultural restrictions and a degree of social freedom could provide a useful safety valve for Iran's youthful populace.

Despite their lofty pledges of creating an industrial economy, the ambitions of the pragmatists soon fell victim to the vicissitudes of Iranian politics. During Rafsanjani's presidency from 1989 to 1997 his initiatives inevitably began to encroach on the ideological imperatives and the power base of the conservatives. As we have seen, for Iran's hard-liners privatization meant a merchant class free of state regulation and intervention. The task of creating a coherent economy with a modern infrastructure, rule of law, and uniform tax policy manned by a technocratic bureaucracy was abhorrent to the conservative bloc. Given the right wing's paranoia about Western cultural influences, they were averse to opening the system to foreign investments, much less implementing the structural measures mandated by the World Bank. For them, the sanctity of private property implied empowering the bazaar and its opaque economic arrangements and not creating a modern economy integrated in global markets.

Beyond his economic measures, Rafsanjani faced an open rebellion on his attempt to loosen the suffocating cultural impositions. Supreme Leader Khamenei led the chorus by claiming, "Some mock religious virtues, but if we spend billions on development projects and ignore moral issues, all achievements amount to nothing." The head of the Guardian Council, Ayatollah Ahmad Jannati, similarly admonished Rafsanjani, stressing that the role of the state is to support "true Islamic culture by reinforcing religious bedrock of the people and fighting all those who are anti-Islamic and Western-stricken."[16] For the Right, the mission of the revolution remained the rigorous enforcement of Islamic tenets. Despite Rafsanjani's professions, moral police and law enforcement officials continued to harass and arrest those seeking a degree of personal and intellectual freedom.

In a pattern that would prove all too familiar, the hard-liners employed their institutional power to thwart reform measures. Under the auspices of Ayatollah Khamenei, the hard-liners systematically undermined Rafsanjani's initiatives. Not for the first time Iran was paralyzed by the core contradiction between factions professing ideology and those pressing the cause of national interest.

In the end, Rafsanjani's presidency failed to achieve its main objectives. Despite some success in denationalization measures, the so-called Era of Reconstruction did not liberalize the economy or resolve its inherent distortions. Borrowing from the international markets placed Iran in the unenviable position of having a huge debt burden. The resulting inflationary pressures eroded the standard of living of the poor and the middle class. The inability of the state to reduce its heavy subsidies, the periodic declines of the petroleum market, and an inability to attract foreign investment curbed the potential of Iran's growth. On the cultural front, Iran remained a largely repressive society, struggling under the burdens of religious impositions that many found objectionable, given the rampant corruption of the clerical class.

The triumph of the Right had much to do with Rafsanjani being unwilling to challenge the fundamental power of the hard-liners. Every time he met resistance, he quickly retreated, shielding himself in a barrage of religious rhetoric. Despite his advocacy of reform and moderation, Rafsanjani reigned over a state that was economically stagnant and socially repressed. And his quest for power led him to abandon his own convictions and betray the nation that had invested so much hope in his presidency.

At first glance it is easy to dismiss Rafsanjani and his pragmatic allies as a fading and unsuccessful phenomenon. However, in a perverse manner, the pragmatists contributed to the long-term transformation of Iran by altering the legitimacy of the republic. During Khomeini's reign, the basis of the regime's authority was its Islamic ideology and the Supreme Leader's overpowering charisma. More than any of his clerical counterparts, Rafsanjani appreciated that the populace that had suffered so much hardship and loss of life during the prolonged war with Iraq would no longer be satisfied with the rhetoric of martyrdom and sacrifice. Rafsanjani's emphasis on economic performance and cultural freedom altered the nature of the relationship between state and society. The declared mission of the government was no longer provision of salvation but delivering on its practical pledges. Thus, Rafsanjani's tenure served as the midwife of the reform movement, which sought to fundamentally alter the political topography of Iran.

TEHRAN SPRING

The Iranian regime in the post-Khomeini years was nothing if not fractious, as a third group, the reformers, also emerged, pressing their own claims and ideological template.[17] The politician who would capture the imagination of the reformers and indeed the larger Iranian society was a midlevel cleric, Hojjat-ol-Islam Seyyed Muhammad Khatami. Despite his position in the clerical establishment, Khatami had long distinguished himself from it, both in his politics and in his intellectual enterprises. In 1992, the future president, who was then the minister of culture, broke with the Rafsanjani administration over his liberal tendencies and his willingness to grant licenses for publications and plays that defied the strictures of the regime. After he was ousted, he immersed himself in Western philosophy as a complement to his Islamic training. In his subsequent writings, Khatami dared to contravene the ruling consensus, declaring that "state authority cannot be attained through coercion and dictatorship. Rather it is to be realized through governing according to law, respecting the rights and empowering people to participate and ensuring their involvement in decision making."[18] Themes of civil society, rule of law, and individual sovereignty permeated his speeches and writings.

Although Khatami was versed in Western political thought, it would be wrong to characterize him as a Western-style democrat in clerical garb. To be sure, he often acknowledged the West's economic progress and pluralistic achievements, but he was also quick to criticize the West for its excessive materialism and insensitivity to man's spiritual needs. In a sense, Khatami can best be seen as following the long line of Islamic reformers, seeking to revitalize their societies by relying on Islam's own traditions and injunctions. Khatami remained a man of the system, however, and once his reforms threatened to undermine the edifice of the Islamic Republic, he quickly retreated and opted for conformity instead of confrontation. As he was preparing to leave office in 2005, Khatami defended his reticence, stressing, "We believed that internal clashes and chaotic conditions were a fatal poison for the country's existence and the Islamic Republic's sovereignty."[19]

The other misconception about Khatami is that he was the sum total of the reform movement, and that his failings foreclosed the possibility of expanding Iran's political parameters. The reform movement was a vast coalition of dissident intellectuals, liberal clerics, middle-class professionals, and hard-pressed students. As with most coalitions, there were always tensions between those pressing for dramatic change and more establishment figures calling for caution and restraint. Given Khatami's impeccable revolutionary credentials and liberal tendencies, he was initially seen by a cross-section of the reform movement as an ideal vehicle for its aspirations. However, there were always many rank-and-file reformers who were uneasy about Khatami's strategy of gradualism. To properly understand the reform movement, with all its complexities and contradictions, it is important to look beyond Khatami and examine the diverse forces that shaped this important faction in Iranian politics.

By the early 1990s, an eclectic group of politicians, seminary leaders, religious scholars, and intellectuals undertook an imaginative reexamination of the role of public participation in an Islamic government.[20] An impressive array of the regime's own loyal soldiers—men who had fought for the clerical state and served in some of its highest posts—found themselves increasingly marginalized by the defenders of strict Islamic orthodoxy and began subtly defecting from the official line. Recognizing that the rigid definition of religious governance was threatening the entire structure of the Islamic Republic, veteran politicians such as Abdollah Nuri, Sa'eed Hajarian, and Abdulvand Musavi-Lari mobilized a counterassault. The academic and journalistic circles they established then served as the precursors for their subsequent campaigns to capture the elections and political institutions.[21]

The challenge for the reformers was to reconcile two competing demands. On one side stood Islam with its holistic pretensions, maintaining how society and individual lives should be governed. On the other side was the movement for political modernity with its democratic claims. The reformers, in essence, claimed that these two realms were not incompatible in principle or in practice. This was a remarkable rebuke to totalitarian Islam, which was increasingly serving as the regime's ideology, providing the ruling clergy with a divine justification for its privileges and power.

The essential basis of the reformers' ideology was that the interpretation of the scriptures cannot remain immutable and must adjust to the changing human condition. For religion to remain vital, they said, it had to address the demands of modern society. Islam was not lacking in traditions that can address this challenge, as the well-established practice of *ijtihad* (interpretation) offered the reformers a path toward an evolved understanding of the sacred texts. In the hands of the reformers, Islam was not merely a system for connecting man to his divine creator, but a force for progressive change. The scriptures call for freedom from tyranny and for human equality, and Islamic civilization's historical legacy of intellectual inquiry was seen as the basis for reconstructing the society along pluralistic lines. Moreover, the Koran's mandate that the community be consulted and rulers be accountable established the platform for collective action and democratic participation.

This reconceptualization of Islam was most effectively articulated by a courageous intellectual who would challenge the foundations of theocratic rule. Abdol Karim Soroush was a professor at Tehran University whose personal journey mirrored the evolution and contradictions of the Islamic Republic. During the initial decade of the revolution, Soroush was an ardent proponent of imposing the regime's cultural restrictions on the universities and dismantling objectionable student organizations. He was active in revising the universities' academic curriculum, establishing new criteria for admission that took into consideration religious commitment, and essentially reducing the university into an ideologically reliable pillar of the state. Soroush was just another functionary of the regime, using a reactionary and exclusivist definition of Islam to combat political diversity and democratic pluralism.

But by the late 1980s, Soroush appeared a changed man, his training in philosophy and science seemingly having reasserted itself, eclipsing his once militant tendencies. In the pages of his publication *Kian,* in lectures around the country, and through his university teaching, he popularized the notion that for religion to inspire devotion it had to embrace rationality, the power of scientific judgment, and the philosophical spirit of reason: "An ideal religious society cannot have anything but a democratic argument."[22] Religious canon and Islamic jurisprudence had to be seen, he argued, as the means of ensuring individual sovereignty and governmental accountability. Through such a liberal reinterpretation of Islam, Soroush argued that it was possible to envision a political order in which religious doctrine and pluralism were reconciled.[23] The once obscure professor suddenly emerged as the backbone of an emboldened movement seeking progressive change.

In his writings Soroush propounded the notion of collective rationality, which can only be ascertained through the democratic process as the best guide for the national government, and he came to differentiate between a "religious state" and a "religious jurisprudence state." The latter was a regime that was governed by the clerical class with its reliance on scriptural sources and indifference to popular mandates. However, a more ideal "religious state" would merely "obligate itself to create an atmosphere that defends believers' free and conscious faith and religious experience."[24] In essence, Soroush argued that a tolerant regime would foster conditions whereby people would wish for religion to have a continuing and important role in society and even in the administration of the state. This stands in stark contrast to Khomeini's perception that the best manner of ensuring the survival of a religious order was to create institutional arrangements designed to thwart, or even subvert, the popular will. Soroush proved a more judicious observer than Khomeini, as he appreciated that once religion became the instrument of an oppressive state it would only provoke contempt for the clerical estate and widespread secularization. Soroush's writings and speeches were an unmistakable challenge to the ruling establishment, securing him the acclaim of the students and other enterprising reformers.

It was not only university professors and political activists who were shaping the reform movement. In one of the paradoxes of the Islamic Republic, the system was being challenged by many within the clerical community. One of Iran's most intellectually imaginative clerics, Hojjat-ol-Islam Mohsen Kadivar, now came forth with his own rebuke of the ruling mullahs.[25] In his critique of the Islamic Republic, Kadivar naturally relied on Shiite theology, demonstrating the extent to which Khomeini's vision had departed from religious norms. Given that in Shiite Islam the occultation of the twelfth Imam in 976 had invalidated all temporal authority until his return, the notion of clerical government seemed peculiar. Kadivar insisted, "There is no blueprint for the management of the society during the time of occultation. No one has a special mission or authority to guide the society." Given that no particular class has a divine right to monopolize political power, the government had to be an expression of the majority opinion. For Kadivar, a democratic government was the only one that can claim religious approbation.

Kadivar's interpretation of Shiite political doctrine soon attracted the attention of Iran's most esteemed and senior clerics. Ayatollah Montazeri joined the fray on Kadivar's side, saying, "I believe that Islam and democracy can coexist because Islam supports freedom. What the conservative leaders are practicing today is not Islam and I oppose it."[26] Ayatollah Jalaleddin Taheri, who resigned in July 2002 as Isfahan's Friday prayer leader, accused the clerical oligarchs of "Genghis-like behavior, acting against the people and the law, isolating thinkers, paralyzing government, and throwing the country in the wind which will lead to an inauspicious end."[27] Given the unpopularity and corruption of the religious state, many influential segments of the clergy were searching for ways to reform and revitalize the stagnant theocratic order.[28]

It is important to note that along with the other factions in the Islamic Republic, the reformers were loyal to the regime and its defining institution, the *velayat-e faqih*. However, the difference between the reformers and the hard-liners was their interpretation of the prerogatives of the office and the extent to which it must accommodate popular imperatives. For the hard-liners the powers of the Supreme Leader were immune from electoral scrutiny, and Ayatollah Khamenei was essentially invested with dictatorial determinations. For the reformers the absolutism of the office contravened the democratic spirit of the constitution. As the main reformist clerical organization, the Association of Militant Clergy, noted, "All pillars of the regime, including the Leader, must draw their legitimacy from republicanism."[29] In this context, the Supreme Leader may exercise a general supervisory role, but his powers must be circumscribed by the constitution and he must defer to the elected branches of the government.

In the end, for the reformers the elected institutions of the Islamic Republic were more important sources of authority than its appointed offices with their mandates from heaven. As the former speaker of the parliament, and a recent presidential candidate, Mehdi Karrubi, stipulated, "Without the vote of the people, the regime does not have legitimacy."[30] The essential argument of the reformers was that a religious order can only retain its authority through persuasion and popular acceptance. A compulsory imposition of religious strictures and a disdain for the collective will would inexorably erode the foundations of the state. Unlike the hard-liners, the reformers exhibited ample confidence in the ability of the populace to sustain a state that was religious in character and yet democratic in its practices. Tensions and contradictions that such an order inevitably provoked would be resolved through compromises that democracies are particularly capable of forging. Such a progressive interpretation of the Islamic Republic would prove fundamentally at odds with the despotic aspirations of the hard-liners.

Into this charged atmosphere stepped Muhammad Khatami, who emerged as the presidential candidate of the reformers for the 1997 election. The hard-liners quickly accepted his petition; they perceived him as a suitable token candidate for their much better organized and funded conservative standard-bearer, Speaker of the Parliament Ali Akbar Nateq-Nuri. To the shock and dismay of the hard-liners, Khatami's expansive vision of a tolerant Islamic government won the hearts and minds of the Iranian public. And it gained the little-known cleric a whopping 69 percent of the vote, a stunning victory over the establishment candidate.[31] Suddenly elections seemed to matter, as they provided the public with an avenue for infiltrating the corridors of power. Khatami's resounding triumph energized the reform movement; its adherents had to make the leap from contemplation to accountability, from theory to practice.

The moment of exhilaration, however, was marked by a degree of caution, if not trepidation. Now the reformers faced a new challenge: how to navigate the treacherous waters of Iranian politics and institutionalize their ideas.[32] This would prove a difficult, if not impossible, task. As their ideas threatened to escape the confines of clerical politics and potentially sweep away the entire system, the reformers faced the challenge of sustaining their loyalty to the regime or joining the popular wave. They ultimately opted for conformity, disillusioning their once ardent supporters.

The perennially cautious Khatami came into office with the determination to choose his battles carefully and avoid open clashes with the conservatives. This was to be the strategy of incrementalism, seeking to gradually reform the Islamic Republic from within its own institutions. Taking the dual approach—characterized by the catchphrase "pressure from below, negotiations from the top"—he responded to the burgeoning public demands for greater freedom. To turn up the pressure from below hundreds of new publications were allowed with censorship guidelines loosened, and permits for reformist groups and gatherings were issued with ease. The reformers, however, refrained from challenging the wide discretionary powers of the Supreme Leader, which the hard-liners jealously guarded. Instead, the reformers focused on expanding their institutional power by establishing a critical media and participating in elections. The reformers' electoral triumphs in the municipal elections of 1998 and in the parliamentary contest of 2000 initially gave credence to this strategy, since Iran's democratic infrastructure was expanding.

During the heady days of the "Tehran Spring," the reform movement proceeded from triumph to triumph, overwhelming bastions of reaction through electoral success. The presence of the conservatives in a variety of institutions was seen as a transient stage before the final exodus of their bankrupt ideology and stagnant movement. Such euphoric expressions engendered a sense of complacency, as the reformers never developed a grassroots organizational network to sustain their momentum and did not conceive a coherent strategy for actually dislodging their well-entrenched nemeses. The reform movement remained a closed circle of intellectuals without connection to other disaffected communities. Labor unions, trade organizations, and the modern business sector, which are the backbone of change in most developing societies, were largely absent from Iran's emerging political struggles. The debates were scintillating, and the innovative attempts to reconcile tradition with modernity were thought-provoking and imaginative. However, the movement did not undertake the organizational effort of institutionalizing its power.

Beyond the constitutional impediments, the reformers mistook the public's patience with approval. The reformers' lofty rhetoric and expansion of civil society had convinced average citizens that they should be the arbiters of important national debates. Once those expectations remained unfulfilled, a more disillusioned public began to question the utility of the reformers' strategy, and eventually the reform movement itself. The fact that Khatami and his cohort confined themselves within the redlines established by the theocratic elite and retreated when confronted by conservative intransigence further estranged them from their constituents. In the end, the reformers simply lacked the courage of their endlessly refined convictions. The reform movement won the battle of ideas, but then had no strategy for the implementation of those ideas.

While the reformers dithered and debated, the hard-liners had a well-delineated stratagem for assuring their political hegemony. In line with the Supreme Leader's blessing, the conservatives cynically deployed the judiciary and the security services to close down newspapers and imprison key reform figures on contrived charges, while the Guardian Council systematically voided parliamentary legislation. Even more brutally, the clerical establishment orchestrated a campaign of terror that targeted intellectuals, writers, and activists, and unleashed vigilante groups on student gatherings and peaceful demonstrations.

At every step of the way, the conservative obstructionism enjoyed the approbation of Ayatollah Khamenei and the hard-line leadership. The Supreme Leader warned his followers soon after Khatami's election to be vigilant, for today "the enemy is striking Islam at home."[33] Khamenei's explicit denunciation of the reformers as enemies of religion emboldened his followers to issue similar threats. The commander of the Revolutionary Guards, Yahya Rahim Safavi, declared, "When I see conspirator cultural currents, I give myself the right to defend the revolution and my commander, the esteemed Leader, has not prevented me."[34] The conservative countermeasures were intended not simply to weaken the reform movement but to demonstrate to the populace the futility of elections in altering the demarcations of the state and the citizenry's irrelevance in the political process. In essence, the conservatives sought to disillusion the public and provoke their retreat from public affairs. And this is where the reformers' strategy of incrementalism faltered—it simply could not overcome the intransigence of a core group of hard-liners who had the power to preclude meaningful change to Iran's political structure.

The other party that must bear its own measure of blame for the failure of the reform movement is the United States. The Bush administration's strategy of democratic transformation and its so-called moral clarity paradoxically contributed to the conservative consolidation of power. The contest between reform and reaction in Iran took a dramatic turn after the terrorist attacks of September 11, 2001, as external events suddenly intruded on Iran's domestic struggles. The bitter lesson of the Islamic Republic remains that hard-liners have historically been the sole beneficiaries of American antagonism. Khomeini, as we have seen, provoked the hostage crisis to inflame the public and displace the moderate provisional government. More than two decades later, his disciples sensed in Washington's bellicosity another opportunity to fend off the reformers and change the nature of the debate. The fact that the reformist government had cooperated with the United States in Afghanistan made it all the more vulnerable. Far from being rewarded for its assistance, Iran was once more castigated, threatened, and lumped with the unsavory states of Iraq and North Korea.

As America's war on terrorism unfolded, the proponents of pluralism were defamed by the conservatives as a "fifth column" undermining national cohesion at a time of maximum peril. Ayatollah Khamenei emphasized this point, stressing, "If they [the United States] see that disgruntled people and adventurers want to cause trouble, and if they can turn them into mercenaries, they will not hesitate do to so by giving them their support."[35] In an even more preposterous assertion, the reactionary cleric Mohiyeddine Haeri Shirazi stated, "Those who weaken the Guardian Council and the Revolutionary Guards are spreading discord among the people and want to promote American influence."[36] Beyond their rhetorical fulminations, the conservatives wrapped themselves in the mantle of national unity to justify their crackdown. They were not engaged in the suppression of democratic rights, they said, but were merely instituting judicious security measures designed to safeguard Iran from foreign intervention.

The self-defeating nature of the American strategy was quickly noted by the democratic dissidents it was designed to aid. Shirin Ebadi, the recipient of the 2003 Nobel Peace Prize, pointedly criticized the U.S. policy: "The fight for human rights is conducted in Iran by Iranian people, and we are against foreign intervention in Iran."[37] In a similar vein, Hamid Reza Jalaiapour, a leading reformist politician, noted, "When Bush named Iran as an axis of evil, our hard-liners became happy. They can then mobilize the part of the country that supports them."[38] The reality remains that the hard-liners required international crisis and conflict with America as a means of deflecting attention from their sagging political fortunes. Sadly, Washington's approach played easily in the hands of the "unelected few" that President Bush and his advisers justifiably abhor.

THE WAY AHEAD

A glance at Iran today seems to suggest that the conservative strategy for reclaiming their power has succeeded. Mahmoud Ahmadinejad's presidential triumph concludes a remarkable resurgence of the Right that has now captured all the relevant elected institutions. In a dramatic realignment of Iranian politics, it appears that after eight years of stalemate, internal discord, and lofty promises of reform and democratization, the Iranian populace has conceded the state to the conservatives in the hope that they can deliver on their promise of economic justice.

Despite the conservative jubilation, their strategy may yet prove self-defeating. The Right's monopolization of power has burdened it with responsibilities that the reformers did not have. The reformers can be absolved for some of their failures by the divided nature of the government and right-wing obstructionism. The conservative consolidation of power over all the relevant organs of the state deprives them of such a pretext. Given their intellectual poverty, corruption, and attachment to anachronistic policies, the hard-liners have no viable solutions to Iran's manifold political and economic troubles. The moderate newspaper E'temad captured the predicament of the hard-liners, warning, "With all the capabilities, and the consolidation of the powers that they enjoy, they should be able to solve all the problems without the slightest excuse."[39] On the eve of their most impressive power grab, the conservatives may yet face a disgruntled public that they can neither appease nor contain.

The alarmist headlines and the astonishing power the conservatives hold should not conceal the fact that the clerical establishment is still divided along factional lines. Indeed, a persistent problem for Western observers is their perception of Iranian politics as static. The reformist triumphs of the 1990s were seen by many as inevitably ushering in a new democratic epoch, while today the conservative assumption of power is seen as necessarily permanent and durable. In Iran, however, politics is a shifting landscape. It is not inconceivable that the reformers may stage yet another comeback and reclaim the parliament in the next election. Nor can it be ruled out that Rafsanjani or one of his pragmatic protégés will assume the office of the presidency yet again. The conservatives have a daunting mandate, namely, fixing Iran's economic ills. Should they prove unable to discharge that burden, they may yet face another populist backlash.

However, for the reformers or the pragmatists to take advantage of such an inevitable reaction, they would have to move beyond their inhibitions and transform themselves into a viable oppositional force. As we have seen, at the core level all attempts by both Rafsanjani and Khatami to revise the parameters of the state have faltered in the face of the absolutism of the Supreme Leader and the determination of the ideologues to employ their institutional power. In the end, no reform movement can succeed and no liberal tendency can predominate without another round of constitutional revisions circumscribing the functions of the Supreme Leader and making the office accountable to the citizenry. For the Islamic Republic to change, it has to subordinate its religious dogma to its republican pillar.

Iran's innovative intellectual class is not without ideas about how to proceed and forge new constitutional arrangements designed to foster a more inclusive regime. After all, Iran's constitution has been amended before, most notably in 1989 when the powers of the Supreme Leader were considerably augmented. The problem so far has been an absence of will, coupled with a refusal to engage in protest and confrontation to achieve political aims. There are signs that the most recent repudiation of the reformers and pragmatists by a sullen electorate has finally injected them with a measure of resolution. The so-called anti-fascist front that began to evolve during the presidential campaign uniting the pragmatists and the reformers is beginning to congeal. A younger generation of activists led by reformers such as Muhammad Reza Khatami, the brother of the former president, and Gholam-Hussein Karbaschi, a former mayor of Tehran and a Rafsanjani protégé, are openly discussing the prospects of a common front and examining ideas about how to alter the fundamental contours of the state. A more determined effort, coalescing Iran's factions against the reactionary Right, may yet belie the notion that the conservative manipulations can perpetuate their political monopoly.

As Iran's liberals and pragmatists plot their future, it is important to stress that the only pathway out of the Islamic Republic's current impasse is the restoration of the original draft of the Islamic Republic's constitution, which pledged separation of powers, a strong presidency, and a clear demarcation of responsibilities for the elected institutions. This would be a viable return to the roots of the revolution, as the 1979 mass uprising was designed to forge a new republic, a political order based on pluralism and individual rights. It was a national effort for democratic empowerment of a citizenry long suppressed by an unelected few. In essence, for Iran to reclaim its democratic spirit it must deconstruct Khomeini's political order and dismantle his innovative but ultimately pernicious legacy.

Should Iran's activists manage to construct a system that accommodates both religious convictions and democratic norms, then the Islamic Republic may still emerge as a model of political development for the region. A social revolution is engulfing the theocratic state with notions of representation and accountability, inspiring political action and defining ideological battles. The Iranian populace—the economically stressed middle class, the disenfranchised youth, the reformist clerics, and the persecuted intelligentsia—are rejecting their revolutionary patrimony and demanding a state whose legitimacy is predicated on popular sanction. The governing order that emerges from Iran's tribulations and struggles may finally offer the region a model that draws on the democratic ideals of the West and the cultural traditions of the Middle East.

3

IRAN'S PLACE
IN THE GREATER
MIDDLE EAST

A state's international orientation is shaped by a variety of factors and historic interactions. Cultural traits, ideological aspirations, demographic pressures, and religious convictions are all critical in determining how a country views its environment and its place within its neighborhood. Iran is no exception, since its unique national narrative and Islamic pedigree define its approach to the Greater Middle East.

As with most revolutionary states, Iran has journeyed from being a militant actor challenging regional norms to being a pragmatic state pursuing a policy based on national interest calculations. However, Iran's journey has been halting, incomplete, and tentative. Through the 1980s, under the stern dictates of Ayatollah Khomeini, Iran thrashed about the Middle East, seeking to undermine established authority in the name of Islamic redemption. Khomeini's successors would wrestle with this legacy, as they sought to integrate the theocracy into the global society. From Rafsanjani to Khatami to Ahmadinejad, Iran's presidents would seek the impossible, balancing Khomeini's vision with the mandates of the international community.

The best manner of understanding Iran's regional policy is to envision three circles: the Persian Gulf, the Arab East, and Eurasia. The Persian Gulf would by far be the most significant, while the Arab East and Central Asian lands would assume less importance. The intriguing aspect of Tehran's policy is that while ideology may define its approach toward one of these circles, in the other, careful national-interest determinations would prove its guide. Thus, while in the 1980s the Saudis would decry Iran as a grave fundamentalist threat, Russian diplomats would just as convincingly testify to Tehran's pragmatism and moderation.

In essence, geography and competing interests would do much to moderate Iran's ideological tendencies. Given the fact that Iran's oil is largely exported through the Persian Gulf, the theocracy eventually appreciated the need for stability in this critical region. As such, ideological crusades and terrorist attacks against the Gulf sheikdoms came to an end, and Iran accepted the prevailing status quo. In a similar vein, the theocratic regime recognized the futility of antagonizing its powerful Russian neighbor, and did not inflame the Islamic sentiments in the former Soviet bloc. As the two powers cultivated favorable economic and strategic relations, Iran was provided further incentives for a policy of moderation. However, in the more distant Arab East that neither bordered Iran nor offered it lucrative commercial opportunities, Tehran behaved in a zealous manner and allowed its animosity toward Israel to condition its strategy. The fact remains that Iran's excessive ideological posture toward this region did not infringe on its tangible interests, limiting the need for caution and pragmatism.

Such a bewildering array of policies and priorities has often confounded the international community, making Iran's foreign policy difficult to comprehend. Through a more detailed assessment of the evolution of Iran's regional policy, one can better appreciate why the clerical state has made the decisions that it has and where it is likely to go from here.

THE SOURCES OF IRANIAN CONDUCT

More than any other nation, Iran has always perceived itself as the natural hegemon of its neighborhood. Iranians across generations are infused with a unique sense of their history, the splendor of their civilization, and the power of their celebrated empires. The Achaemenid Empire of the sixth century B.C.E. was, after all, the first global power, reigning over lands that stretched from Greece to India. Subsequent Persian dynasties of Sassanians and Safavids displayed similar imperial reach as they intricately managed vast domains. A sense of superiority over one's neighbors, the benighted Arabs, and the unsophisticated Turks, would define the core of the Persian cosmology. The empire shrank over the centuries, and the embrace of Persian culture faded with the arrival of more alluring Western mores, but a sense of self-perception and an exaggerated view of Iran have remained largely intact. By dint of its history and the power of its civilization, Iranians believe that their nation should establish its regional preeminence.

Yet Iran's nationalistic hubris is married to a sense of insecurity derived from persistent invasion by hostile forces. The humiliating conquests by the Mongol hordes and Arabs have left Iran profoundly suspicious of its neighbors' intentions and motives. Few nations have managed to sustain their cultural distinction and even absorb their conquerors as effectively as the Persians. In due course, Persian scholars, scribes, and bureaucrats would dominate the courts of Arab empires and define their cultural landscape. Nonetheless, such unrelenting incursions with their prolonged periods of occupation have had a traumatic impact, leading Iranians to simultaneously feel superior to and suspicious of their neighbors.

By far, the one set of imperial conquerors that proved the most formidable challenge to Iran were the Western powers. These states could neither be absorbed as the Arabs were, nor did they necessarily defer to Persians for the management of their realm. In a sense, Iran became another victim of the "Great Game," played by the British and the Russians for the domination of Central Asia, and later the intense

Cold War rivalry between America and the Soviet Union. While it is true that Iran was never formally colonized as was India, nor did it undergo a traumatic national liberation struggle as did Algeria, it was still dominated and its sovereignty was still usurped by imperial intrigue. Behind every Shah lay a foreign hand that could empower or humble the Peacock Throne with ease. The Shahs and the parliaments debated and deliberated, but all Iranian politicians had to be mindful of the preferences of the imperial game masters. At times a degree of autonomy would be secured by manipulating great-power rivalries, but this was a precarious exercise, since accommodation usually proved a better path toward self-preservation. The Islamic Republic's stridency and suspicions of the international community can better be understood in the context of Iran's historic subjection and manipulation by outside powers.

However, to ascribe Iran's foreign policy strictly to its sense of nationalism and historical grievances is to ignore the doctrinal foundations of the theocratic regime. Khomeini bequeathed to his successors an ideology whose most salient division was between the oppressors and the oppressed. Such a view stemmed from the Shiite political traditions as a minority sect struggling under Sunni Arab rulers who were often repressive and harsh. Thus the notion of tyranny and suffering has a powerful symbolic aspect as well as practical importance. Iran was not merely a nation seeking independence and autonomy within the existing international system. The Islamic revolution was a struggle between good and evil, a battle waged for moral redemption and genuine emancipation from the cultural and political tentacles of the profane and iniquitous West. Khomeini's ideology and Iran's nationalist aspirations proved reinforcing, creating a revolutionary, populist approach to the regional realities.[1]

The Islamic Republic's inflammatory rhetoric and regional aspirations conceal the reality of Iran's strategic loneliness. Iran is, after all, a Persian state surrounded by non-Persian powers, depriving it of the ethnic and communal ties so prevalent in the Arab world. If durable alliances are predicated on a common vision and shared values, then Iran is destined to remain somewhat insulated from the rest of its region. Nor, until the emergence of the Shiite bloc in Iraq, has religion necessarily mitigated Iran's isolation. Historically, the persecuted Shiites have been held at arm's length by the Sunni Arabs, who harbor their own suspicions of their coreligionists. In a standard Persian self-justification, Iran has tried to turn its isolation into an advantage, since notions of self-sufficiency and self-reliance have had an emotive appeal to a beleaguered populace. Nonetheless, as Iran's rulers look over the horizon, they seldom see a placid landscape or ready-made allies.

Iran is a country of contradictions and paradoxes. It is both grandiose in its self-perception yet intensely insecure. It seeks to lead the region while remaining largely suspicious and disdainful of its neighbors. Its rhetoric is infused with revolutionary dogma, yet its actual conduct is practical, if not realistic. A perennial struggle between aspirations and capabilities, hegemony and pragmatism has characterized Iran's uneasy approach to the Greater Middle East.

FIRST CIRCLE: THE PERSIAN GULF

Despite the mullahs' often-declared pan-Islamic pretensions, the Persian Gulf has always been Iran's foremost strategic priority. The critical waterway constitutes Iran's most direct link to the international petroleum market, the life blood of its economy. Although the issue of Iraq will be addressed later, it is important to note here that Tehran's concerns and aspirations in the Gulf transcend Iraq. The Islamic Republic, as with all its monarchical predecessors, perceived that Iran by the virtue of its size and historical achievements has the right to emerge as the local hegemon. The changing dimensions of Iran's foreign policy are most evident in this area, as revolutionary radicalism has gradually yielded to pragmatic power politics.

Soon after achieving power, Khomeini called on the Gulf states to emulate Iran's revolutionary model and sever relations with the "Great

Satan," the United States. The profligate princely class, the hard-pressed Shiite populations, and these states' dependence on America were all affronts to Iran's revolutionaries. The theocratic state unambiguously declared the monarchical order a source of oppression and tyranny. "Monarchy is one of the most shameful and disgraceful reactionary manifestations," Khomeini declared.[2] An authentic Islamic society could not prevail under the banner of monarchy, because the proper ruling elite were the righteous men of God. Thus, beyond their foreign policy alignments, the character of the Gulf regimes proved a source of objection to Iran's new rulers.[3]

As Iran settled on its course of enmity and radicalism, the Kingdom of Saudi Arabia emerged as the subject of particularly venomous attacks. In a sense, the two states had much in common, as they both predicated their legitimacy on a transnational mission of exporting religion and safeguarding Islam. The natural competition between their contending interpretations of Islam was sufficient to ensure a tense relationship. To this pressure was added Saudi Arabia's close ties to the United States, further fueling Khomeini's already intense antagonism toward the House of Saud. "In this age, which is the age of oppression of the Muslim world at the hands of the U.S. and Russia and their puppets such as al-Sauds, those traitors to the great divine sanctuary must be forcefully cursed," he said.[4] The Iranian revolutionaries saw the Saudis as not just sustaining America's imperial encroachment of the Middle East, but also employing a reactionary interpretation of Islam to sanction their hold on power.[5]

Tehran's mischievous efforts were not without success; in the early 1980s, demonstrations rocked Kuwait, Saudi Arabia, and Bahrain. In the end, however, Iran's revolutionary message proved attractive only to a narrow segment of the minority Shiite population. Even the sporadic Shiite demonstrations were not designed to emulate Iran's revolution, but rather were an expression of the Shiites' economic and political disenfranchisement. The protesters used the specter of Iranian subversion to press their claims and extract needed concessions from the ruling elite. The prevailing regimes, for their part, seemed to appreciate this reality and, after putting down the demonstrations by force, opted for economic rewards as a means of restoring quiescence. This strategy essentially ended Iran's attempt to exploit Shiite grievances to launch a new order. Tehran would subsequently rely on violence and terrorism, practices that were bound to alienate the local populace.

A campaign of bombings, targeting embassies, industrial plants, and even oil installations, was soon attributed to Iranian-sponsored opposition groups. The states that were particularly targeted by Iran's new tactics were those with substantial Shiite populations, namely, Kuwait, Bahrain, and Saudi Arabia. In many cases, the instrument of Iranian terrorism was the al-Dawa Party, which has since become part of the ruling coalition in the post-Saddam Iraq. All this is not to point out the irony of the United States empowering an Iranian-terrorist client, but to suggest that Iran's revolutionary élan faded rapidly, forcing it to rely on terrorist tactics that would succeed in neither overthrowing the incumbent regimes nor enhancing its standing in the international community.[6]

By the time of Khomeini's death in 1989, Iran's revolutionary foreign policy had not achieved any of its objectives. Tehran's attempt to export its revolution had not merely failed, it had led the Gulf states to solidify against Iran. Leading regional actors such as Saudi Arabia severed diplomatic ties with the Islamic Republic, while the sheikdoms put aside their historic enmities and came together in the Gulf Cooperation Council, an organization largely devoted to containing Iranian influence. Along these lines, the Arab princes and monarchs further solidified their security ties to the United States and generously subsidized Saddam Hussein's military in his war with Iran. The revolution without borders seemed uneasily confined within Iran's boundaries.

The 1990s will stand as one of the most important periods of transition for the Islamic Republic. The end of the prolonged war with Iraq and Khomeini's death suddenly shifted focus away from external perils to Iran's domestic quandaries. The specter of invading Iraqi armies had ensured a remarkable degree of political conformity and allowed the regime to mobilize the masses behind its exhortations of national resistance. Khomeini's undisputed authority and his hold on the imagination of the public allowed the state to deflect attention from its domestic deficiencies and feel safe from popular recrimination. The basis of the regime's legitimacy and authority would now have to change; the Islamic Republic had to offer a reason for its rule beyond the catastrophic invasion of its territory and the moral claims of its clerical founder.

Along these lines, Iran's new pragmatic rulers, led by Akbar Hashemi Rafsanjani, began discussing a regional security arrangement whereby the stability of the Gulf would be ensured by the local regimes as opposed to external powers. After Saddam's eviction from Kuwait in 1991 and the deflation of his power, the mullahs perceived a unique opportunity to establish their hegemony in the region. Instead of instigating Shiite uprisings and exhorting the masses to emulate Iran's revolutionary model, Tehran now called for greater economic and security cooperation. However, the success of this ambition was predicated on the withdrawal of American forces. This was to be hegemony on the cheap, with Iran's preeminence recognized, the U.S. presence lessened, and a permanent wedge drawn between Iraq and the Arab Gulf states. The only problem with this proposal was that it remained fundamentally unacceptable to the sheikdoms for whom Saddam's invasion of Kuwait had conveyed the danger of relying on imperious local regimes for their security.[7]

In essence, Iran's new stratagem conflicted with the Gulf states' survival tactics. The sheikdoms, with their perennial concern about the designs of their more powerful and populous neighbors, viewed Tehran's penchant toward collective security with apprehension. Although relations between Iran and the Gulf states did improve in terms of establishment of formal diplomatic ties and volume of trade, the local princes were not about to sever ties with the United States in order to appease Iran. In line with their long-standing historic practice, they sought the protection of external empires against neighboring states that have often coveted their wealth and resources. In the aftermath of the Gulf war, the level of defense cooperation between the United States and the Gulf regimes significantly increased, with America enforcing the containment of Iraq and the no-fly zones from military bases in Saudi Arabia and Kuwait. Whereas in the 1980s Iran's revolutionary radicalism had polarized the Gulf, in the 1990s its insistence that these states share its opposition to the American presence proved a source of division and tension.

Once more, the failure of Iranian ambitions triggered reliance on terrorism and intimidation. If the Gulf leaders refused to sever ties with America, then perhaps violence directed against U.S. troops would lead Washington to voluntarily withdraw from the region. For the clerical regime, as well as much of the Middle East, the American departure from Lebanon after the 1983 bombing of the marine barracks was an indication that the United States was unwilling to accept casualties and that a spectacular act of violence could trigger America's exit. The presence of U.S. troops in Saudi Arabia proved tantalizing to the mullahs, as Riyadh had remained largely aloof from Iran's blandishments. The 1996 bombing of the Khobar Towers, housing American military personnel, has been attributed to Tehran by Washington.[8] Given Iran's policy of pressing for eviction of U.S. forces through acts of violence, this claim has a degree of credibility. As with the Islamic Republic's previous acts of terrorism, once more its strategy of selective violence failed to achieve its ambitions.

In the end, Rafsanjani and his pragmatic allies did not fundamentally harmonize Iran's ties with its neighbors. To be sure, the Islamic Republic did dispense with much of its revolutionary radicalism and began to project the image of a judicious state, basing its policies on careful calculations of national interest. However, Tehran's tense relationship with the United States and its insistence that the Gulf states share its antagonism undermined its own gestures of goodwill. Once Iran fell back on its predictable response of terrorism, it essentially ended the possibility of emerging as a critical player in its immediate neighborhood.

The most momentous change in Iran's regional policy came with the election of the reformist president Muhammad Khatami in 1997. As we have seen, Khatami's international perspective grew out of the debates and deliberations prevalent in Iran's intellectual circles. Many dissident thinkers and clerics were uneasy about the static nature of Iran's foreign policy and its evident inability to respond to the changing global and regional realities. The reformist perspective was not limited to making the theocracy more accountable to its citizenry, but also sought to end the Islamic Republic's pariah status and integrate Iran into global society. As with his political reforms, Khatami was drawing on the works of intellectuals outside a power structure that had grown stagnant and complacent.

In terms of his approach to the Gulf, Khatami appreciated that previous attempts at reconciliation with the sheikdoms had failed due to Iran's dogmatic insistence that they share its hostility to America. In essence, Khatami compartmentalized Iran's relations. Tehran continued to object to the U.S. military presence in the Gulf and persisted in calling for an indigenous network to displace the American armada. The refusal of the Gulf states to embrace Iran's proposals did not, however, trigger a counterreaction and an unleashing of terror. Khatami was willing to normalize relations with the Gulf states despite their attachment to the United States. For all practical purposes, Iran was prepared to live in a Gulf whose balance of power was determined by the United States.

In a remarkable gesture, Ayatollah Khamenei endorsed Khatami's initiative. In a speech to the gathering of Arab dignitaries at the Organization of Islamic Conference's 1997 meeting in Tehran, Khamenei plainly declared, "Iran poses no threat to any Islamic country."[9] Tehran's "Vision Statement," which was approved by Khamenei, recognized the sovereignty of local states and the inviolability of borders, and it pledged noninterference in the internal affairs of the incumbent regimes. The mystery lingers of why Khamenei so fundamentally departed from his established antagonism toward the Gulf princely elite. Certainly, the popular appeal of Khatami in his honeymoon period must have impressed the Supreme Leader to adjust his positions. Despite the fact that Khamenei's powers are not contested by elections or plebiscites, he has always been somewhat sensitive to public opinion and shifts in the popular mood. Moreover, despite his stern ideological predilections, Khamenei has historically exhibited sporadic bouts of pragmatism and may well have sensed that Iran's lingering isolation in its immediate neighborhood was ill serving its interests. Gazing across the region, the Leader may have perceived that Khatami's election offered Iran certain opportunities for mending fences and reconciliation with important states, such as Saudi Arabia. At any rate, Khamenei provided the essential backing that Khatami's diplomacy of reconsideration required.

Khatami's "Good Neighbor" diplomacy finally managed to rehabilitate Iran's ties with the local regimes. An entire range of trade, diplomatic, and security agreements were signed between the Islamic Republic and the Gulf sheikdoms. In this way, Khatami managed finally to transcend Khomeini's legacy and to displace his ideological antagonisms with policies rooted in pragmatism and self-interest. This is the impressive legacy that Iran's unnecessarily maligned president has bequeathed to the reactionaries who have succeeded him.[10]

Today, as a hard-line government consolidates its power and proclaims a desire to return to the roots of the revolution, dire warnings are on the horizon. Both Washington policymakers and their European counterparts seem to suggest that the new regime will once more resort to violence and terror to subvert its neighbors and export its Islamic revolution. Such alarmism overlooks Iran's realities. Under Khatami's auspices, Iran's Gulf policy underwent a fundamental shift, with national interest objectives its defining factor. Irrespective of the balance of power between conservatives and reformers, Iran's regional policy is driven by fixed principles that are shared by all of its political elites.

This perspective will survive Iran's latest leadership transition. Although Ahmadinejad and his allies are determined to reverse the social and cultural freedoms that Iranians have come to enjoy during the reformist tenure, with regard to Persian Gulf issues the new president has stayed within the parameters of Iran's prevailing international policy. In his August 2005 address to the parliament outlining his agenda, President Ahmadinejad echoed the existing consensus, noting the importance of constructive relations with "the Islamic world, the Persian Gulf region, the Caspian Sea region, and Central Asia."[11] Moreover, the most important voice on foreign policy matters, the head of the Supreme National Security Council, Ali Larijani, has reiterated the same themes.[12] Unlike the Iran of the 1980s, Ahmadinejad's Iran has not embarked on attempts to subvert the sheikdoms and has not revived its links to the Gulf terrorist organizations unleashing violence as a means of fostering political change.

Although the assertive nationalists who have taken command of Iran's executive branch have dispensed with their predecessor's "dialogue of civilizations" rhetoric and display a marked suspicion of America, they are loath to jeopardize the successful multilateral détente that was the singular achievement of the reformist era. As far as the Gulf is concerned, Iranians seemed to have finally buried Khomeini's dictates and moved to an era of uncontested pragmatism.

SECOND CIRCLE: THE ARAB EAST

One of the more enduring ideological aspects of the Islamic Republic's international relations has been its policy toward the Arab East. The defining pillar of Iran's approach to this region has been its intense opposition to the state of Israel and the diplomatic efforts to normalize relations between the Jewish state and its neighbors. Iran's strident ideological policy has been buttressed by strategic incentives, as its support for militant groups such as Hezbollah gives it a power to influence the direction of politics in the Levant and inject its voice in deliberations that would otherwise be beyond its control. Unlike the Gulf where geographic proximity compelled Tehran toward a pragmatic search for stability, in the more distant Arab East, Iran feels free to be mischievous and injudicious. Along this path, Iran has made common cause with the radical Syrian regime that shares its antipathy to Israel, while alienating the key Egyptian state that has often sought to resolve the divisive Arab-Israeli conflict. So long as Iran's policy toward the Arab East remains immured in its conflict with Israel, Tehran is unlikely to edge toward the type of pragmatism that it has demonstrated in the Gulf.

On the surface, the high-profile visits and the wide variety of compacts and accords may give the impression that Iran and Syria are intimate allies sharing the same vision and embracing similar priorities. However, the ties between the two states are at best an alliance of convenience based on shared fears and apprehensions. For the past two decades, Iran's persistent animosity toward Israel has coincided with Syria's quest to exert pressure on the Israelis as a means of recovering lands lost during the 1967 war. However, while Iran's policy is driven by Islamist determinations, Syria is propelled forward by cold, strategic calculations. Tehran may view Hezbollah as a vanguard Islamist force struggling against the "Zionist entity," while for Damascus, the Lebanese militant party is just another means of coercing Israel. As such, potential disagreement between the two states looms large. Syria may yet accept an agreement that exchanges recognition of Israel for the recovery of the Golan Heights, while Iran's more ideologically driven hostilities are not predicated on territorial concessions.[13]

Beyond the issue of Israel, Iraq also constitutes a potential source of division between Syria and Iran. During Saddam Hussein's reign, the two powers shared yet another antagonist. The Syrian Ba'ath Party long condemned the so-called revisionism of its Iraqi counterpart and viewed itself as the legitimate representative of the Arab socialist cause. The very secular objections of the Syrian regime were shared by the Iranian mullahs, whose own war with Saddam made them equally hostile to the Iraqi dictator. However, once more there are indications that Iran's lone Arab alliance may not survive the changing politics of the Middle East. Unlike the Iranian theocracy, Syria does not wish to see a further empowerment of religious forces, particularly Shiite actors, in Iraq. As a secular state that has waged a merciless war against its own Islamists, Syria finds the ascendance of religious parties in Iraq particularly disconcerting. As with most of the dynasties and republics of the region, Syria had hoped that Saddam's demise would somehow bring to power yet another Ba'athist amenable to the predilections of the secular Arab bloc. The intriguing aspect of Iraq's current tribulations is the extent to which Iran and Syria are on the opposite sides, with Damascus fueling the largely Sunni insurgency, while Tehran lends its support to the ruling Shiite parties. One state is hoping to destabilize Iraq through continued violence, while the other views the conventional political process as the best means of securing its national objectives.

In yet another paradox of the Middle East, what is increasingly binding Damascus and Tehran together is the Bush administration. The inability or unwillingness of Washington to substantively engage in the Arab-Israeli peace process and craft an agreement acceptable to Syria has made Iran an indispensable partner for Damascus. The relentless pressure brought on both parties by the Bush White House has compelled them to rely on each other as they face yet another common enemy. Nonetheless, developments in the region during the next several years may yet disentangle ties between these two unlikely allies. In the end, as a state that neighbors Israel, Syria will one day have to accept a territorial compromise with the Jewish state and end its prolonged and self-defeating conflict. However, an Iran that is beyond the reach of Israeli armor can afford its militancy and persist with its ideologically determined policies. In the meantime, as a secular state Syria may find Iran's new Shiite allies in Iraq as objectionable as do the Saudis and Jordanians, who are loudly decrying the emergence of the "Shiite Crescent." As the Middle East increasingly polarizes along sectarian lines, Syria will have to choose between its contentious alliance with Iran and its alignment of interest with the larger Arab bloc.

Whatever the vagaries of the Iranian-Syrian alliance, Egypt remains the epicenter of Arab politics. Egypt's population now exceeds that of the rest of the Arab East, and its geographic size dwarfs peripheral states such as Lebanon and Jordan. Moreover, Egypt's encounter with modernization is the longest, its industrial and educational structures the most extensive, and its cultural and intellectual output the most prolific. Cairo's influence has ebbed and flowed over the years, but it is hard to imagine Arab cohesion without its active leadership. Iran's tense relation with Egypt has drastically limited its influence in the Arab East. No alliance with Syria or patronage of Hezbollah can compensate for Tehran's estrangement from the most pivotal state in the region.[14]

Although many in the United States are accustomed to perceiving Iran as unrelentingly hostile to America, during the early part of the revolution, Iran's animosities were distributed more widely. For Khomeini and his followers, no leader symbolized the pusillanimity of the Arab political class more than the Egyptian president, Anwar al-Sadat. The Camp David Accords ending Egypt's hostility toward Israel were bitterly denounced by Iranian clerics as a gesture of un-Islamic behavior, even apostasy. For Khomeini, the accords proved that Sadat was the purveyor of "false Islam" and an agent of Zionism. Sadat's warm embrace of the exiled Shah (who spent the last days of his life in Egypt) further enraged the reigning Iranian clerics. Tehran's crass celebration of Sadat's assassin by naming a prominent street after him and even issuing a stamp commemorating the occasion in turn infuriated an Egyptian ruling elite that was already anxious about the potential of Iran's revolutionary Islam. These early policies established a certain legacy for Iran's relations with Egypt that would prove difficult to surmount. In the intervening decades, other events would intrude, buttressing the legacy of mistrust and animosity.[15]

The Iran-Iraq war further added fuel to the Iranian-Egyptian antagonism. For Cairo, which was ostracized by the Arab bloc because of its reconciliation with Israel, the war offered a unique opportunity to reassert its Arabism and to mend ties with its erstwhile allies. Soon after the war began, Egypt started furnishing arms to Iraq despite the fact that the two powers had spent decades bitterly vying for the leadership of the Middle East. Beyond exploiting an opportunity to return to the Arab fold, Cairo's policy was designed to contain Iran's revolution within its borders. An Iran that was preoccupied with the daunting challenges of a prolonged war was bound to be a less mischievous state. For the Islamic Republic, such policies were tantamount to Egypt effectively joining the war, congealing the clerical class's enmity toward Cairo.

The aftermath of the war did not necessarily lead to a thaw in relations. The 1990s witnessed yet another radical divergence of perspectives between Tehran and Cairo. For the United States and Egypt, the defeat of Saddam's armies constituted an ideal time to resolve the Arab-Israeli conflict, while Iran perceived the time ripe for the advancement of its Islamic model. Militant Islam seemed an ideology on the ascendance, with Islamic Jihad challenging the Egyptian regime, Hezbollah assuming a greater prominence in Lebanese politics, and the Islamic Salvation Front triumphing in democratic elections in Algeria. The Palestinian resistance that had historically been led by secular leftist parties was increasingly being spearheaded by violent Islamist organizations such as Hamas. For the Iranian mullahs, it seemed that the region was finally embracing Khomeini's message. While the Egyptian state was seeking to stabilize its domestic situation and persuade the Arab states to follow its path of reconciliation with Israel, Iran was actively promoting the fortunes of the emboldened Islamists.

In a sense, Egyptian president Hosni Mubarak's blaming of Iran for the surge of fundamentalism in Egypt and the wider Middle East was self-serving and convenient. Egypt has long struggled with Islamic radicalism and the roots of the Islamist rage lay deep in the Egyptian society. After all, the most significant fundamentalist party in the Middle East, the Muslim Brotherhood, was born in Egypt in the 1930s, and since then has found a ready audience across the region.[16] The fascination with Wahhabi Islam ought not obscure the fact that the intellectual and tactical architects of al-Qaeda are mostly Egyptians, led by the notorious second-in-command, Ayman al-Zawahiri.[17] Nonetheless, even the modest support that Iran offered Egypt's religious extremists was sufficient to antagonize an Egyptian state that in the early 1990s was battling a serious Islamic insurrection.

During the Khatami era there were attempts to relax the tensions with Egypt. However, it appeared that such normalization was not a top priority for either state. Khatami's internal struggles and his attempts to reach out to the United States were sufficiently contentious to preclude yet another provocative diplomatic foray. In the meantime, the Mubarak regime was struggling with its own domestic challenges and with a foundering peace process, and so it was also disinclined to move forward aggressively.

Today the relations between the two states may not be as inflammatory as during the early periods of the revolution, but they seem frozen in time, as neither side seems inclined to press ahead. The hard-line Ahmadinejad regime is unlikely to seek a new opening, as many conservatives in Iran have yet to forgive Egypt for the Camp David Accords. The reactionary newspaper *Jomhuri-ye Islami* captured the sentiment of many on the Right: "Any form of political relations with Hosni Mubarak is tantamount to getting digested into the system prepared and designed by America and Zionism in the region."[18] Given such sentiment within his support base, it is unlikely that Ahmadinejad can move forward toward more proper relations, even if he were so inclined.

In the Persian Gulf, the Islamic Republic finally appreciated after years of revolutionary radicalism that it could not have suitable relations with the Gulf sheikdoms unless it first came to terms with Saudi Arabia. Such lessons have yet to be fully absorbed by the Iranian elite when it comes to the Arab East. The reality is that Iran cannot be part of the larger Middle Eastern landscape until it rationalizes its relations with Egypt. Tactical alliances with a beleaguered Syrian regime and patronage of terrorist organizations such as Hezbollah will not ease Iran's path to the heart of the Arab world. Tehran can be mischievous and use terrorism and violence as a means of attracting attention to its claims and obstructing peace initiatives between Israel and the

Arab bloc. But for Iran to assert its influence in the region it has to have a more constructive agenda than prefabricated Islamist slogans and hostility to the Jewish state. Hovering over all this is the gradual fracturing of the Middle East along sectarian lines, with Shiite Iran increasingly pitted against the alarmed Sunni powers. The Islamic Republic may emerge as a critical player in its immediate neighborhood, but as a non-Arab, Shiite state it is unlikely ever to become a significant actor in the Arab East.

THIRD CIRCLE: EURASIA

In contrast to its policy toward the Persian Gulf and the Arab East, Iran's approach toward its northern and eastern neighbors has been one of sustained realism. The proximity to a strong Russian state and the prospect of commercial contracts and important arms deals has always injected a measure of pragmatism in Iran's policy. In a curious manner, despite its declared mission of exporting the revolution, the Islamic Republic has seemed perennially indifferent to the plight of the struggling Muslims in Central Asia. A beleaguered Iranian state requiring arms and trade and an aggrieved former superpower seeking profits and relevance have forged an opportunistic relationship that eschews ideology for the sake of tangible interests. Nor is such pragmatism unique to Russia; as when the theocracy looked to Afghanistan, its priority was always stability, not Islamic salvation. In essence, the fears of being isolated in the international arena and having Afghan troubles seep over its borders have compelled Iran's theocratic oligarchs to transcend their ideological exhortations and focus on achieving their practical objectives in the vast Eurasian landmass.

On the eve of the Islamic Revolution, Iran's prevailing foreign policy slogan was "Neither East nor West." Khomeini was as contemptuous of Soviet Communism as he was of Western liberalism, and he often denounced the Soviet Union in harsh and unyielding terms. Iran vocally condemned the Soviet invasion of Afghanistan and materially assisted the mujahedin's resistance to the occupation. On the domestic front, the mullahs relentlessly persecuted the Communist Tudeh Party and other leftist forces attracted to the Soviet model. For its part, Moscow proved a generous supplier of arms to Saddam Hussein, as he waged his war of aggression against Iran, and often supported Iraq against Iran in various international forums.

Yet even as tensions were simmering, both sides seemed to veer away from active confrontation as trade between the two powers continued to increase, and the Soviet Union was never without an extensive diplomatic representation in Tehran. In a manner radically different from its approach to the United States, the theocratic regime seemed to appreciate that its geographic proximity to the Soviet Union and its estrangement from the West required a more realistic relationship with Moscow. The two sides would often differ, as they did on critical issues of Afghanistan and Iraq, yet somehow Khomeini managed to suppress his ideological animosities and pursue ties with the Soviet state that seemed beneficial to Iran's overall interests.[19]

The collapse of the Soviet Union in 1991 and the rise of the Russian Federation ushered in a new regional policy in Moscow. The Soviet state had been inordinately invested in the fortunes of radical Arab regimes and shared their concerns regarding developments in the Arab-Israeli arena. For the new masters of the Kremlin, the direction of the newly independent Central Asian republics and the nature of Islamic awakenings in that region were far more relevant than the plight of the Soviet Union's Arab clients. The stability of the Russian frontier was now partly contingent on Tehran resisting the impulse to inflame Islamic sentiments in Central Asia. Moreover, with its imperial reach dramatically contracted and the country in dire need of hard currency, Russia began to auction off its military hardware to the highest bidder. Iran proved a tempting market for Russian arms merchants, since it possessed both cash and a seemingly insatiable appetite for military equipment.[20]

The Islamic Republic had to make its own set of adjustments to the collapse of the Soviet Union and the emergence of Central Asia. During the Soviet era, Iran propagated its Islamic message over the airways in a variety of local languages without evident anticipation that it would have any impact. Such limited propaganda effort satiated its ideological imperatives without unduly straining its relations with its powerful neighbor. But the collapse of the Soviet empire and the independence of the Central Asian republics presented Iran with the need for circumspection. The Islamic Republic had to balance its strategic ties with Russia with its declared mission of exporting its revolutionary template to new, fertile grounds. In a unique display of judiciousness, Iran largely tempered its ideology, essentially denoting the importance of trade and stability over propagation of its Islamic message.[21]

The full scope of Iran's pragmatism became evident during the Chechnya conflict. At a time when the Russian soldiers were indiscriminately massacring Muslim rebels and aggressively suppressing an Islamic insurgency, Iran's response was a mere statement declaring the issue to be an internal Russian affair. At times, when Russia's behavior was particularly egregious, Iran's statements would be harsher. However, Tehran never undertook practical measures such as dispatching aid to the rebels or organizing the Islamic bloc against Moscow's policy. Given that Iran had calculated that its national interests lay in not excessively antagonizing the Russian Federation, it largely ignored the plight of the Chechens despite the Islamic appeal of their cause.[22]

The Chechnya issue reveals that during the past decade, a tacit yet important bargain has evolved between Russia and Iran. The Islamic Republic has emerged as Russia's most important partner in the Middle East and as a valuable market for its cash-starved defense industries. Although in recent years the nuclear cooperation between the two states has garnered much attention, the more significant fact is that Russia has also been willing to sell Iran a vast quantity of conventional arms, including sophisticated aircraft and submarines. Iran, on the other hand, has kept a low profile in Central Asia and has refrained from destabilizing a region critical to Russia's security. This important relationship has led Moscow to provide Iran indispensable diplomatic support, particularly at a time when its nuclear portfolio is being addressed in a variety of international organizations. The United States, hoping to garner Russian support for its policy of sanctioning and ostracizing Iran, would be wise to consider the overall nature of relations between Moscow and Tehran. Given that reality, the notion that Russia would assist in applying significant economic pressure on Iran for its nuclear infractions is far-fetched and fanciful.

A similar penchant toward national interest calculations has defined Iran's policy toward Afghanistan, its neighbor to the east. Despite Iran's close linguistic and cultural ties to Afghanistan, relations between the two countries have not always been simple. The fiercely independent Afghan tribes have historically resisted Persian encroachment and have jealously guarded their rights. Tehran's most natural allies are found in the province of Herat, where proximity to Iran and a large Shiite population have encouraged the establishment of close relations. But for Tehran the issue in Afghanistan has not been ideological conformity but stability. Since assuming power, the theocracy has looked warily upon its neighbor with its war against the Red Army, the rise of Taliban fundamentalism, and, finally, the American invasion. Afghanistan's tribal identity, ethnic diversity, and largely Sunni population have made it an uneasy place for implanting the Islamic Republic's revolutionary message. And, to its credit, Iran has not been active in seeking to export its governing template to its troubled neighbor.

During much of the 1980s, Iran's policy toward Afghanistan was opposition to the Communist regime and assisting forces battling the Soviet occupation. In yet another uneasy paradox, this decade saw a rough coincidence of objectives between Iran and the United States as both parties had an interest in holding back Soviet power in Southwest Asia. Although Khomeini attempted to justify this policy on Islamic grounds, the instability of the war and the extension of Soviet influence southward offered sufficient strategic justification for Iran's conduct. At a time when Iran was housing nearly two million Afghan refugees, the clerical state understood that it could not afford a failed state next door.[23]

In a similar manner, Iran had to endure the prolonged years of Taliban rule. The radical Sunni regime that waged a merciless war against Afghanistan's intricate tribal system and routinely massacred Shiites provided a formidable challenge for the Islamic Republic. In the summer of 1998, the killing of ten Iranian diplomats by Taliban forces in Mazar-i-Sharif nearly led the two states to go to war. Beyond active confrontation, Iran was extraordinarily alarmed by the puritanical Taliban regime's reliance on the drug trade and on Sunni terrorist organizations such as al-Qaeda to sustain its power. Today a large portion of Afghan drugs end up in Iran, creating its own addiction crisis; it is estimated that the Islamic Republic may have as many as two million drug addicts. Given these realities, Iran soon emerged as the most durable foe of the Taliban. Indeed, despite the presence of American forces in Afghanistan since 2001, the theocratic regime finds the existing configuration of power whereby Sunni militancy is largely tempered and a benign government reigns in Kabul an acceptable outcome.[24]

While Iran's relations with Afghanistan have improved over the years, its ties to Pakistan have at times been problematic. The Pakistani policy of using Afghanistan as a conduit for assertion of influence over Central Asia has greatly troubled Iran.[25] At a time when the Bush administration loudly proclaims Pakistan a valuable ally in its "war against terror," it conveniently neglects the fact that it was Islamabad that sustained the Taliban and tolerated its al-Qaeda ally. The cynical Pakistani policy of unleashing the Taliban upon the hapless Afghan nation as a means of securing a bridge to Central Asia confronted Iran with a pronounced strategic threat. Since the demise of the Taliban, the relations between the two powers have markedly improved, since the issue of Afghanistan no longer divides them. However, Iran remains concerned about the internal stability of the

Pakistani state, with its ample nuclear depositories. From Tehran's perspective, the prospect of a radical Sunni regime coming to power in Pakistan with its finger on the nuclear button is nearly an existential threat. As such, once more stability is the guide of Iran's policy toward yet another unpredictable neighbor.

It may come as a shock to the casual observer accustomed to American officials' incendiary denunciations of Iran as a revisionist ideological power to learn that, in various important regions, the Islamic Republic's policy has historically been conditioned by pragmatism. Iran's approach to the Persian Gulf sheikdoms and its Eurasian neighbors today is predicated on national interest designs that are largely devoid of Islamic content. The need for stability on its frontiers and the recognition of the importance of its strategic relationship with Russia have pressed Tehran toward behaving with moderation in its immediate environment. The same cannot be asserted in the case of the Arab East; the theocratic state's dogmatic opposition to the state of Israel has deprived its policy of the nuance and flexibility that has characterized its approach to many of its neighboring states. It is likely that this central contradiction in Iran's regional policy will persist, as Tehran may continue with its perplexing mixture of radicalism and moderation, pragmatism and defiance.

In formulating its regional vision, the Islamic Republic has tried to marry two disparate strands of Iran's identity: Persian nationalism and Shiite Islam. As a great civilization with a keen sense of history, Iran has always perceived itself as the rightful leader of the Middle East. For centuries, Persian empires dominated the political and cultural landscape of the region, inspiring a national narrative that views Iran's hegemony as both beneficial and benign. At the same time, as a persecuted religious minority, Shiites in Iran have always been suspicious and wary of their neighbors. The reality of rising Arab states, domineering Western empires, and Iran's religious exceptionalism has not ended Tehran's perception of itself as the "center of the universe," a society that should be emulated by the Arab masses. Successive Persian monarchs and reigning mullahs would subscribe to this national self-perception, giving Tehran an inflated view of its historic importance.

A final important factor that has intruded itself uneasily in Iran's international orientation is pragmatism. Iran may perceive itself as uniquely aggrieved by the great powers' machinations and it may nurse aspirations to emerge as the regional leader. However, the limitations of its resources and the reality of its actual power have sporadically led to reappraisal and retrenchment. The intriguing aspect of Iran's policy is that it can be both dogmatic and flexible at the same time. The Islamic Republic may take an ideologically uncompromising position toward Israel, yet pragmatically deal with its historic Russian nemesis. The tensions between Iran's ideals and interests, between its aspirations and limits, will continue to produce a foreign policy that is often inconsistent and contradictory.

4

TURNING POINTS
IN U.S.–IRANIAN
RELATIONS

——————

At the height of the hostage crisis, President Jimmy Carter's chief of staff, Hamilton Jordan, was having another secret meeting with Iran's foreign minister, Sadeqh Ghotbzadeh, in the suburbs of Paris. After a series of talks, both men instinctively knew that their delicate diplomatic dance was coming to an end. As the two jaded officials departed for the last time, Ghotbzadeh turned to Jordan and breezily declared, "You know, we came close." Indeed, relations between the United States and Iran have often come close, but somehow never managed to transcend the enduring animosities and suspicions.

A look back at the entangled ties between Iran and the United States reveals a series of critical turning points, watershed events whose impact would persist. The relationship between America and Iran has witnessed its fair share of tension, drama, and missed diplomatic opportunities. However, in selecting events that have fundamentally transformed this relationship, one must choose more carefully and focus on incidents that have left a permanent imprint. I have identified four such episodes, leaving behind many others that, although crucial, were not of enduring significance.

One of America's first acts as a great power in the Middle East was the overthrow in August 1953 of the nationalist Iranian prime minster Muhammad Mossadeq in the name of Communist containment. Over the decades, as history faded into mythology, Mossadeq would assume a commanding presence in the Iranian imagination. To this day, many Iranians believe that an opportunity to forge a new independent and nonaligned foreign policy, employ natural resources for national development, and build a democracy were all lost due to the machinations of a rapacious superpower. The charge, however exaggerated, is not without merit, as American intervention did obstruct the progressive trajectory of Iranian politics. The events of 1953 have created an emotional barrier for Iran's masses and have made them inherently suspicious of American motives and conduct. The United States was once genuinely seen as a depository of idealism, a great power that resisted temptations of imperial aggrandizement. After August 1953, few Iranians would hold such a pristine image of America.

A quarter-century later, Iran's populist revolution ushered in a theocracy determined to confront and defy the "Great Satan." Such defiance soon manifested itself through the hostage crisis, as the revolutionary regime held captive fifty-two American diplomats for fourteen months. The ferocity and ambition of Iran's revolutionaries was a new phenomenon for the American people. To be sure, the United States had grown used to being demonized in Third World capitals, but the mullahs fundamentally challenged the paradigm of interstate relations. During 1979, Americans seemed transfixed by daily images of clerics denouncing their country as sacrilegious, while frenzied crowds routinely commemorated their national events with chants of "Death to America." The American public could not comprehend the turbaned Old Testament–like figures who repudiated their country, its values, and its traditions. A certain perception of the Islamic Republic soon congealed in the popular imagination, transforming Iran from a strategic quandary to a hated country that had managed to emasculate the American colossus with impunity.

The one sustained attempt by the United States to reach out to Iran, the infamous Iran-Contra affair of the mid-1980s, was simplistic in its assumptions and undermined by the connection to the Nicaraguan rebels. The scandal of arms for hostages tainted the reputation of one of the most popular presidents in the postwar period, destroyed the careers of many officials, and greatly embarrassed the United States. The Iran-Contra affair is no passing episode, as subsequent administrations have been particularly gun-shy about approaching Iran, a nation generally regarded by the American people as poisonous. Any notion of engagement with Iran was sacrificed on the altar of bureaucratic expediency and self-preservation. It was simply convenient to sustain a policy of containment, however flawed and ineffective that approach may have been. It was such politically sensitive caution that caused the Clinton administration to miss one of the rare opportunities to fundamentally alter the parameters between the two countries.

The tragedy of the current impasse in U.S.–Iranian relations is that despite half a century of intrigue and acrimony, the Iranian people still admire American values, ingenuity, and industrial prowess. Americans with firsthand knowledge of Iran have similarly come to appreciate the generosity of the Persian culture and the many lures of this ancient land. In yet another paradox, the hostile relations between the two powers often conceals the extent to which their strategic objectives coincide in the region. From the stabilization of Afghanistan and the volatile Persian Gulf region to diminishing Sunni militancy, the two antagonists at times find themselves uneasily on the same side. Should the diplomats and politicians ever manage to dismantle the "wall of mistrust" separating these two nations, they can take an important step toward creating a new Middle East.

MOSSADEQ AND THE POLITICS OF INTERVENTION

In August 2005, Iranian newspapers reported yet another gathering of historians to discuss the ramifications of the 1953 coup that overthrew the nationalist prime minister Muhammad Mossadeq.[1] The specific theme to be explored was whether the coup retarded the development of democracy in Iran. The fact that a meeting of historians dealing with an event that took place five decades ago would garner such prominent news coverage may seem incomprehensible to an American audience, with its limited historical memory. For Iranians, however, history is a living enterprise, and no event has been more repeatedly assessed than the American complicity in the demise of Mossadeq's government. The 1953 coup stands as a formative event, as myth and history have combined to concoct a narrative that continues to bedevil U.S.–Iranian relations.

In the years following World War II, Iran was a devastated country, barely recovering from famine and starvation and subsisting on meager American handouts.[2] Ironically, Iran was also a wealthy country, with ample oil reserves that were fueling the engines of the British Empire. Much of Iran's oil was controlled by the Anglo-Iranian Oil Company (AIOC), whose majority shareholder was the British government. By 1950, the AIOC's annual profits from Iranian oil amounted to 200 million pounds while Iran's share of the revenues was a mere 16 million.[3] The AIOC's oil concessions had been negotiated in the early twentieth century, when the British lion imperiously roamed the Middle East, coaxing local monarchs and princes to acquiesce to its whims. In the early 1950s, when assertive nationalism was sweeping the emerging Third World, such anachronistic colonial arrangements seemed not only iniquitous but undignified.[4]

Iran's original demands were modest and focused on a more generous profit-sharing arrangement and better working conditions for Iranian laborers living in squalid conditions. At a time when the American oil firms were offering 50-50 profit-sharing deals to the governments of Saudi Arabia and Venezuela, Iran perceived that it could demand no less.[5] Accustomed to their profits and fearing that such concessions would establish an improper precedent for their global holdings, the AIOC and the British government demurred. The best that Iran could get was an additional four million pounds per year and further pledges for improvement of working conditions. Before World War II,

Britain could have dictated terms like this with impunity, but the problem in the early 1950s was that nationalism was now the defining ideology of the developing world, a fact the British failed to recognize in dealing with Iran. This failure to acquiesce to the prevailing winds of change would embroil Britain in a crisis that a more imaginative policy may have averted.

The oil controversy inevitably provoked a political crisis inside Iran. The young Shah, eager to consolidate his rule and perennially in search of Western benefactors, was inclined to accept the British proposal. An array of conservative forces, ranging from large landlords to court politicians on the British payroll, similarly seemed amenable, giving AIOC's executives the illusion of control. This was a grave misreading of the popular and parliamentary mood, as Iran was about to enter one of the most acute crises in its history.

The provocative and callous British conduct only managed to unite the differing strands of Iranian opposition into a remarkable coalition, the National Front.[6] The National Front was essentially composed of liberal reformers, the intelligentsia, elements of the clerical class, socialist activists, and middle-class professionals. It is important to appreciate that the demands of the National Front soon transcended the oil issue as the party pressed for a more representative government with constitutional demarcations of power. The National Front government that emerged sought to improve public education and establish an accessible health system. Its proposed judicial reforms were designed to ensure equality before the law, while its efforts to broaden the prerogatives of the local governments were intended to decentralize power. This was not just a movement to reclaim Iran's resources, but a new progressive alliance seeking to revamp Iranian society and government.[7]

The politician who emerged at the heart of this movement was the prominent parliamentarian Muhammad Mossadeq. Born into an aristocratic family and educated in Switzerland, Mossadeq belonged to a narrow class of Iranian elite that considered high government office its patrimony. Respectful of the monarchy and the traditions of its class, this cohort would constitute the cabinets, parliaments, and civil service that ruled Iran. An ardent nationalist, Mossadeq was dubious of foreign control and came to articulate the concept of "negative equilibrium," under which Iran would preserve its autonomy by playing off one empire against another. A man prone to the histrionics of Persian politics, he would weep while making speeches, feign illness, and play the part of a fragile old man. To Iranians such theatrics were comprehensible, but to an international audience accustomed to a more stoic class of politicians, Mossadeq appeared eccentric, even bizarre. All this should not discount the fact that Mossadeq was a genuine patriot seeking to emancipate his country from the clutches of the British Empire.[8]

The continued British obstinacy further antagonized Iranian nationalistic feelings, eroding the consensus behind the 50-50 profit-sharing arrangement. The minority position in the parliament, led by Mossadeq, had been pressing for outright nationalization of the oil industry, and now it gained strength. On April 30, 1951, the Iranian parliament passed the nationalization bill, defying the monarch and propelling Mossadeq to the post of the prime minister. Had Britain been more imaginative in its recognition that it was impossible to rebuff Iran's demands—particularly in light of the arrangements that the United States was offering to countries where it operated its oil industry—and embarked on a more generous package, the crisis might have been averted. But the imperial arrogance of the British government and the rapacious nature of the AIOC had inexorably radicalized Iranian politics.

In terms of dealing with Mossadeq's challenge, the British contemplated a policy of what we would now call "regime change." Britain imposed a stringent embargo on Iran's oil, depriving Tehran of much of its revenues. The AIOC's announcement that it would take legal action against anyone seeking to purchase Iran's oil proved a sufficient deterrent to many international oil firms, who were already wary of Tehran's nationalization act. In the meantime, the departure of British technicians essentially crippled the Iranian oil industry. It was hoped in Whitehall that by undermining Iran's fragile economy and depriving it of its oil revenues, sufficient popular pressure could be generated, leading in due course to Mossadeq's overthrow. For good measure, the British intelligence services also began covert planning and mobilizing their ample assets in Iran.

The notion of a malevolent America plotting against Iran conceals much about the actual course of events in the Mossadeq crisis. The Truman administration appreciated the shortcomings of the British strategy and pressed London to accept Iran's legitimate demands. As for Iran, successive American diplomats led by the indefatigable Averell Harriman sought to similarly adjust Mossadeq's positions and make the prime minister realize that a dogmatic assertion of Iran's rights was unlikely to resolve the dispute. In the initial stages, America played the role of mediator, pressing both sides toward accommodation and compromise. The Truman administration sustained its assistance to Iran, which helped ease the pain of British economic sanctions, and it was instrumental in dissuading Britain from precipitous military action, seeking instead to craft a negotiated solution somehow acceptable to both parties.[9] The United States has much to account for in its later behavior during the nationalization crisis, but Truman's efforts on behalf of Iran should also be acknowledged.

Despite ample efforts, the American mediation diplomacy was increasingly frustrated by the political ferment that was sweeping Iran. As Mossadeq proceeded to galvanize the public, the prospects of a compromise vanished. The prime minister's absolutist rhetoric and his pledges to end British influence created political conditions militating against a judicious resolution of the crisis. The reality was that the British had the capacity to shut down Iran's oil industry, depriving the country of its essential source of revenue.[10] Unlike today, the Iranian oil was not critical to the global petroleum market, making the British sanctions policy more tolerable for the international community. At any rate, Mossadeq had a great capacity for mobilizing diverse national forces, but only a limited ability for crafting a negotiating position that could be acceptable to his powerful and increasingly unyielding adversary. Both parties in the conflict proved inflexible in their views, parochial in defining their interests, and overly sensitive to the political ramifications of any deal. For Britain, Iran's nationalization act remained an illegal expropriation of private property, while for Iran it was a legitimate reclamation of a natural resource long exploited by a greedy foreign company. As both sides became entrenched in their principles, the prospect of mutual agreement seemed far-fetched. The only difference was that the British could better afford their intransigence than a poverty-stricken country deprived of its indispensable source of subsistence.

As the crisis enveloping Iran intensified, Mossadeq behaved in an increasingly autocratic manner, extending his powers through contrived referendums, dispensing with the parliament, seeking the assumption of the war ministry, and usurping the prerogatives of the monarchy. At his core, Mossadeq was a principled politician with deep reverence for Iran's institutions and constitutional arrangements. But the pressure of governing at a time of deepening crisis accentuated the more troubling aspects of his character. Suddenly the champion of democratic reform and accountable government seemed to indulge in a type of arbitrary behavior that he had spent much of his political career condemning.

Iran's escalating economic crisis also began to fracture the National Front coalition. The middle-class elements, concerned about their declining economic fortunes, gradually began to abandon Mossadeq. In the meantime, the intelligentsia and the professional classes were also increasingly wary of the prime minister's autocratic tendencies and looked for an alternative leadership. A number of smaller political parties that had been associated with Mossadeq's movement were also contemplating their own exit. Even more ominous, the armed forces that had stayed quiet despite Mossadeq's periodic purges of the senior officer corps now grew vocal and began to participate in political intrigues.

Among Mossadeq's coalition partners, the clergy would play the most curious role. As with most historical events, the Islamic Republic has been conveniently selective in its recapitulation of this episode and has neglected the role that the clerical community played in Mossadeq's demise. The senior clerics' approach toward the enveloping nationalist struggle was always one of disengagement.[11] The clergy were traditionally uneasy about the modernizing penchants of secular politicians such as Mossadeq and their quests for republican rule and liberalization of the existing institutions. The mullahs preferred the deference of a conservative and uncertain monarch than the secular enterprise of Mossadeq and the National Front. However, given the popularity of the nationalist cause, they recoiled from outright opposition, remaining diffident. To be sure, not all clerical leaders would accept such quietism, as Khomeini chafed under such restrictions, but still acceded to the determinations of the senior clergy. The banner of clerical opposition would be led by the opportunistic Ayatollah Abdolqasem Kashani, who sensed a chance for self-aggrandizement. In due course, Kashani would switch his allegiances and prove instrumental in Mossadeq's downfall. The Islamic Republic's perennial demand for an American apology over its complicity in the 1953 coup ought not to obscure the fact that the clerical community was either indifferent or actively conspired against Mossadeq.

As Mossadeq increasingly stood isolated, in yet another miscalculation he invoked the Communist threat as a means of extracting American concessions. In a dramatic note to the United States, Mossadeq implored, "If prompt and effective aid is not given this country now, any steps that might be taken tomorrow to compensate for negligence of today might well be too late."[12] The premier perceived that as Iran's economy suffered and fears of Communist takeover gripped Washington, the United States would abandon Britain and rescue him from his predicament. Perversely, he now brandished the Communist threat as a means of compelling assistance from the United States. Mossadeq failed to appreciate that Communist subversion would only lead the United States to embrace Britain, its intimate Cold War ally, and oppose Iran's nationalistic intransigence. For Mossadeq, as for many of his countrymen, Iran was the center of the universe, and he assumed that the great powers would gladly accede to his country's demands. Indeed, such a distorted sense of Iran was not limited to Mossadeq but is an enduring Persian conceit.

By 1953, as the oil crisis entered its third year, a combination of events would lead the United States to contemplate Mossadeq's overthrow. A new president, Dwight D. Eisenhower, came to power with a determination to wage a more aggressive Cold War, and his administration displayed a marked suspicion of Third World neutralism.[13] Eisenhower and his hawkish secretary of state John Foster Dulles proved more sensitive to the British assertion that only a change in the Iranian regime could resolve the impasse.[14] This claim seemed even more compelling as the economic situation deteriorated, which seemed to empower the Communist Tudeh Party that the prime minister was both brandishing as a threat and increasingly relying on as a coalition partner. In retrospect, Tudeh had little capacity to dislodge Mossadeq, since its radicalism remained unacceptable to many parts of Iranian society.[15] But in America's zero-sum Cold War rivalry with the Soviet Union, Third World nationalist struggles were too often subsumed in the framework of the containment policy. Mossadeq became just one more victim of the stark Cold War duality—that every government was either "with us or against us."

The drama of CIA officers clandestinely plotting the coup against Mossadeq has been breathlessly told many times, and further repetition is not needed here. The cast of characters is indeed bewildering: Kermit Roosevelt, the scion of America's foremost political family, paying street thugs to agitate against the hapless Mossadeq; American operatives shoring up an indecisive monarch to return to Tehran from his exile in Rome and reclaim his throne; Communist agitators and clerical firebrands struggling under the same banner and participating in demonstrations financed by the United States and Britain. As Iran veered from crisis to crisis, the armed forces finally stepped in and ended Mossadeq's brief but momentous tenure. The famed Operation Ajax would stand as one of the most effective of CIA's covert enterprises, leading Washington to perceive that it could easily replicate its success elsewhere.[16]

As with most political narratives, there exists a gap between the historical figure of Mossadeq and the evolved myth. Mossadeq was indeed a principled politician, yet the temptations of power at times led him to electoral manipulations. He was a determined nationalist whose quest for popular acclaim blinded him to a compromised solution that might have resolved the stalemate with Britain and sustained Iran's economy. Mossadeq was certainly toppled due to American machinations, yet by 1953 his coalition had so frayed that it was hard to see how he could maintain his hold on power. As with most politicians, he was a complex, contradictory figure who was shaped by historical forces not all his choosing. However, in the contemporary Iranian political imagination he remains a promising democrat, subverted by a malicious America. Iranians continue to believe that their country may have forged a nationalist path, reclaimed its resources from foreign exploitation, and escaped the tentacles of a despotic monarchy had it not been for American manipulations. Such claims are not entirely fanciful, as an expeditious resolution of the oil crisis may have averted the coup and even propelled Iran toward a more progressive political path. It is impossible to say with certainty how history would have evolved, yet such certainty is the mainstay of the Iranian memory of 1953.

In a sense, the coup of 1953 made the Islamic Revolution of 1979 possible, even predictable. Having survived a pronounced threat to his rule, the Shah proceeded to create a rigid authoritarian state, relying on an extensive secret police apparatus to maintain order. The coup essentially destroyed the delicate internal balance of power, with the monarchy coexisting with assertive parliaments and prime ministers. The National Front that was the main engine of the modern middle class's aspirations was effectively crushed when the monarchy proved relentlessly hostile to leftist and moderate political parties. As the secular opposition was repressed and its leaders and politicians imprisoned, the clerical establishment emerged as the main venue of opposition politics. As we have seen, the clerical community largely stayed out of the 1953 nationalization crisis, while at critical junctures it even assisted the restoration of the monarchy. However, by the 1960s more militant mullahs such as Khomeini were coming to the forefront and mobilizing the impressive clerical network against the regime. Given the fact that the secular forces were largely decimated, the mullahs with their privileged mosque sanctuaries managed to appropriate the leadership of the evolving anti-Shah opposition and finally the revolution itself.

The current state of U.S.–Iranian relations obscures the fact that during the first half of the twentieth century, Iranians looked to America as a source of their release from Russian machinations and British imperialism. Successive Persian prime ministers implored the United States to be more involved in Iran, hoping to employ its idealism to fend off European encroachment. The crucial legacy of the 1953 coup is the creation of not just a deep-seated suspicion of foreign powers but of the United States in particular. The fact that subsequent to the coup America had become the main patron of an unaccountable and dictatorial monarchy reinforced its image of obstructing democratic change to protect its economic and strategic interests. A mythologized but still powerful historical narrative would erect a "wall of mistrust" between the Iranian populace and the United States. To be sure, Iranians would remain optimistic about American values, but the events of 1953 would provide a cautionary note that the United States was not always true to its declared principles and often abandoned the democratic cause when confronted with countervailing pressures. The relationship between the two nations would never again be uncomplicated, without historical grievances. It was possible before 1953 for Iranians to see America as a fundamentally benevolent power, but after the coup that image would be forever tarnished.

In this complex drama, the Americans would also have their own grievances and impressions. While the 1953 coup would condition successive generations of Iranians' perceptions of America, it would be the events of 1979 and the tortuous hostage crisis that shaped

Americans' views of Iran, reinforcing the formidable "wall of mistrust" separating the two nations.

444 DAYS

During August 2005, American newspapers and television screens were unexpectedly filled with images of 1979. The scene of the U.S. embassy in Iran being taken over by radical students, effigies of Uncle Sam being burned, and angry mobs desecrating the American flag seemed the order of the day. The latest crisis in U.S.–Iranian relations was sparked by five former American hostages who identified the newly elected Iranian president, Mahmoud Ahmadinejad, as one of their captors.[17] The Iranian denials did not diminish the anger of the hostages and their demands for justice and recompense. The revival of the dramas of 1979 reveals that the hostage crisis is hardly a stale historic episode; its images and emotions continue to shape the collective conscious of the American public. For a generation of Americans, the hostage crisis remains an open wound, transforming Iran into an unsavory state unfit for rehabilitation.

Sunday, November 4, 1979, began as any other day in revolutionary Tehran, with protests engulfing the streets of the capital. But then a group of demonstrating students suddenly took a different route, breaching the walls of the formidable U.S. embassy and announcing the arrest of the perplexed diplomats. The ostensible purpose of the hostage taking was the students' alarm that the Shah's admission to the United States for medical treatment was an attempt by Washington to orchestrate a coup against Iran's nascent revolution.[18] Initially, all the parties involved assumed the crisis would be short-lived. The students themselves hoped to deliver what they called a propaganda of deed, and then return to their universities; the Carter administration, accustomed to Iranian transgressions, sensed yet another momentary crisis soon to be resolved; and the officials of Iran's provisional government seemed more annoyed than exulted by the students' militancy. Yet the embassy takeover would soon be entangled in Iran's vicious factional politics, prolonging the incarceration of the hapless diplomats.[19]

The memories of 1953 should not be discounted in understanding the hostage crisis. In November 1979, the Iranian revolution was truly under threat: its contending factions were battling each other, ethnic minorities in Kurdistan and Khuzestan were agitating for autonomy, and the imperial army was still largely intact. From the perspective of Iranians, whose country had been subject of persistent foreign intervention for much of the twentieth century, it was not unreasonable to perceive that the United States and its allies were conspiring against the new regime.[20] Was it irrational to believe that the embassy that plotted the 1953 coup was not concocting a similar scheme in 1979?

A look back at the Iran of 1979 reveals a revolutionary elite that really did see itself as under siege, struggling against enemies, real and imagined. Despite their flamboyant rhetoric and defiant posture, the Islamic Republic's leaders were extremely anxious about U.S. intervention. An Iranian generation accustomed to believing that American machinations lay behind all of their country's misfortunes found it impossible to believe that the Carter administration would passively accept the demise of its reliable ally in the strategically critical Persian Gulf. As such, the takeover of the embassy was a strike against the nefarious American plot, a nonexistent one at that. Still, Iran's insecure revolutionaries came to perceive that by taking over the embassy, they would necessarily prolong their new mission.

As we have seen, for Ayatollah Khomeini the hostage crisis offered a tantalizing opportunity to outflank his domestic political rivals, particularly the moderates. In the Islamic Republic's first days in February 1979, Khomeini recognized that it was an inopportune time to unleash the Islamic order, as he and his disciples were still insufficiently organized to assume complete power. And so Khomeini agreed to the appointment of the moderate Mehdi Bazargan as prime minister. A devout leader with impeccable nationalistic and religious credentials, the new premier was acceptable to the bewildering factions that waged the revolution. As a leader of the Freedom Movement,

Bazargan was part of a generation of Iranian intellectuals who sought to harmonize their religious values with modern transformations. He was an engineer of some accomplishment, a political activist often jailed by the Shah, and a man of absolute integrity. More important, Bazargan was a man of order, reassuring those who were put off by the rash conduct of the revolution and who sought to sustain existing institutional arrangements.[21]

The provisional government signaled its intention to pursue a pragmatic foreign policy, even maintaining ties with the United States. To be sure, it did not envision an alliance as under the Shah, but the two powers could still maintain normal relations and avoid unnecessary antagonism. This was the message that Bazargan and his foreign minister, Ibrahim Yazdi, conveyed to Carter's national security adviser, Zbigniew Brzezinski, when they met in Algiers shortly after the revolution.[22] Far from seeking to revamp the international norms along ideological lines, Bazargan sought to assert Iran's sovereign rights without provoking the animosity of the Western powers.

The stage was set for an all-out battle between the secular and religious forces, as each side sought to shape the revolution in its own image. During the pivotal period of 1979–81, numerous institutions and ruling documents were crafted, and the foundations of the Islamic Republic were defined. In the realm of foreign policy, Khomeini was appalled by Bazargan's essential moderation; resisting the "Great Satan" was a defining and enduring tenet of Khomeini's ideology. The revolution had been waged not just for the Islamic redemption of Iranian society but also as a strike against America's imperial encroachment in the Middle East. The network of the mosques, the revolutionary committees, and the vast organizational structure of the clerical militants now went to work agitating against Bazargan and his provisional government. However, Iran's revolutionaries needed a crisis to arouse the population, discredit their foes, and consolidate their power. The radical students and their impulsive conduct offered the plotting Khomeini his chance.

Shortly after the takeover of the embassy, Khomeini quickly endorsed the students' action, noting, "Today underground plots are being hatched in these embassies, mostly by the Great Satan."[23] The Iranian demands for ending the hostage crisis seemed equally fantastic as Tehran called for the return of the Shah and his assets, the end of American interference in Iran's internal affairs, and an apology for past U.S. misdeeds. Khomeini's stance ensured that unlike previous assaults on the embassy immediately after the revolution, the current crisis would be prolonged. Khomeini's embrace of the embassy take-over stiffened the resolution of the students, who now saw themselves as a vanguard of a great revolutionary struggle seeking the emancipation of Iran, if not the entire Third World.

Jimmy Carter's response to the hostage crisis reflected the dilemma of an administration caught between limits of its power and rising popular dissatisfaction with its conduct. The Carter administration truly had no viable option for quickly ending the crisis, entangled as it was in the vagaries of Iran's domestic politics. The president's legitimate insistence that the hostages must be kept alive and safely released further narrowed his options. The prevailing military contingencies focused on punitive strikes against Iran's military and economic targets. However, such strikes were quickly shelved because they could trigger a terrible Iranian retaliation—the killing of the hostages. The alternative measure of imposing a naval blockade on Iran would similarly lead to the loss of American and Iranian lives without necessarily bringing about a peaceful resolution of the crisis. Moreover, such a strategy could have provoked Iranian retaliation against the oil traffic in the Persian Gulf, leading to catastrophically high gas and oil prices.[24]

In the absence of viable options, the United States fell back on its customary default position, economic sanctions. Washington imposed a ban on further purchases of Iran's oil and on all trade, with the exception of food and medicine. The Carter administration also froze Iran's assets in the United States, which amounted to $12 billion.[25] Such economic measures were unlikely to stay the determination of a revolutionary regime that was indifferent to the cost of its militancy. Moreover, Tehran had already announced its refusal to sell oil to the

"Great Satan" and was not eager for the expansion of other commercial ties.

The pressure on the Carter administration was accentuated by the fact that the hostage drama was one of the first international crises to become part of the daily political debates and discussions in America. The tribulations of the captive diplomats evoked a powerful emotional response from the American people, a response that was nurtured by the saturated media coverage. The venerable CBS anchorman Walter Cronkite closed every broadcast with the tally of the number of days the hostages had spent in captivity, and television screens continuously broadcast images of bearded mullahs denouncing the United States. Thus did the Iranian revolution come into every home in America. President Carter, for his part, reinforced the American public's fixation, as the president naturally made the plight of the hostages his most pressing priority, remaining in the Oval Office until late at night to micromanage the crisis. As the hostage crisis lingered, it began to epitomize America's struggle in the post-Vietnam period. Once more, America appeared abused and victimized, without an ability to respond in an effective manner. The hostages' continued detention led their fellow citizens to demand action and ultimately to blame Carter for his seeming lack of resolution.[26]

In the meantime, Iran's militant mullahs were busy garnering the benefits of a nationalistically aroused populace. A beleaguered Bazargan and his cabinet resigned in November 1980 after its inability to gain the release of the hostages, paving the way for the further consolidation of power by Khomeini and his disciples. The clerical cadre now triumphed in parliamentary elections and oversaw the passage of a referendum that affirmed the revised constitution with its privileged position for the Supreme Leader. The battered secular opposition was castigated as agents of America, and their criticism of the mullahs' dictatorial tendencies were dismissed as fracturing national unity at a time of confrontation with the "Great Satan." In the meantime, a cultural revolution that was to purify Iran's institutions was also launched under the stern purview of the revolutionaries. Under the shadow of conflict with America, Iran was being transformed into a new society, governed by a reactionary cohort in the name of Islamic militancy.

It is important to note that while the United States condemned Iran's conduct as a breach of international law, it was a violation of Shiite Islam's own traditions as well. Historically, Shiite clergy have been generous in assuring safe passage to non-Muslim emissaries. The great Islamic empires were at pains to accommodate diplomats from all countries and treated them with respect and deference. These traditions were sanctified by a clerical class that was the guardian of law. An entire legal corpus soon evolved on the need to grant protection to representatives of all states. As a learned Shiite scholar, Khomeini must have been familiar with these traditions and must have known that his conduct was contravening the established norms of the Islamic order he was purportedly committed to constructing.[27]

As diplomacy and economic pressure failed to resolve the crisis, an increasingly desperate Carter administration opted for a military rescue mission, Operation Eagle Claw. The planned operation was logistically complex. Using eight helicopters, a crew of 118 men would fly into Iran, refuel in the central desert, and proceed to a location close to Tehran. At that time, using pre-positioned trucks, they would embark toward the embassy and assault the compound. This would be a challenging task under the best of circumstances, but the unpredictable desert weather and lack of coordination forced commanders to abort the operation not long after it began. The mechanical problems arising from the desert storm and the crash of a helicopter with a refueling plane led to the deaths of eight American servicemen.[28] The United States stood utterly humiliated, a superpower that could neither compel Iran to free its diplomats nor mount a credible rescue effort. Suddenly, Khomeini's persistent slogan, "America cannot do a damn thing," appeared eerily true.

By the fall of 1980, Khomeini appeared ready to end the ordeal of the American captives. By that point, he and his disciples had assumed control over all the key institutions of power and his vision of a rigid theocratic order had overcome the opposition of his erstwhile coalition partners. As a close aide, Behzad Nabavi, confessed, "The hostages were like a fruit from which all the juice had been squeezed out."[29] Even more dramatic, Iraq's invasion of Iran on September 22, 1980, altered the national priorities, since the theocratic regime had to mobilize its resources behind a war effort that would prove daunting. However, Khomeini still had one last score to settle, refusing to release the hostages until Carter had been defeated in his reelection bid and formally relinquished power to his successor, Ronald Reagan. Khomeini perceived that a resolution of the crisis prior to the election might redound to Carter's advantage, and thus he slowed the process to erode the president's domestic support base. In a sense, Khomeini succeeded in overthrowing an American president, as Carter was decisively defeated. But this would prove an empty victory, as the Islamic Republic now had to contend with a more hawkish Reagan administration.[30]

The conflicting Iranian and American perceptions of the hostage crisis reflect its differing impact on the two nations. For the Iranians, the embassy was the "den of spies," the embodiment of a superpower that had sustained a cruel monarchy. For the Americans, the hostages were fellow citizens, ordinary individuals held against their will by an inhuman regime. Iranians saw the crisis as a triumphant blow against a superpower, while the Americans perceived it in terms of suffering of families whose loved ones were unjustifiably held captive. For one audience it was a political gesture of Third-Worldist defiance. For the other, it was a personal story of tragedy befallen their innocent countrymen.

In a curious manner, Khomeini's fertile imagination failed him. The hostage crisis may have been useful in removing his internal rivals, but it also secured him the enmity of the American public, which would prove costly for his beleaguered nation. Iran paid a high price for its conduct, as the resulting international opprobrium forced it to deal with Saddam Hussein's aggression in isolation. The Islamic Republic was a victim of Saddam's invasion and his indiscriminate use of chemical weapons, but given Iran's own violations of international law, not many states were willing to side with the mullahs and legitimize their claims. Moreover, Tehran paid another price as the most powerful economic and military power in the world subtly but effectively sided with Iraq as it waged its eight-year war against Iran.

Beyond the Iran-Iraq war, the legacy of the hostage crisis continues to extract a price from Iran. An indelible image of the Islamic Republic was imprinted on the collective psyche of the American people. Iranians were seen as fanatical, reactionary fundamentalists enchanted by their peculiar culture of martyrdom and impervious to reason. To a cross-section of the public, a theocratic anachronism steeped in its ossified ideology had managed to humiliate America with impunity. The chants of "Death to America," mullahs in their strange clerical garb, and a population seemingly united in its hatred of America would be the enduring picture of Iran.

To be sure, the United States was no stranger to ideological adversaries, having contained and engaged the Soviet Union for over four decades. But the hostage crisis was fundamentally different. The anger and anguish that the Americans feel toward Iran is never far below the surface. The crisis led the Americans to build their own "wall of mistrust" that further estranged the two societies. Such popular disdain for the Islamic Republic has hampered prospects of rapprochement and has restricted the diplomatic moves of any U.S. administration seeking to engage Iran. The irony is that in the intervening quarter-century, the two powers would often have interests in common, but the emotional barrier to dealing with the other would preclude meaningful cooperation.

The twin crises of 1953 and 1979 would ensure that U.S.–Iranian relations would always transcend the strategic realm and would play themselves out at a visceral, emotional level. However, it would be the scandal of the Iran-Contra Affair that would frighten both elected officials and the diplomatic corps from embarking on an imaginative policy toward the Islamic Republic. The resolution of the U.S.–Iran imbroglio requires considerable skill and a willingness to assume risks. After Iran-Contra, there were not too many ambitious officials willing to endorse a creative policy with its potential perils.

A BIBLE, A CAKE, AND MISSILES

The resolution of the hostage crisis did not alter the established pattern of U.S.–Iranian relations. Tehran continued on its path of defiance and hostility to America, while the Reagan administration embraced a punitive policy of coercion and containment. From the bombing of American marine barracks in Beirut in 1983 to Washington's attempt to internationalize its economic sanctions against Iran, the two countries seemed locked in an enduring pattern of animosity. In a sense, Iran's radical posture created a self-generating and self-sustaining momentum of antagonism. Given the centrality of the Middle East to America's security concerns, the United States was not about to abandon the region to Iran's ideological enterprise. Indeed, the more mischievous Iran became, the more Washington grew determined to sustain its allies and bolster its presence. It would be America's policy to continually inflict setbacks and defeats on Iran as a lesson to its ruling elite and to those in the region attracted by the theocracy's intransigence.

At times, America's obsession with negating Iran's influence would lead it to make common cause with unsavory allies, such as Saddam Hussein's Iraq. The Reagan administration did much to prop up the Iraqi regime, which it increasingly saw as a bulwark against Iran's revolution. Through the provision of economic assistance and sensitive battlefield intelligence, Washington tilted in favor of Iraq during its war against Iran. Even more egregious was America's indifference to Saddam's employment of chemical weapons against Iranian civilians and soldiers.[31] All the aspects of Saddam's behavior that the two Bush administrations would later find so objectionable, such as aggression against neighboring states and the use of weapons of mass destruction, the Reagan team not only tolerated but implicitly encouraged. Blinded by its suspicion of Iran, Washington essentially ignored its own rhetoric, principles, and self-interest in cultivating the genocidal Saddam Hussein.[32]

The pattern of recrimination and suspicion seemed to have been broken by the infamous Iran-Contra Affair, an unsavory deal between Washington and Tehran to trade arms for American hostages held in Lebanon—and then funnel Iranian money to Nicaragua where it would fund the Contra rebels fighting the Marxist government there.[33] Once the plot was revealed, many in the Reagan administration defended their conduct by stressing that the entire enterprise was motivated by a desire to bolster the power of the moderates within the Iranian clerical hierarchy.[34] Despite various congressional investigations and published memoirs, there is still much about the Iran-Contra Affair that eludes the average analyst. Was the United States government discerning enough to differentiate among the bewildering factions within Iran and determine who the moderates were? How could the transfer of arms to Iran buttress the power of such moderates? Was Khomeini, with his well-honed anti-American instincts, prepared to dispense with his ideology and embark on a new relationship with the United States? And, of course, what were the lasting ramifications of one of the most dramatic failures in U.S. diplomacy toward Iran?

Although the Islamic Republic's approach to Israel will be examined later, it is important here to note that to an extent the origins of the Iran-Contra Affair are mired in the complex web of Iranian-Israeli relations. The war between Iran and Iraq offered the Israeli state a unique set of opportunities and challenges. On the one hand, the assumption of power by a theocratic regime determined to strengthen Islamic forces battling Israel confronted Jerusalem with a pronounced threat. On the other hand, by the early 1980s the Israelis still defined Iraq as their greater enemy. The Ba'athist regime, with its quest to lead the Arab world, had embraced a stridently anti-Israeli posture and was busy mobilizing the region against the Jewish state. Moreover, Iraq had emerged as the leader of the Arab bloc that was seeking to isolate Egypt subsequent to Anwar al-Sadat's acceptance of the Camp David Peace Accords with Israel. For Israeli officials, who hoped that the peace treaty with Egypt would lead to similar compacts with other Arab states, Iraq's conduct was particularly disturbing. Saddam's unpredictable rule and his quest for nuclear arms (which in 1981 led to a successful Israeli preemptive strike on Iraq's atomic installations) were seen as a more immediate threat than the theocratic regime in Iran. For Israel, the idea of assisting Iran in a war that was preoccupying Saddam and draining his treasury was not entirely unwelcome.[35]

Beyond the issue of Iraq, there has always been a strain in Israeli foreign policy that has sought to craft relations with the "outer ring" of the Middle East, namely, the non-Arab powers of Turkey and Iran. Given these countries' own tense and problematic relations with the Arab world, the possibility of establishing an alignment among the region's non-Arab states has long intrigued Israeli politicians. The establishment of such ties could enable Jerusalem to escape its isolation and even pressure the recalcitrant Arab regimes into accepting its legitimacy. In a peculiar manner, this argument discounted the intensity of the clerical regime's anti-Zionist convictions, since Khomeini was not about to suppress his disdain for a state he had spent much of his life castigating.[36]

Nowhere is the amorality of politics more pronounced than in the Middle East. Under the banner "the enemy of my enemy is my friend," Jerusalem began selling arms to Iran soon after Iraq's invasion.[37] The Israelis saw much to commend a policy that prolonged the war, exhausted Saddam's resources, and diverted Iran's attention. However, given that much of Israeli military arsenal was furnished by the United States, they could not sell such arms to a third party without American permission. Thus, the continuation of Israeli policy was contingent on American approbation, even complicity. Israeli officials would do much to entangle the United States in their dealings with Iran and were critical in brokering the arms-for-hostages deal.

Adding to this complex brew was the reality of southern Lebanon in the early 1980s. The raging civil war among Lebanon's different religious groups had destroyed one of the most progressive societies in the Middle East. A number of American missionaries, journalists, and academics were caught in the cross-fire of Lebanese animosities and were taken hostage by Iran's Shiite client, the Hezbollah. The fate of these hostages proved a heavy burden for President Ronald Reagan, who was genuinely anguished about their continued captivity. The distressed president persisted in pressuring his intelligence operatives and policy advisers to liberate the hostages, and he could not fathom why a superpower was incapable of freeing a handful of its citizens in southern Lebanon. In the meantime, developments in Iran were also making the trading of hostages for U.S. arms possible.

By the mid-1980s, Iran was in shambles; its stalemated war with Iraq was not only draining its economy but also disenchanting its once-revolutionary masses. Saddam's war machine was inflicting heavy damage on the Iranian populace and the country's military, leading to fears within the clerical regime of popular discontent, even a coup. Given Khomeini's absolute determination to pursue the war, Iran required weapons and spare parts that could only be obtained from the United States, and the perennially pragmatic Rafsanjani and his allies were now the key Iranian officials searching for American arms. A bewildering cast of Israeli officials, unscrupulous middlemen, cunning mullahs, and gullible U.S. functionaries would now come together to craft a deal that would meet Reagan's desire to free the hostages and Iran's quest for weapons. Perhaps only in the Middle East could such disparate events involving covert Israeli-Iranian arms dealings, hostage taking in southern Lebanon, and an American president's anguish over his countrymen's captivity fit seamlessly into the same narrative.

The comical aspects of the operation mirror its intellectual misconceptions. The former national security adviser, Robert "Bud" McFarlane, arrived in Tehran with a cake and a Bible signed by Reagan as a gesture of goodwill, hoping to meet the moderates he had come to empower. McFarlane was relegated into seeing second-tier foreign ministry officials and quickly dismissed. In the meantime, as shipments of sophisticated American weapons arrived in Tehran, particularly the antitank TOW missiles (Tube-launched Optical-tracking

Wire-guided), a few of the hostages were released, but this led to more being captured since they were proving a valuable commodity of exchange for the mullahs.

The different parties involved in the deal had varying motives. Israel was merely sustaining its existing policy of aiding Iran in its war against its more immediate enemy, Iraq. Reagan was in a desperate search for release of the hostages and evidently acquiesced to an arrangement that contradicted his own administration's policy of prohibiting arms to Iran. A few American officials, such as McFarlane, seemed to hope that the arms deal would pave the way for a more normalized relationship with Tehran. However, yet another group of officials involved in the deal, such as the unscrupulous National Security Council aide Oliver North, were enchanted not so much by the prospect of reconciling with Iran, but by aiding the Contra rebels waging war against the Marxist Nicaraguan government. It was not long before North and his boss, national security adviser John Poindexter, were diverting the profits from the arms sales to the rebels in contravention of congressional mandates. Given such differing ambitions and the unsavory nature of so many of the actors involved, it was inevitable that the arms deal would end in scandal.

Were there moderates in Iran willing to normalize relations with the United States if only they obtained a cache of arms? To be sure, the Islamic Republic had factions and divisions of opinion on foreign policy issues. The more pragmatic politicians such as Rafsanjani bemoaned the Islamic Republic's self-imposed and debilitating isolation, and stressed that Iran's economic quandaries required developing links with international markets.[38] This was pragmatism born out of compulsion, as Iran could not wage war or deal with its economic burdens and growing population with strained international relations. However, it would be a misreading of the domestic situation to suggest that such pragmatic redefinition of interests constituted ascendance of a moderate faction willing and able to normalize relations with the United States.

The many U.S. officials who pressed the idea of theocratic moderates also failed to appreciate that Ayatollah Khomeini was still the central actor in Iran's decision-making process. For Khomeini to achieve his goal of toppling Saddam, his forces required weapons that only the United States could provide. Thus his willingness to trade arms for hostages was not so much a desire to begin a new relationship with the United States but an appreciation that his maximalist war aims necessitated a retreat on the issue of America. America still remained the "Great Satan," but one with an arsenal that could be used against the more immediate danger of Saddam. In the end, it was not so much the rise of the moderates but the requirements of a desperate regime waging a costly war that governed Tehran's approach to the arms deal.

The Iran-Contra Affair continues to exercise a subtle yet perceptible influence on U.S. policy. The primary imperative of politics is caution, which has usually translated into unimaginative and banal policies. It is easy to be derisive of McFarlane and the other American officials who arrived in Tehran with their Bible and cake. At every step of the way, the Reagan administration made the wrong calculation and substituted its flawed impressions for reasoned analysis. However, if there is to be a solution to the U.S.–Iran imbroglio, it will require imagination and a propensity to think outside the box. After the Iran-Contra Affair came to light, ending many careers and blemishing an entire administration's reputation, not too many American officials were willing to assume risks and move forward with provocative ideas. The foreign policy establishment was to remain firmly and instinctively in its enclosed box when it came to the issue of Iran.

An even more dramatic legacy of Iran-Contra is the discrediting of the concept of moderate Iranians. Even after Khomeini's death, successive U.S. administrations mired in the so-called lessons of the Iran-Contra Affair would dismiss the notion of Iranian pragmatism. This would prove particularly tragic when Muhammad Khatami arrived in power in 1997 and was initially ignored by the Clinton administration as just another Iranian politician with mere soothing words. As we have seen, there were moderates in Iran during the 1980s who may even have been interested in forging a different relationship with the United States. But the ponderous shadow of Khomeini stifled all such initiatives. For many Americans that shadow has never lifted.

Subsequent to the revelations of a deal that contradicted so many of the administration's public pronouncements, official declarations, and wars on terrorism, Washington grew determined to prove its resolution and toughness. There would be more tilts toward Iraq and further attempts to contain and isolate the Islamic Republic. Such policies were viewed not just as strategically necessary but politically convenient. As a result of the Iran-Contra Affair, the paradigm of hostility and recrimination that initially guided the Reagan administration remained intact. It was too politically costly and bureaucratically hazardous to consider alternative approaches to Iran.

The Iran-Contra Affair also had implications for the Islamic Republic's internal factional politics. While high-profile congressional investigations and sensationalist press accounts characterized the American reaction to the deal, a quieter but just as serious struggle took place within the Islamic Republic's corridors of power. The sensitivity of trading with the "Great Satan" provoked its own uproar in Tehran. After all, as the Bazargan episode reveals, dealing with the Americans does not usually contribute to political longevity in the Islamic Republic. The sordid affair first came to public knowledge when an Iranian extremist faction leaked it to a Lebanese newspaper. The hard-line parliament even called for an investigation to "determine which authorities and officials decided to establish links with Washington."[39] The pragmatists, such as Rafsanjani, were now in the militants' crosshairs for their duplicitous stance toward America. The pandemonium ended when Khomeini personally intervened and admonished the parliamentarians, "You should not create schism. This is contrary to Islam."[40] It was only through Khomeini's intervention that Rafsanjani and the pragmatists were saved.

After Khomeini's death, Rafsanjani and his allies assumed greater power, but their increased stature did not diminish their anxiety about dealing with America. The hard-liners, led by the new Supreme

Leader Ali Khamenei, would watch carefully and be ready to obstruct any enterprising attempts to reach out to the "Great Satan." The ideologically vulnerable Rafsanjani would at times entertain ideas about new relations with America, but mindful of his past and cautious of his power, would quickly recoil when meeting resistance from the Right. In a sense, the Iran-Contra Affair became part of the theocracy's vicious factional politics, militating against moderation toward the United States.

Two decades later, the ghost of Iran-Contra still haunts Washington and Tehran. Though there would be occasional shifts to reduce animosities, both parties were too aware of their past failings to move decisively forward. In both countries, politicians proved too feckless and bureaucracies too cautious for bold initiatives. And it would be such circumspection that would undermine one of the rare opportunities to fundamentally realign U.S.–Iranian relations.

DIALOGUE OF CIVILIZATIONS

It is customary, even conventional, to assess President Muhammad Khatami's tenure as an utter failure. To be sure, Khatami did not achieve his lofty ambition of creating an Islamic democracy, a regime that would seamlessly amalgamate religious convictions and pluralistic precepts. In the realm of foreign policy, however, Khatami's achievements were considerable—he fundamentally altered Iran's international orientation. In a dramatic twist, a president often castigated for his lack of courage managed to compel an influential segment of the conservative bloc to support a variety of his progressive foreign policy initiatives.

In formulating his strategy, Khatami perceived a clear nexus between domestic liberalization and international relations. Addressing a gathering of Islamic states in 1997, the new president emphasized that a government whose legitimacy was based on popular mandate would "recognize the right of other nations to self-determination and access to the necessary means for honorable living."[41] Foreign minister Kamal Kharrazi echoed this theme, claiming, "We hope with the international reaction to the large turnout in the elections, we will see a major change in Iran's relations with the regional nations and the entire world."[42] In essence, a regime seeking to democratize its governing order would pursue a responsible foreign policy predicated on cooperation and interdependence, conceding the sovereignty of its neighbors, the norms of the international system, and the need for dialogue. The president's policy was a clear repudiation of Khomeini's divisive diplomacy, as it implicitly recognized that Iran's predicament was its own fault. A policy of confrontation and spreading the revolution through terror had succeeded only in marginalizing Iran in the Middle East and the larger international community.

Soon after his election, Iran's intellectual president stunned both his domestic and international audiences by stressing that Iran's mission was no longer the export of its revolution and the destabilization of its neighborhood. "Foreign policy does not mean guns and rifles, but utilizing all legitimate means to convince others," declared Khatami.[43] Along these lines, the new president emphasized that "any country that recognizes our independence and does not have an aggressive policy toward us can be our friend."[44] Such gestures became the foundation of Khatami's "Dialogue of Civilizations" proposal, which called for intellectuals, artists, writers, and politicians from different countries to get together and address the commonalities of their seemingly disparate cultures. Gone were the days of incendiary rhetoric and calls for preservation of Iran's Islamic identity through confrontation with sinister global forces.[45]

In yet another departure from the norms of the ruling clerical elite, Khatami did not view the West as a pernicious agent seeking to undermine the cohesion of the Islamic civilization through its cultural intrusions. As with many Muslim reformers, Khatami had a more nuanced view of the West and stressed that its scientific achievements and democratic heritage were worthy models of emulation. "Our revolution can give rise to a new civilization if we have the ability to absorb the positive aspects of Western civilization," he declared.[46] For the first time since the revolution an Iranian politician acknowledged that pluralism, democracy, and other products of Western political heritage should be embraced by an Islamic government seeking the empowerment of its citizenry.

The foundation of the hard-liners' foreign policy had always been a relentless struggle on behalf of revolutionary ideals. But by the late 1990s, burdened by Iran's costly isolation and challenged by Khatami's popularity, the conservatives conceded the need for mending fences with key global actors. In his role as the Supreme Leader, Khamenei sanctioned such compromises as necessary for the vitality of the nation. Soon after his election, Khatami scored a series of impressive victories as he managed to reconcile with the Saudi regime, long the bête noire of the Islamic Republic, as well as the European Union, which had grown weary of Iranian terrorism on its territory. It was Khatami who transcended Iran's factionalism and prodded the Supreme Leader into accepting the necessity of abandoning Iran's hostility to states that Ayatollah Khomeini had routinely castigated as immoral. It was at this point that terrorism as an instrument of Iranian policy toward the Gulf sheikdoms and European states essentially ceased.

It would be over the issue of the United States that Khatami's policy of engagement experienced its most pronounced setback. In a bold move, Khatami reached out to the United States. In a famous January 1998 interview with CNN, he praised "the great American people" and the civilization that rested "upon the vision, thinking, and manner of puritans who desired a system which combined the worship of God with human dignity and freedom." For an American audience accustomed to clerical fulminations and chants of "Death to America," Khatami must have seemed like a remarkable change. The new Iranian president invited discussion between the two peoples, "especially scholars and thinkers." Despite his unwillingness to call for an official dialogue, Khatami left the door ajar for a potential normalization of relations with the United States.[47] However, Khatami's enterprising diplomacy fell victim to the Iranian hard-liners' hostility and to American indifference.

The conservative counterattack was swift and decisive. Supreme Leader Khamenei set the tone by denouncing the West as "targeting our Islamic faith and character."[48] The influential hard-line cleric Ayatollah Muhammad Mesbah Yazdi followed suit by claiming, "It is natural that one cannot establish links with the likes of America, whose aim is merely to exert its hegemony and whose policies and actions we have witnessed in history."[49] A former foreign minister, Ali Akbar Velayati, chimed in with his objections, stressing, "The issue of talks with America is a prelude to America reopening its 'den of spies' in Iran and carrying out its plans to overthrow the Islamic Republic."[50] Given the conservatives' institutional power and suspicions, the only manner that Khatami could have pressed the hard-liners into acquiescing to his diplomacy was to garner significant American concessions. Alas, such an imaginative diplomacy would elude a Washington establishment mired in its anachronistic containment policy.

During much of the 1990s, America's foreign policy was guided by the Democratic administration of Bill Clinton. Although the Clinton team disparaged various aspects of its Republican predecessors' international policies, it still continued to approach Iran with alarm and dismay. Secretary of State Warren Christopher—who had served in the Carter administration and was the chief negotiator in the final months of the hostage crisis—quickly denounced Iran as an "international outlaw" and a "dangerous country."[51] Anthony Lake, the national security adviser, was no less charitable, chastising Iran as one of the "reactionary backlash states" that "seek to advance their agenda through terror, intolerance and coercion."[52] Moreover, given the collapse of the Soviet Union and the military defeat of the radical Iraqi regime in the first Gulf war, the Clinton team perceived an ideal opportunity to resolve the Arab-Israeli conflict and usher in a "new Middle East" that would be politically stable and economically integrated. The resolution of the Israeli-Palestinian dispute was seen as having an impact beyond the Levant, leading to the transformation of the entire region. Under the banner of "dual containment," the United States sought to prevent the potential resurgence of Iraq and to prolong the policy of isolating and coercing Iran.[53] Trade prohibitions, attempts to limit Iran's access to international lending organizations, and even the imposition of secondary sanctions on European firms doing business with Iran became the order of the day.

The extraordinary aspect of America's position was that even the election of the dynamic and forthcoming Khatami did not provoke a change in policy. The specter of the Iran-Contra Affair continued to haunt the Clinton White House, restraining its options and removing the prospect of a creative diplomacy. Moreover, an administration that had made the resolution of the Israeli-Palestinian conflict the center-piece of its regional policy was prone to look at Iran through the prism of the peace process, focusing on terrorism as the essential barometer of change in Iran. Although the administration did express a willing-ness to "test the possibilities for bridging the gap between the two nations," Clinton maintained his commitment to the policy of "dual containment."[54] The U.S. position was encapsulated by UN ambassa-dor Richard Holbrooke, who said, "If the Iranian government responds positively to the American position on issues of state sponsorship of terrorism and cooperating in solving regional problems and sources of instability in which Iran plays a big role, then the road will be open for a major development in the relationship."[55] In essence, instead of de-vising a negotiation process that could resolve such disputes, the onus was placed on Iran, with any improvement of relations contingent on Tehran embracing America's priorities.

Three years after Khatami's election, Washington finally responded with an important speech delivered by Secretary of State Madeleine Albright. In a unique gesture of contrition, Albright apologized for America's role in the overthrow of Mossadeq in 1953, acknowledging that "the coup was clearly a setback for Iran's political development." In another magnanimous move, the secretary noted that "U.S. policy toward Iraq during its conflict with Iran now appeared to have been regrettably shortsighted."[56] The administration then moved beyond rhetoric and lifted sanctions on Iranian carpets, pistachios, and caviar, which along with oil are among Iran's most lucrative exports. However, the intent of the speech was mired when Albright declared, "Despite the trend toward democracy, control over the military, judiciary, courts, police remain in unelected hands, and the elements of its foreign policy, about which we are most concerned, have not improved."[57] A speech that began by apologizing for intervention in Iran's internal affairs ended up meddling in Iran's domestic conflicts. It was inevitable that the conservatives would retaliate by obstructing a positive Iranian response.

Tehran's reaction was predictable, as the theocratic regime pushed aside Albright's positive gestures and denounced the speech as a crass intervention in its internal politics. To be sure, the reformist government did appreciate the historic significance of the speech and was inclined to respond positively, but the dreadful phrase "unelected hands" offered the hard-liners sufficient ammunition to thwart any such efforts. Iran's official response came when the Supreme Leader pointedly asked, "What good does this admission—that you acted in that way then—do us now? Admission years after the crime was committed, while they might be committing similar crimes now, will not do the Iranian nation any good."[58] Iran's secretary to the National Security Council, Hassan Rowhani, also castigated the speech, emphasizing, "From their point of view they are offering a piece of chocolate to what they see as developments inside Iran. This is a very ugly and unacceptable move."[59] Tehran's reaction essentially ended a belated effort by Washington to forge a more rational relationship with the Islamic Republic.

The Albright speech and the partial lifting of sanctions should not be dismissed as mere symbolic gestures, as these constituted an important change in America's behavior and a significant revision of the dual containment policy. Nonetheless, America's gesture was still too little and, more important, too late. The crucial time for embracing Khatami would have been immediately after his election, certainly by the time of his historic CNN interview. A more substantial offer of sanctions relief at that time, including allowing U.S. investments in Iran's critical energy sector and an offer to discuss the return of Iran's frozen assets, might have tipped the balance in favor of the reformers. Such relaxation of sanctions need not have been conditioned on Iran's behavior, as its mere offering might have manipulated the internal balance of power in favor of those inclined to diminish the Islamic Republic's militancy. At a time when the conservatives were still in shock, struggling to regain their footing, this offer might well have allowed Khatami to breach the "wall of mistrust" and assist the reformers in consolidating their power. But by 2000 the conservative counterattack was in full force, and the American concessions went largely unheeded. In a relationship that has witnessed so many missed opportunities, the inability of the Clinton administration to forge a timely and imaginative policy stands as one of its most tragic failures.

In many ways, Iran and the United States appear as two ships that always seem to pass in the night. At the rare moment when Iran was ready to improve relations, America was unresponsive. When the Americans were prepared to move beyond their hostility, Iranians were quick to demur. The emotional legacy of the Mossadeq coup and the hostage crisis, and the bureaucratic paralysis in both countries, have led to a relationship that seems immured in its pattern of antagonism and suspicion. The timing of positive gestures is usually bad, the contemplated offers always too little, and the domestic political scene in both countries often unprepared for the end of conflict. It is rare in international diplomacy to be given a second chance. Yet, in the aftermath of the September 11 tragedies, Washington was once again offered an opportunity to rationalize its relationship with the Islamic Republic. And, not unsurprisingly, the United States failed to take advantage of that opportunity.

5

UNDER THE SHADOW
OF SEPTEMBER 11

It is often stated that the terrorist attacks of September 11, 2001, for-ever changed America. In an even more dramatic fashion, al-Qaeda's nefarious plot also changed the Middle East. The region's pathologies, its ideology of wrath, and a political culture that too often condoned suicide bombing could no longer be concealed by its oil wealth. Perhaps more than any other regional actor, the Iranian mullahs appreciated that a certain epoch had ended and that previous arrangements were no longer tenable. As we have seen, President Muhammad Khatami had gradually pressed the clerical oligarchs toward a substantial revision of Iran's foreign policy along pragmatic lines. The issue of normaliza-tion of relations with the United States, though, had persistently eluded him. With the arrival of the American imperium in the Middle East, the recalcitrant hard-liners became convinced that it was time to set aside their long-standing antagonisms toward the United States. For a brief, fleeting moment, a consensus evolved among the clerics on the need to have a more rational relationship with America. However, in a pattern that has so often bedeviled U.S.–Iranian relations, just when one party was ready for accommodation, the other was moving in the opposite direction. The Bush administration had arrived in the Middle East not to reconcile with old foes but to foster a new order.

The tragedies of September 11 led the Washington establishment to reevaluate the traditional concepts of statecraft. Containment and deterrence were now viewed as dangerously naive in the era of terrorism and weapons of mass destruction. America no longer sought merely to contain rogue regimes and to press for their disarmament through negotiations, but to actively alter the political culture of the region by ushering in a democratic dawn. Regime change, preemptive war, and coerced democratization were the new currencies of American policy. As the administration of President George W. Bush gazed across the Middle East, it perceived a unique opportunity to reformulate the dysfunctional political topography of the region and finally ensure the stability that all empires crave. In this context, Iran was no longer a problem to manage, but a radical, unsavory regime to topple.

As the fractious theocracy came close to accepting the need for a changed approach to America, Washington proved not only indifferent but hostile. The brief interlude between the U.S. invasion of Afghanistan in October 2001 and President Bush's State of the Union address in January 2002 represented a unique opportunity to fundamentally alter relations between the two states. And once more that opportunity was squandered. A year later, as America became entangled in the Iraq quagmire, a more consolidated conservative government in Iran was no longer eager to normalize relations with the United States. The power of ideologues in both Washington and Tehran essentially precluded an imaginative revision of U.S.–Iranian relations.

NEW THINKING

As the American empire arrived in the Middle East brandishing its new doctrine of preemption, the most critical debate within the Islamic

Republic was how to approach its new neighbor. As we have seen, the reactionary elements within the Iranian state had long objected to any normalization of ties with the "Great Satan," reasoning that the benefits garnered by such militancy outweighed its costs. The American colossus was too distant, its leaders too fickle, and its struggles against terrorism more symbolic than real. However, the Bush administration's expansive vision for the Middle East confronted the Iranian Right with realities that it could no longer ignore and responsibilities that it could no longer evade.

More than any other international event, America's response to the September 11 attacks exposed the fault lines among Iranian conservatives. As with most political movements in contemporary Iran, the conservative bloc is riddled with its own factions and contradictions, chiefly over foreign policy. For the ideologues among Iran's hard-liners, the Islamic template remains a model worthy of export, and the necessity of resisting America and its regional surrogates has never been greater. Moreover, a confrontational foreign policy has the advantage of reinvigorating a revolution whose popularity has long waned. By contrast, Iran's pragmatic conservatives stress that given the proximity of the American presence, Iran has to tread carefully and cultivate cooperative relations with its neighbors. They also argue that given Iran's economic pressures, dogmatism does not serve the cause of attracting foreign investment. Such debates were once more polarizing Iran's clerical rulers as competing factions of ideologues and realists battled each other over national security issues.

Iran's hard-line ideologues view themselves as the most ardent disciples of Ayatollah Khomeini and his revolutionary mission. These stalwarts of the revolution, such as Ayatollah Jannati and Ayatollah Shahroudi, control powerful institutions such as the Guardian Council and the judiciary, and they command key coercive instruments such as the Revolutionary Guards and Ansar-e Hezbollah. Their worldview is framed by a vision of the Islamic Republic as more than a rebellion against an iniquitous monarch but rather an uprising against a host of forces—the imperial West, Zionist encroachment, and Arab despots, to name a few—that have sustained America's presence. As such, their hostility to the United States is immutable and a function of their "revolution without borders." As Ayatollah Shahroudi, the judiciary chief, exclaimed in 2001, "Our national interests lie with antagonizing the Great Satan."[1] For the ideologues, international isolation, ostracism, and sanctions are necessary sacrifices on the path of revolutionary affirmation.

Khomeini's more pragmatic partisans may share the ideologues' disdain for popular sovereignty, but they recognize that the survival of the regime is contingent on a more judicious international course. Even at the height of its revolutionary fervor, the Islamic Republic never renounced the imperatives of the international economy and has always remained a participant in the global financial order. For the first time, the conservative wall of solidarity against America was fractured. In an important move, former president Rafsanjani, in his new role as the head of the powerful Expediency Council responsible for resolving disputes within the state, led the chorus by stressing, "We have lost opportunities in the past. We have made inappropriate measures or never made any measures. Our ideology is flexible and we can choose expediency on the basis of Islam."[2] Another stalwart of the revolution, Bahzad Nabavi, a prominent member of the parliament, similarly noted, "Normalizing ties with the U.S. does not contradict our values—the conditions today require different policies."[3] The realities of the post–September 11 international system were also starkly noted by Ayatollah Muhammad Emami-Kashani, a Friday prayer leader when he stressed, "In the absence of a rival superpower, America is relying on guns and its economic power to play with the fate of the world. Unfortunately, some European countries are going along with it."[4] Iran's conservative clerics did not suddenly alter their perception of America as an iniquitous state, but given the changing realities, they perceived a limited utility in continuing the conflict.

It is important to stress that it was not just the projection of American power that was pressing Iran's pragmatists toward a readjustment of their policy toward the United States. The persistent domestic deadlock and the inability of the state to formulate a cohesive economic plan had effectively obstructed much-needed reforms. This paralysis was coming at a time when the regime was failing to meet half the unemployment needs of 700,000 new job seekers every year or to generate $70 billion needed over the next decade to refurbish the country's dilapidated oil industry. Double-digit unemployment and inflation rates, falling standards of living and a bloated bureaucracy were eroding the prospects of a massive younger generation demanding material wealth. Daunting economic challenges and the demographic bulge were finally leading some within the clerical class to focus on the best means of alleviating a potentially explosive political problem. Given their reluctance to enact structural economic reforms, which at least in the initial stages would lead to a degree of dislocation and thus popular anger, the theocracy opted for foreign investment to rescue it from its predicament. Khatami captured Iran's dilemma by noting, "The government cannot come up with the money needed to create a million jobs a year. We need private and foreign investments."[5] It would be difficult for Iran to generate the necessary level of external investments while still embracing a militant defiance of the international community.

The compelling economic realities reinforce security arguments for a more normalized relationship with the United States. Rafsanjani once more acknowledged, "Iran has never banned economic, technological, and scientific relations with America."[6] Khatami has also weighed in, stipulating, "From our point of view there are no obstacles preventing economic cooperation with the U.S."[7] Iranian conservatives similarly endorsed such commercial relations. Muhammad Javad Larijani, an adviser to Ayatollah Khamenei, emphasized, "We and the U.S. have many differences. But this does not mean that we cannot adopt a regular policy in view of our national interests."[8] Economic imperatives were finally leading Iran to subordinate its revolutionary zeal to pragmatic considerations, and deal with a state that it has long demonized.

Hovering over this debate was Khamenei, the Supreme Leader and thus the ultimate arbiter of Iran's policy deliberations. As the theocracy's foremost ideologue, Khamenei shared the hard-liners' revolutionary conviction and their confrontational impulses. However, as the head of state he also bore the responsibility for safeguarding Iran's national interests and tempering ideology with the mandates of statecraft. The traditionally rigid and obstructionist Khamenei seemed to grasp the urgency of the times and the dangers that Iran's previous path now entailed. Through Iran's actions in the months following the September 11 attacks, he seemed to signal his willingness to explore a different relationship with the United States.

The first test of Iran's new policy came in Afghanistan. In October 2001, after fruitless negotiations with the Afghan leadership, the United States launched a military invasion designed to topple the Taliban and apprehend Osama bin Laden. For Iran, which had had bitter and acrimonious relations with the militant Sunni regime of the Taliban and its Wahhabi terrorist allies, this was an ideal opportunity. During much of the 1990s, as the international community remained indifferent to developments in Afghanistan, Iran actively assisted opposition groups such as the Northern Alliance and sought to draw attention to the peculiarities of the Taliban regime and its problematic guests. Once U.S. military operations commenced, subtle signs were soon sent to Washington. Foreign minister Kamal Kharrazi publicly declared, "We have some common points with the U.S. over Afghanistan."[9] The head of the parliamentary commission overseeing the war, Hadi Salam, reinforced this message, stressing that dialogue with the United States was critical "due to the crisis prevailing in the region and safeguarding our national interests."[10]

Such Iranian gestures were soon given tangible expression. The underreported story of the first episode of America's war on terrorism is that it could not have succeeded as easily as it did without Iranian support. The fact remains that by 2001 America's links with the Northern Alliance were fragmentary, and its long years of neglect had led many Afghan opposition groups to be suspicious of the United States. Tehran's mediation proved essential as Iran actively pressed the Northern Alliance and other opposition groups to cooperate with American forces. Iran also provided intelligence to the Northern Alliance, agreed to rescue American pilots in distress, and allowed some 165,000 tons of U.S. food aid to traverse its territory into Afghanistan. The speedy collapse of the Taliban acclaimed by the Bush administration had in fact enjoyed substantial Iranian assistance.

The pattern of cooperation persisted after the military campaign ceased and Washington focused on reconstruction and stabilization of a war-torn Afghanistan. Iran was instrumental in crafting the interim Afghan government at the Bonn Conference in December 2001, pressing its ally and longtime leader of the Northern Alliance, Burhanuddin Rabbani, to relinquish his claims to power in favor of the American candidate, Hamid Karzai. At the January 2002 Tokyo Conference, Iran pledged $530 million for Afghan reconstruction. To be sure, Iran was concerned about the possibility of a permanent American military establishment next door and was hoping for a quick withdrawal of U.S. forces. Iran was also active in attempting to assert its influence, particularly in western Afghanistan. Although, in all such cases, Iran's policy was motivated by critical national security considerations, rather than the export of an Islamic revolution. The paradox of the Afghan war was the extent that the American and Iranian interests actually coincided.

On the surface, Tehran's decision to assist the United States could be seen as a clever attempt to dislodge the Taliban government it had almost gone to war with in 1998. If the United States insisted on removing a regime hostile to Iran, why not be helpful? Such calculations certainly provided Iran with incentives to be cooperative. However, it does appear that Tehran's objectives transcended the immediate issue of deposing the Taliban, since the theocracy genuinely hoped to reach out to the United States. Khatami eagerly noted that "Afghanistan provides the two regimes with a perfect opportunity to improve relations."[11] The exigencies of September 11 and Iran's debilitating economic condition seemed to have finally shattered old taboos and engendered a new consensus within the theocracy behind a foreign policy of "New Thinking." A powerful coalition of reformers and pragmatic conservatives now coalesced around the understanding that in the altered regional landscape, Iran must come to terms with the United States on issues of common concern.

As we have seen in the last chapter, the period between 1997 and 1998 was the first occasion when U.S.–Iranian relations could have been reconciled. The second such time was the period between September 11, 2001, and January 29, 2002. Once President Bush addressed the joint session of Congress for his momentous State of the Union speech, the opportunity all but vanished. It is to American calculations during this period that we must now turn.

NEW WINE IN NEW BOTTLES

When the Bush administration first assumed power, it appeared to follow the cautious realism that had essentially characterized much of America's post–World War II foreign policy. On the issue of Iran, the new national security adviser, Condoleezza Rice, captured the tone of the administration by stressing in the pages of *Foreign Affairs,* "All in all changes in U.S. policy toward Iran would require changes in Iranian behavior."[12] Such a statement could have been uttered by officials of both Republican and Democratic administrations that had wrestled with the Iranian conundrum for a quarter of a century. Missile defense, preoccupation with a rising China, and transatlantic relations seemed to define the new administration's international priorities. The fact that the reform movement in Iran had failed to usher in a democratic breakthrough diminished any incentive that Washington may have had in devising an imaginative policy toward Iran. The Islamic Republic had essentially receded from the scene, left to indulge its grievances and sense of self-importance.

The September 11 tragedies fundamentally altered the Bush administration's international perspective, as it sought to revise, if not discard, the traditional American reliance on diplomacy and deterrence to deal with threats. Curiously, President Bush now stated:

"After September 11, the doctrine of containment just doesn't hold water."[13] Traditional conservatives such as Vice President Dick Cheney and Secretary of Defense Donald Rumsfeld perceived that the credibility of American power was contingent on its demonstration in the Middle East. By October 2002, the administration went so far as to enunciate a new national security doctrine that flamboyantly pledged the preemptive use of force as a tool of counterproliferation and regime change as a means of ensuring disarmament.[14] Beyond such provocative assertions, it became increasingly clear that the character of the regime—as opposed to its actual conduct—would determine the degree of American antagonism. Rice best captured this sentiment in 2005:

> Our experience of this new world leads us to conclude that the fundamental character of regimes matters more today than the international distribution of power. Insisting otherwise is imprudent and impractical. The goal of our statecraft is to help create a world of democratic, well-governed states that can meet the needs of their citizens and conduct themselves responsibly in the international system. Attempting to draw neat, clean lines between our security interests and our democratic ideals does not reflect the reality of today's world. Supporting the growth of democratic institutions in all nations is not some moralistic flight of fancy; it is the only realistic response to our present challenges.[15]

Under this framework, despotic regimes would inevitably seek and use weapons of mass destruction, promote terrorism, menace their neighbors, and plot against American interests. In the Bush administration's reformulation of traditional concepts of security, Iraq and Iran were threats not just because of their nuclear ambitions but because they oppressed their citizens. Such recalcitrant regimes could be neither contained nor deterred, leaving regime change as the only viable option.[16]

The president's missionary impulse was actively buttressed by a powerful cohort of neoconservatives who had assumed key posts in the administration. From their perch in the Pentagon and in the vice president's office, the neoconservatives now found a president receptive to their postulations. Deputy Secretary of Defense Paul Wolfowitz, Under Secretary of Defense Douglas Feith, and Vice Presidential Chief of Staff I. Lewis "Scooter" Libby all became household names as they invoked Wilsonian assertions as a means of stabilizing a turbulent Middle East.

Neoconservatism was an intellectual movement of significance long before Iraq commanded international attention. Since their emergence in the 1970s, the neoconservatives had always disparaged the realists' penchant for managing problems rather than solving them, especially when dealing with nonrepresentative regimes. As prime critics of the détente policy toward the Soviet Union, they created organizations with ominous-sounding names such as the Committee on the Present Danger and filled their magazines and journals with articles disparaging arms control treaties and U.S.–Soviet summitry. The demise of the Soviet Union led many neoconservatives to focus on the Middle East, particularly the tyrannical regime of Saddam Hussein in Iraq with its efforts to develop weapons of mass destruction and its aggressive wars.

In many ways, however, the neoconservatives' critique of U.S. policy in the Middle East transcended Saddam, as they never perceived the region as a bastion of stability, even before September 11. As with their advocacy against the Soviet Union, they called for a muscular policy of imposing American values on a reluctant part of the world. Although Iraq would always remain central to their obsessions, Iran was never far behind. The Islamic Republic, which persistently denounced the United States as the "Great Satan," humiliated America during a prolonged hostage crisis, and proved relentlessly hostile to Israel, was seen as an ideal candidate for the imposition of America's will.

For the neoconservatives, the Islamic Revolution of 1979 was a watershed event—it had not just displaced a reliable American ally, it had ushered in an ideology of radical Islam that was to challenge America's power and threaten the security of America's ally, Israel.

William Kristol, the editor of the *Weekly Standard,* employed typically inflated rhetoric in claiming, "We are in a death struggle with Iran," and called for "measures ranging from public diplomacy to covert operations."[17] James Woolsey, the former director of the CIA, proclaimed the arrival of World War IV (the third evidently being the Cold War) and Iran as America's central antagonist in that conflict. For Woolsey, Iran was a "fanatical theocratic totalitarian state ripe for the ash heap of history."[18]

In many ways, the neoconservative's image of Iran was frozen in time as Ayatollah Khomeini and his anti-American fulminations continued to disturb and agitate them. The evolutionary changes that Iran had undergone, the transformation of its political system, and its international outlook were simply ignored or dismissed as clerical ploys. Moreover, Iran's attempt to reach out to the United States in the aftermath of September 11 was disregarded to benefit the new strategy of displacing nonrepresentative regimes. Richard Perle, one of the leading neoconservative thinkers and an architect of the Iraq war, took the lead: "The U.S. should do everything to encourage the centrifugal forces in Iran that, with any luck, will drive that miserable government from office."[19] Even a distinguished scholar of the Middle East such as Bernard Lewis could not resist the ideological pull; he assured his audience that once the invasion of Iraq was complete, the Iranian people would beseech us, "Come this way."[20] In the neoconservative conception, Iran was a country ripe for a revolution, and limited American pressure could easily push it over the brink. History and reality would now be twisted to accommodate the distorted neoconservative predilections.

Although much has been written about how the neoconservatives hijacked American foreign policy in the aftermath of September 11 in order to institute their intellectual speculations about the nexus between democracy and stability, the fact remains that their influence stemmed from the coincidence of their ideology with President Bush's own instincts. Ultimately the president establishes both the rhetoric and the strategy of his administration's foreign policy. A president with an inadequate understanding of the complexities of regional politics and a propensity to view events in stark black-and-white terms spearheaded a foreign policy that was often self-defeating. The precipitous American invasion of a dispossessed and essentially partitioned Iraqi state on the spurious grounds of searching for nonexistent weapons of mass destruction led many in the international community to question Bush's judgment and whether American power can still be a force for good. Iran, with its many shades of gray, would prove an insurmountable challenge for Bush's simplistic ideological paradigm.

Every crisis requires a catalyst, and in the case of Iran that trigger was a shipment of arms to Palestinian groups resisting Israel. Although Iran's hard-liners had grudgingly accepted an accommodation with the United States, the issue of Israel was still beyond the pale. By 2002, the collapse of the Oslo peace process and the Palestinian uprising once more seemed to validate the Iranian hard-liners' strategy and provided them with allies in distress. Tehran's inflammatory rhetoric was buttressed by the provision of arms to the Palestinian resistance, and it was the Israeli interception of one such ship, the *Karine-A,* in January 2002, that focused Washington's attention on Iranian terrorism, as opposed to its constructive assistance in Afghanistan. The contradictions of Iranian foreign policy may have diminished, but they were still very much evident in the case of Israel. Tehran simply could not divest itself from the Israeli-Palestinian conflict. The clerical leaders failed to appreciate that Washington would not acknowledge their help so long as they strenuously sought to obstruct America's attempts to broker peace between Israel and its neighbors. Cooperation on Afghanistan, high-level negotiations, and international conferences could not balance Iran's opposition to the Jewish state.

In his 2002 State of the Union address, President Bush effectively closed off the possibility of a new chapter in U.S.–Iranian relations, denouncing the Islamic Republic as a member of an axis of evil, along with Saddam Hussein's Iraq and Kim Jong Il's North Korea. Bush described Iran as a "major sponsor of terrorism," and once more condemned the "unelected few" who suppress a restive populace. The incendiary language entailed a palpable threat. The United States of America, Bush proclaimed, "would not permit the world's most dangerous regimes to threaten us with the world's most dangerous weapons." In the post–September 11 and post-Afghanistan atmosphere, this was not an idle threat. Iran was once more in America's crosshairs.

Soon the administration officials began echoing the president, essentially calling for a change of Iranian regime. Vice President Dick Cheney expressed his "disappointment" with Iran, invoking a litany of American objections, such as "Iran's apparent commitment to destroy the Israeli-Palestinian peace process and unstinting efforts to develop weapons of mass destruction."[21] The new U.S. policy was spelled out in most detail by senior White House aide Zalmay Khalilzad in a speech: "Our policy is not about Khatami or Khamenei, reform or hardline; it is about supporting those who want freedom, human rights, democracy, and economic and educational opportunity for themselves and their fellow countrymen and women."[22] The administration would no longer preoccupy itself with the intricacies of Iranian politics but would instead substitute simplistic slogans such as "support for freedom" for an actual policy. This was to be regime change on the cheap, as an administration reluctant to commit its own troops hoped that by simply advocating democracy it could somehow trigger a revolution in Iran.

Iran's response was predictably incendiary and uncompromising. Ayatollah Khamenei proclaimed that the "drunkard shouts of American officials reveals the truth that the enemy is the enemy."[23] Even the mild-mannered President Khatami forcefully rejected Bush's remarks as "war mongering and insulting toward the Iranian nation."[24] Bush's strident rhetoric even alienated the Iranian masses who were to be the vanguard of progressive political change. The Iranians may have detested the corruption and inefficiency of the theocracy, but as a deeply nationalistic population they resented being defamed by an American politician and equated with the unsavory states of Iraq and North Korea. A nation that sees its rich culture as the epicenter of the world's civilization would not easily forgive a petulant U.S. president.

The issue that seemingly eluded the president and his speechwriters was that the Iranian nation could disdain both its rulers and the insulting Americans at the same time.

Was it Iran's shipment of arms that derailed a prospective U.S.–Iranian rapprochement that began in the rugged mountains of Afghanistan? Indeed, questions still linger about the *Karine-A* episode. Was the dispatch of arms a national decision or a freelance activity undertaken by hard-liners to undercut Iran's nascent cooperation with America? Were the arms actually intended for the Palestinians or for Iran's longtime Lebanese ally, Hezbollah? All these questions are relevant if one believes that an emerging reconciliation between America and Iran was fatally wounded by the shipment of arms. The more complex reality is that September 11 had generated such a dramatic shift in America's international orientation that an antagonistic approach to Iran was nearly inevitable. The Bush administration could not deal with a regime whose complicated foreign policy defied the simple characterization of "with us or against us."

The four months between September 2001 and January 2002 stand as a watershed in U.S.–Iranian relations. In a sense, this period reflects the tragedy of this relationship; the Iranian theocracy and the United States could not transcend their mutual animosities. During this brief period, the clerical regime had moved far in its readiness to embrace a different relationship with the United States, should America have been willing to reciprocate. However, the Iranian overture came at a time when a besieged America was recovering from a devastating attack on its homeland and contemplating the uses of its awesome power. After hopeful signs of rapprochement, U.S.–Iranian relations had returned to the typical realm of antagonism and emotion.

OLD THINKING

The American invasion of Iraq in 2003 once more confronted the Islamic Republic with a daunting set of challenges. The intricacies of

Iran's approach to Iraq will be examined in chapter 7, but it is important to stress that unlike September 11, the latest American military intervention was not viewed by Iranian officials as an opportunity to forge new ties with the United States. Washington's harsh rhetoric and its aversion to diplomacy had already closed off the opening that had appeared in the aftermath of September 11. To be sure, there was a degree of tactical Iranian cooperation in that Tehran appreciated that the American displacement of Saddam was in its interests. Nonetheless, the early success of the invasion deeply concerned the clerical elite—an emboldened America might decide to turn its sights on Iran next. That sense of unease soon evaporated as the United States became entangled in a bloody quagmire, and the task of pacifying and stabilizing Iraq began to drain American power. The theocracy rebounded and regained its sense of confidence. The clerical oligarchs assured themselves that an America preoccupied with its strained alliances, drained treasury, and discredited intelligence services would have a limited appetite for further military incursions. Given the tense U.S.–Iranian relations and persistence of calls for regime change in Washington, Iran had no incentive to press for an opening to America.

In the meantime, important changes were taking place within the theocratic state that further diminished prospects of a rapprochement. The reformers and pragmatic conservatives who had called for cooperation with the United States in Afghanistan seemed increasingly under pressure within the corridors of power. The United States had not only failed to reward Iran's constructive behavior but was once more beating the drums of regime change and pressing the international community to embrace its sanctions policy. Washington's new reliance on democratization as a means of dealing with security challenges like proliferation of weapons of mass destruction and terrorism did not bode well for an Iranian regime whose politics were distinctly reactionary. The hard-liners, who had always claimed that America's hostility toward Iran was immutable and that the core American objective remained the overthrow of the theocracy, seemed validated by the course of events.

After twenty-six years in power, the face of the Iranian regime was also changing, as a new generation of conservatives came to the surface with their own distinct views and ideologies. For the aging mullahs such as Khamenei and Rafsanjani who had been present at the creation of the Islamic Republic, America remained the dominant actor in Iran's melodrama. For the hard-liners, the United States was the source of all of Iran's problems, and for the pragmatists it was the solution to the theocracy's mounting dilemmas. In either depiction, America was central to Iran's affairs. Given that this generation came to political maturity during the reign of the Shah and his close alliance with United States, engaged in a revolutionary struggle defined by its opposition to America, and then led a state often in conflict with Washington, it was perhaps natural that they were obsessed with the United States.

For the new generation of conservatives it was the war with Iraq in the 1980s—not the revolution—that defined their political experience. Their isolation from the United States, their suspicion of the international community (which had tolerated Iraq's use of chemical weapons against Iran), and their continued attachment to Khomeini's dogmatic vision defined their ideology. In the meantime, the corruption of many of the founding leaders of the republic and their lack of revolutionary resolution affronted the austere war veterans. It is to Khamenei, another stern, uncorruptible ideologue, that they pay tribute. The younger conservatives are unyielding in their ideological commitments, earnest in their belief that the Government of God has relevance, and persistent in their simplistic claim that all problems would be resolved if Iran were to return to the roots of the revolution.

In terms of their international perspective, the young conservatives do not share their elders' preoccupation with the United States. Throughout the 2005 presidential campaign, the striking aspect of the younger hard-liners' message was the notion of an "Eastern orientation." As Ali Larijani, a conservative presidential candidate and the current head of the Supreme National Security Council, noted, "There are certain big states in the Eastern Hemisphere such as Russia, China, and India. These states can play a balancing role in today's world."[25] In a similar vein, another stalwart of the new conservatives, the former Revolutionary Guard commander and the current mayor of Tehran, Muhammad Qalibaf, stressed, "In the current international arena, we see the emergence of South Asia. And if we do not take advantage of that we will lose."[26] In the perspective of the new Right, globalization does not imply capitulating to the United States but rather cultivating relations with emerging power centers on the global landscape. They hope such relations might obviate the need to come to terms with the United States at all.

The war generation also displays a degree of indifference and passivity toward America. Iran's president Mahmoud Ahmadinejad emphasized this point, stressing, "Our nation is continuing the path of progress and on this path has no significant need for the United States."[27] The notion that Iran should offer substantial concessions on critical national issues, such as its nuclear program, for the sake of American benevolence or European investments has a limited utility to them. After a quarter-century of hostility, war, and sanctions, Iran's emerging leadership class is looking east, where its human rights record and proliferation efforts are not particularly disturbing to its prospective commercial partners. All this is not to suggest that the new regime cannot have tactical dealings with America, but a fundamental transformation of U.S.–Iranian relations is unlikely to be achieved by Ahmadenijad and his allies.

The younger conservatives' perception that expanding trade with China and India can resolve Iran's economic predicament reflects their lack of understanding of the complexity and interconnections of the global economy. Although it is true that Iran has signed a handful of blockbuster energy deals with China and India, the rosy headlines often obscure a starker economic reality. These deals represent only the most preliminary phases of projects that, particularly in the case of a proposed natural gas pipeline to India, entail enormous political, commercial, and geological risks. In addition, projects of this scale are unlikely to move forward without significant Western capital and technical expertise—precisely the sort of assistance that the West could withhold. It is such a realization that may eventually lead the younger conservatives to appreciate the centrality of America to the global economy and the international investment community. The hard realities of actually governing may in time temper their ideological designs and lead them in the direction of their more pragmatic elders.

Today, a new consolidated conservative government has the national charge to chart Iran's international course. The melodramatic depictions of the new president ought not to obscure the reality that this is still a coalition government, with many competing centers of power and levers of influence. To be sure, the hard-line faction of the conservative bloc has assumed a preponderance of influence, diminishing the power of pragmatic conservatives whose patron saint Rafsanjani was defeated in the presidential election. Ayatollah Khamenei, the Supreme Leader, has to once more balance these contending voices, determining Iran's approach to sensitive issues such as nuclear weapons and terrorism. It is to these issues that we now turn.

6

ALONG THE
NUCLEAR PRECIPICE

The Iranian regime is defying the world with its nuclear ambitions, and the nations of the world must not permit the Iranian regime to gain nuclear weapons," proclaimed President Bush in his 2006 State of the Union address.[1] As the debate still lingers regarding the vanished Iraqi weapons of mass destruction, yet another proliferation crisis is looming in the Middle East. Washington and much of the international community fear that under the guise of a civilian research program Iran is gradually accumulating the technology and expertise necessary for the construction of nuclear weapons. The question that has bedeviled successive U.S. administrations is how to prevent Iran from crossing the nuclear threshold.[2]

Why does Iran want the bomb? Has the theocracy settled on its course, or are there contending factions that can still be influenced to temper Iran's nuclear ambitions? Who are the proponents of the nuclear option within the theocratic regime, and how influential are they in terms of pressing their case? What impact has the presidency of

Mahmoud Ahmadinejad had on Iran's nuclear deliberations? The answer to these questions requires a better understanding of the interlocking calculations that have propelled Iran toward the nuclear option in the first place.

REVELATIONS

Iran's nuclear ambitions did not begin with the onset of the Islamic revolution in 1979. The nuclear program actually started in the early 1970s under the Shah, who with the assistance of West Germany, France, and South Africa sought to construct an infrastructure of nuclear power plants. Approximately $40 billion was earmarked for this ambitious project, whose purpose was the construction of at least twenty reactors. Suspicion lingered that behind the Shah's declared desire for nuclear energy lay a determination to construct a nuclear weapon. Indeed, the Shah's former foreign minister, Ardeshir Zahedi, has all but confirmed such concerns:

> The Iranian strategy at that time was aimed at creating what is known as surge capacity, that is to say to have the know-how, the infrastructure, and the personnel needed to develop a nuclear military capacity within a short time without actually doing so. But the assumption within the policymaking elite was that Iran should be in a position to develop and test a nuclear device within 18 months.[3]

Akbar Etemad, the director of Iran's nuclear program at the time of the monarchy, similarly endorses Zahedi's claim that the Shah's program was designed to grant him the option of assembling the bomb should his regional competitors move in that direction.[4]

As the theocratic regime is quick to point out, Washington was not only complicit in the Shah's program but never asked, as it persistently does today, why an oil-rich state requires nuclear power. Moreover, the European states that currently are calling on Iran to suspend its enrichment activities were busy selling the Shah the needed technology for the construction of an elaborate network of nuclear plants that could have been easily misused for military purposes. The belated Western concerns regarding Iran's proliferation tendencies adds to Tehran's arguments regarding the hypocrisy of the great powers and the iniquitous nature of the Nuclear Non-Proliferation Treaty (NPT).

During the initial decade of the Islamic Republic, the regime's preoccupations with consolidating power, the war with Iraq, and its international isolation precluded it from aggressively pursuing the nuclear option. Indeed, for Khomeini and many others within the clerical elite, the indiscriminate nature of such weapons was seen as inconsistent with Islamic canons of war. A more detailed focus on the nuclear infrastructure began during Rafsanjani's presidency in the early 1990s and was sustained by Khatami's reformist government.

Successive U.S. administrations have sought to thwart Iran's nuclear ambitions. Over the years, Washington has scored some impressive gains and managed to delay and frustrate Tehran's quest for nuclear technology. The Reagan administration succeeded in obtaining Europe's agreement to rigorous export controls with respect to dual-use technologies and in getting Germany to abandon its cooperation with Iran's nascent nuclear program. Given Europe's unwillingness to assist in Iran's nuclear research activities, Tehran turned to a new source, Russia.

The Russian Federation soon began to fill the void left by the Europeans and assisted Iran in building its two nuclear reactors at Bushehr, which suffered from neglect during the Iran-Iraq war. Over the years Russia has also provided Iran with fuel fabrication technology and, possibly, even uranium enrichment centrifuge plans. Throughout the 1990s, the administrations of George H. W. Bush and Bill Clinton attempted to deter Russia from this course by means of warnings, selective sanctions, and promises of expanded economic ties. A number of compacts were negotiated between the United States and Russia, most notably the December 1995 accord hammered out by Vice President Al Gore and Prime Minister Viktor Chernomyrdin, in which Russia agreed to limit its cooperation with Iran to work on one unit of the Bushehr plant. Russia in essence agreed not to provide additional reactors or fuel-cycle assistance to Iran. By 2000, this arrangement had unraveled, as the lure of profits and strategic cooperation between Tehran and Moscow began to dissuade President Vladimir Putin from a more robust cooperation with the United States.

Despite energetic American diplomacy, throughout the 1990s the international community appeared complacent regarding Iran's nuclear program. The successful efforts by the Clinton administration to prevent substantial international cooperation with Iran's nascent nuclear industry, coupled with Iranian corruption and mismanagement, led to perceptions that the program had stalled. Issues such as terrorism, Iran's opposition to the peace process, and its quest for missile technology and chemical weapons tended to overshadow the nuclear issue. The international community's sporadic expressions of concern did not necessarily trigger diplomatic sanctions or multilateral pressure.

All this changed in August 2002, as a series of revelations forced the Washington establishment to revise its previous intelligence assessments. The first shock came when an opposition group revealed the extensive facilities for uranium enrichment in Natanz, approximately 200 miles south of Tehran. The installations demonstrated Iran's mastery of the complex process of enriching uranium. The Natanz facilities contained 160 centrifuges needed for enrichment purposes, with another 1,000 under construction. The plan was to reach 50,000 completed centrifuges within two years, which would give Iran the capability to produce several bombs a year.

In addition, it appeared that Tehran had been similarly active in the development of a plutonium route to nuclear capability. The heavy-water facilities in Esfahan and the nearly completed plants in Arak point to the fact that Iran's plutonium enrichment capabilities were more advanced than initially anticipated. Even more ominous is an indication that Tehran's program is reaching the point of self-sufficiency. Although Iran's nuclear industry at various stages has benefited from external assistance, particularly from Russia and even more from the Abdul Qadeer Khan network in Pakistan, the sophisticated nature of these facilities reveals that Iran may have reached the point of self-reliance, whereby traditional counterproliferation measures, such as more rigorous export controls and curtailment of external assistance, will not measurably slow down its nuclear time line. Iran's former president Rafsanjani confirmed, "That we are on the verge of nuclear breakout is true."[5] Ali Akbar Salehi, the former Iranian representative to the International Atomic Energy Association (IAEA), similarly stressed, "We have found the way and we do not have any scientific problems."[6]

In April 2006, Iran appeared to take another important step toward nuclear self-reliance. Amid much fanfare, President Ahmadinejad announced that Iran had succeeded in assembling 164 centrifuges and actually enriching uranium. The latest Iranian announcement made clear that the nuclear program was aggressively moving forward with Iran overcoming many technological hurdles on its path toward creating a sophisticated nuclear network.

Despite such revelations, it is still difficult to predict with any degree of accuracy when Iran will be in a position to construct a deliverable nuclear device. Once Iran completes the necessary infrastructure from mining to enriching uranium at the suitable weapons-grade level and masters the engineering skill required to assemble a bomb, it could cross the threshold in a short period of time. All this would depend on the scope and scale of the program and the level of national resources committed to this task. Iran today has an accelerated program, but not a crash one similar to Pakistan's in the early 1970s when the entirety of national energies were mobilized behind the task of constructing a nuclear device. In this context, Iran's persistent determination to complete the fuel cycle—a right it does possess under the NPT—brings it close to a weapon's capability.

Having stipulated the importance of paying attention to Iran's scientific progress, an excessive focus on technological dimensions of the nuclear program can offer a distorted time line. Historically, as a state develops its nuclear program, it creates political and bureaucratic constituencies and nationalistic pressures that generate their own proliferation momentum. As India and Pakistan demonstrated, once a nuclear program matures, it attracts political patrons invoking national prestige, military officers attracted to the weapons of awesome power, and a scientific establishment seeking to perpetuate a program that generates profits and jobs. As such alliances and constituencies develop, a state can cross the point of no return years before it can actually assemble a single bomb. Although Iranian nationalistic pressure has not yet reached the same level of India and Pakistan when they embarked on their crash programs, indications that this phenomenon is becoming all too evident appear in the case of Iran. Thus, time is not necessarily on the side of the United States and the international community.

Although it is customary to suggest that Iran is determined to manufacture the bomb, there is a subtle debate taking place within the theocratic state on the direction of the program. The critical question thus becomes: What are the security factors driving Iran's proliferation tendencies? As constituencies and alliances shift, and policies and positions alter, the United States still has an opportunity to influence Iran's internal deliberations.

WHY DOES IRAN WANT THE BOMB?

Contrary to many Western assumptions, Iran's quest for nuclear weapons does not stem from irrational ideological postulations, but from a judicious attempt to craft a viable deterrent posture against a range of threats. It is often argued that Iran's dangerous and unpredictable neighborhood grants it ample incentive for acquiring nuclear weapons. But it is hard to see how the possession of such weapons would ameliorate the persistent volatility on Iran's frontiers. Instabilities in Afghanistan and Central Asia may be sources of significant concern for Iran's defense planners, but nuclear weapons can scarcely defuse such crises. A more careful examination reveals that Iran's nuclear program has been conditioned by a narrower but more pronounced set of threats. Historically, the need to negate the American and Iraqi threats has been the primary motivation for Iran's policy-makers. In more recent times, the simmering concerns regarding the stability of a nuclear-armed Pakistan have similarly enhanced the value of such weapons to Iran's planners.

From the outset, it is important to place the question of Israel in its proper context. It is often assumed that the hostile relations between Iran and Israel, which possesses nuclear weapons but will not acknowledge that capability publicly, inexorably propel Tehran toward the nuclear option. Indeed, Iran's animus toward the Jewish state has led it to support terrorist organizations and Palestinian rejectionist forces plotting against Israel. However, both Iran and Israel have been careful to regulate their low-intensity conflict and have assiduously avoided direct military confrontation. Ayatollah Khamenei has characterized Iran's controlled rage by stressing that "the Palestine issue is not Iran's Jihad."[7] The alarmist Iranian rhetoric regarding the immediacy of the Israeli threat is more an attempt to mobilize domestic and regional constituencies behind an anti-Israel policy than a genuine reflection of concern. For the Islamic Republic, Israel may be an ideological affront and a civilizational challenge, but it is not an existential threat mandating the provision of nuclear weapons.

To the extent that Israel's nuclear arsenal figures in the Iranian debate, it is to condemn the hypocrisy of the international community—and the United States in particular—for being perennially critical of Iran's nuclear efforts yet retaining a strange silence when it comes to Israel's formidable depository of atomic bombs. Rafsanjani captured the frustration of the clerical class: "When they talk about nuclear weapons, they don't even mention the Zionist state."[8] And yet Iran's antagonism toward Israel is not truly part of a motivation for the bomb. Iranian officials and military officers routinely stress that they do not need nuclear arms to wage their current low-intensity campaign against Israel. Terrorism and reliance on militant Islamic forces have always been Iran's preferred method of conducting its conflict with Israel. All this may change should Israel embark on a precipitous action such as military strikes against Iran's facilities. In essence, such an action would finally lead the Iranian-Israeli confrontation to move beyond its existing limits, transforming Israel into a military challenge that Iran needs to safeguard against.

While Israel may be peripheral to Iran's aspirations for unconventional weapons, developments in the Persian Gulf are of immense importance. From the Islamic Republic's perspective, the Gulf is its most important strategic arena, and its most reliable route of access to the international petroleum market. For a long time, it was Iraq that spurred the theocratic elite toward the nuclear option. Saddam Hussein's Iraq not only sought hegemony over the Gulf, and indeed the larger Middle East, but also waged a merciless eight-year war against Iran. It is the developments in the Gulf that will likely condition Iran's defense posture and nuclear ambitions for the foreseeable future.

The impact of the Iran-Iraq war on Tehran's nuclear calculations cannot be underestimated. Iraq's employment of chemical weapons against Iranian civilians and combatants has permanently scarred Iran's national psyche. The Iranian government estimates that the country suffered 34,000 casualities as a result of Iraq's chemical weapon attacks. Whatever their tactical military utility, in Saddam's hands chemical weapons were tools of terror, since he hoped that through their indiscriminate use he could frighten and demoralize the Iranian populace. To an extent this strategy proved effective. Iraq's determination to target Iranian cities during the latter stages of the war did much to undermine the national support for the continuation of the conflict. Two decades later, the war and its legacy are still debated daily in the pages of Iranian newspapers, in the halls of Iranian universities, and on the floor of the Iranian parliament. As the newspaper *Ya Lesarat* observed, "One can still see the wounds of our war veterans that were inflicted by poison gas as used by Saddam Hussein that were made in Germany and France."[9] The dramatic memories of the war have led to cries of "Never Again," uniting a fractious public behind the desire to achieve not just a credible deterrent but also a convincing retaliatory capability.

Beyond the human toll, the war also changed Iran's strategic doctrine. During the war, Iran persisted with the notion that technological superiority cannot overcome revolutionary zeal and a willingness to offer martyrs. To compensate for its lack of weaponry, Iran launched human wave assaults and used its young population as a tool of an offensive military strategy. The devastation of the war and the loss of an appetite for "martyrdom" among Iran's youth has invalidated that theory. As Rafsanjani acknowledged, "With regard to chemical, bacteriological, and radiological weapons, it was made clear during the war that these weapons are very decisive. We should fully equip ourselves in both offensive and defensive use of these weapons."[10] Moreover, the indifference of the international community to Saddam's crimes also left its mark, leading Iran to reject the notion that international treaties and compacts can ensure its security. As Mohsen Rezai, the former commander of the Revolutionary Guards, said in 2004, "We cannot, generally speaking, argue that our country will derive any benefit from accepting international treaties."[11] Deterrence could no longer be predicated on revolutionary commitment and international opinion, as Iran required a more credible military response.

The overthrow of Saddam's regime has diminished but has by no means eliminated the Iraqi challenge. The unpredictable nature of developments in Iraq has intensified Iran's anxieties and further enhanced the utility of the nuclear option. Should Iraq emerge as a close U.S. ally policing the Gulf at the behest of its superpower benefactor, Iran will stand marginalized and isolated. Indeed, the long-standing ambition of successive Iraqi governments to assert predominance in the Gulf may finally be nurtured by a superpower seeking local allies to contain recalcitrant states such as Iran. A revival of the Nixon Doctrine, whereby the United States sought to ensure the stability of the Persian Gulf by arming its pliant Iranian ally, with Iraq now assuming the role once played by the Shah, would seriously constrain Tehran's options. A presumptive nuclear capability would grant Iran a greater ability to assert its interests and press its claims. Although today Iraq appears far from such a position, the theocratic regime still must formulate a range of contingencies, and one such option is to sustain a robust nuclear research program.

Iraq is not the only potential problem that Iran faces; looking east lies a nuclear-armed Pakistan with its own strain of anti-Shiism. Although General Pervez Musharraf is routinely celebrated in Washington as a reliable ally in the war against terrorism, Pakistan's past is more checkered and problematic. Throughout the 1990s, Pakistan perceived the demise of the Soviet Union as a unique opportunity to exert its influence in Central Asia and to capture the emerging markets in that critical area. Afghanistan was viewed as an indispensable bridge to Central Asia, and Pakistani intelligence services did much to ensure the triumph of the radical Taliban movement in the ensuing Afghan civil war. The rise of the Taliban and the eventual establishment of the al-Qaeda camps in Afghanistan had much to do with Pakistan's cynical strategy. Throughout the 1990s, such Pakistani machinations caused considerable tensions with Iran, which was uneasy about the emergence of a radical Sunni regime on its northeastern border.

Although Pakistan's relations with Iran have improved since September 11, with Pakistan's final abandonment of the Taliban, the specter of instability in Islamabad haunts Iran's leadership. The possibility of the collapse of the current military government and its displacement by a radical Sunni regime with access to nuclear weapons is something Iran feels it must guard against. Pakistan's nuclear test in 1998 caused considerable anxiety in Tehran, with Rafsanjani stressing, "This is a major step toward proliferation of nuclear weapons. This is a truly dangerous matter and we must be concerned."[12] Foreign minister Kamal Kharrazi also mused, "This was one genie that was much better to have stayed confined in the bottle."[13] Along with Iraq, Pakistan is a potential threat that Iran must take into consideration as it plots its defense strategy.

Although both Iraq and Pakistan constitute long-term sources of concern, today the United States stands as Iran's foremost strategic challenge. U.S.–Iranian relations have become even more strained in recent years, with the Bush administration routinely calling for a change of regime in Tehran. The massive projection of American power on all of Iran's frontiers since September 11 has added credence to the Iranian claim of being encircled by the United States. The conservative newspaper *Jomhuri-ye Islami* captured Tehran's dilemma: "In the contemporary world, it is obvious that having access to advanced weapons shall cause deterrence and therefore security, and will neutralize the evil wishes of great powers to attack other nations and countries."[14] In a rare note of agreement, the leading liberal newspaper, *Aftab-e Yazd,* similarly stressed that, given the regional exigencies, "in the future Iran might be thinking about the military aspects of nuclear energy."[15]

The remarkable success of Operation Iraqi Freedom in overthrowing Saddam cannot but have made an impression on Iran's leadership. The reality remains that Iraq's anticipated chemical weapons did not deter Washington from military intervention. As an Iranian official confessed, "The fact that Saddam was toppled in twenty-one days is something that should concern all the countries in the region."[16] Conversely, North Korea offers its own lessons and possibilities. Pyongyang's presumed nuclear capability has not only obviated a preemptive invasion, but actually generated potential security and economic benefits. President Bush may loathe Kim Jong Il, but far from contemplating military action, the United States and its allies are considering an economic relief package and security guarantees to dissuade North Korea from its nuclear path. The contrasting fates of Iraq and North Korea certainly elevate the significance of nuclear weapons in the Iranian clerical cosmology.

Post–September 11 developments in the Middle East have had a paradoxical impact on the Islamic Republic. Two of Iran's formidable foes, the Taliban and Saddam Hussein, have been overthrown by the United States. In the meantime, Iran's American nemesis is entangled in an Iraq quagmire, draining its resources and tempering its ambitions. Nevertheless, the Iranian clerical elite expect a turbulent future, which accentuates their sense of insecurity. Iran remains in

America's crosshairs, at a time when the U.S. military presence in the region has never been greater. The influential *Iran News* emphasized this point in an editorial: "Based on Bush's record after 9/11, one can only conclude that the U.S. did not invade our two immediate neighbors to the east and the west just to fight al-Qaeda. Consequently, astute political observers warn that Iran is next on the U.S. list of direct targets."[17] Such anxieties enhance the apparent strategic utility of nuclear weapons to Iran and validate the claim that the Islamic Republic requires such a capability to ensure both regime survival and territorial integrity.

Hovering over all these threats is the reality of Iran's strategic loneliness. Iran does not have true allies; rather it has convenient relationships with states such as Syria that are often based on mutual animosities. True alliances based on shared values and common vision have largely eluded the Islamic Republic. Iran is still surrounded by states with important security ties to the United States and continues to possess conventional arms that cannot deter its more powerful adversaries. Such a precarious strategic environment has led to a search for a deterrent power predicated on indigenous resources. In essence, the inability of Iran to integrate itself into the regional landscape and to craft conventional forces sufficient for dealing with all its potential threats makes nuclear weapons even more compelling. However, this is still the Islamic Republic, a fractious, divided state that can rarely forge a consensus on key issues. Even on an important topic such as nuclear weapons, voices of dissent within the clerical establishment are still sufficiently influential to have an impact on Iran's nuclear deliberations.

THE DEBATE

More than any other issue, the nuclear question has exposed the divisions within the clerical establishment over Iran's international orientation. Iran's contending factions are united on the need to sustain a vibrant nuclear research program that, in due course, will offer

Tehran the option of assembling a bomb. However, the prospect of actually crossing the nuclear threshold in defiance of the international community and in violation of Iran's long-standing treaty commitments has generated a subtle yet robust debate. Effective American diplomacy can still condition this debate in favor of the more pragmatic elements within the theocratic elite.

From the outset it must be emphasized that for all the factions involved in this debate, the core issue is how to safeguard Iran's national interests. The Islamic Republic is not an irrational rogue state seeking such weaponry as an instrument of an aggressive, revolutionary foreign policy designed to project its power abroad. This is not an "Islamic bomb" to be handed over to terrorist organizations or exploded in the streets of New York or Washington. The fact is that Iran has long possessed chemical weapons, and has yet to transfer such arms to its terrorist allies. Iran's cautious leaders are most interested in remaining in power and fully appreciate that transferring nuclear weapons to terrorists could lead to the type of retaliation from the United States or Israel that would eliminate their regime altogether. For Iran this is a weapon of deterrence, and the relevant question is whether its possession will serve its practical interests.

The primary supporters of the nuclear breakout option are hard-line elements associated with the Supreme Leader, Ayatollah Khamenei. Through command of key institutions such as the Revolutionary Guards and the Guardian Council, Iran's reactionary clerics have enormous influence on national security planning. A fundamental tenet of the hard-liners' ideology is the notion that the Islamic Republic is in constant danger from predatory external forces, necessitating military self-reliance. This perception was initially molded by a revolution that sought not just to defy international norms but to refashion them. The passage of time and the failure of that mission have not necessarily diminished the hard-liners' suspicions of the international order and its primary guardian, the United States. *Jomhuri-ye Islami*, the conservative newspaper and the mouthpiece of Khamenei, sounded this theme:

The core problem is the fact that our officials' outlook on the nuclear dossier of Iran is faulty and they are on the wrong track. It seems they have failed to appreciate that America is after our destruction and the nuclear issue is merely an excuse for them.[18]

In a similar vein, *Resalat,* another influential conservative paper, sounded the themes of deterrence and national interest by claiming, "In the present situation of international order whose main characteristics are injustice and the weakening of the rights of others, the Islamic Republic has no alternative but intelligent resistance while paying the least cost."[19] Given its paranoia and suspicions, the Iranian Right does not necessarily object to international isolation and confrontation with the West. Indeed, for many within this camp, such a conflict would be an effective means of rekindling popular support for the revolution's fading élan.

Iran's nuclear calculations have been further hardened by the rise of war veterans, such as President Ahmadinejad, to positions of power. Although the Iran-Iraq war ended nearly twenty years ago, for many within the Islamic Republic it was a defining experience that altered their strategic assumptions. Even a cursory examination of Ahmadinejad's speeches reveals that for him the war is far from a faded memory. In his defiant speech at the UN General Assembly in September 2005, Iran's president pointedly admonished the assembled dignitaries for their failings:

For eight years, Saddam's regime imposed a massive war of aggression against my people. It employed the most heinous weapons of mass destruction including chemical weapons against Iranians and Iraqis alike. Who, in fact, armed Saddam with those weapons? What was the reaction of those who claim to fight against WMDs regarding the use of chemical weapons then?[20]

The international indifference to Saddam's war crimes and Tehran's lack of an effective response have led Iran's war-veteran president to perceive that the security of his country cannot be predicated on global opinion and treaties.

At the core, all disarmament agreements call upon a state to forgo a certain degree of sovereignty in exchange for enhanced security. Once a state renounces its weapons of mass destruction programs it can be assured of support from the international community should it be threatened by another state possessing such arms. This implied trade-off has no value for Iran's hard-liners. Once more, the prolonged war with Iraq conditions their worldview and behavior. Iraq's use of chemical weapons against Iran—with impunity, if not the tacit acceptance of Western powers—has reinforced Iran's suspicions of the international order. *Jomhuri-ye Islami* observed, "As a rule, it is futile to enter any deal with the West over issues related to the country's independence and national security."[21] For many of the Islamic Republic's reactionary leaders, the only way to safeguard Iran's interests is to develop an independent nuclear deterrent.

Beyond the legacy of the war, America's demands that Iran relinquish its fuel cycle rights under the Nuclear Non-Proliferation Treaty has aroused the leadership's nationalistic impulses. As a country that has historically been the subject of foreign intervention and the imposition of various capitulation treaties, Iran is inordinately sensitive to its national prerogatives and sovereign rights. The rulers of Iran perceive that they are being challenged not because of their provocations and previous treaty violations, but because of superpower bullying. In a peculiar manner, the nuclear program and Iran's national identity have become fused in the imagination of the hard-liners. To stand against America on this issue is to validate one's revolutionary ardor and sense of nationalism. Ali Hussein-Tash, deputy secretary of the Supreme National Security Council, stressed this point, saying, "A nation that does not engage in risks and difficult challenges, and a nation which does not stand up for itself, can never be a proud nation."[22] Thus, the notion of compromise and acquiescence has limited utility to Iran's aggrieved nationalists.

After decades of tension, Iranian reactionaries perceive that conflict with the United States is inevitable and the only means of tempering America's ambitions is through the possession of the bomb. Although today the United States may seem entangled in an Iraq quagmire, for Iranian hawks it is still an aggressive state whose power cannot be discounted and whose intentions must not be trusted. The arch-conservative *Keyhan* newspaper pointedly advised the regime "to plan for acquiring the knowledge and ability to make nuclear weapons, which is necessary in preparation for the next phase in the future battlefield."[23]

Despite their bitterness and cynicism, the theocratic hard-liners are eternal optimists when it comes to their assessment of how the international community will respond to Iran's nuclear breakout. Many influential conservative voices insist that Iran will follow the model of India and Pakistan, with the initial international outcry soon followed by an acceptance of Iran's new status. Thus, Tehran would regain its commercial contracts and keep its nuclear weapons. The former Iranian foreign minister Ali Akbar Velayati noted this theme, stressing, "Whenever we stand firm and defend our righteous stands resolutely, they are forced to retreat and have no alternatives."[24] The Right thus rejects the notion that Iran's mischievous past and its tense relations with the United States will militate against the international community's accepting Iran's nuclear status.

Should their anticipations prove misguided, however, and Iran become the subject of sanctions, it is a price the hard-liners are willing to pay for an important national prerogative. Ahmadinejad has pointedly noted that even if sanctions were to be imposed, "the Iranian nation would still have its rights."[25] In a similar vein, Ayatollah Jannati has stated, "We do not welcome sanctions, but if we are threatened by sanctions, we will not give in."[26] The notion of the need to sacrifice and struggle on behalf of the revolution and resist imperious international demands is an essential tenet of the hard-liners' ideological perspective.

In the Islamic Republic's informal governing structure, the national security decisions are subject to input by many figures, even those not necessarily with a portfolio. For instance, the former prime minister Mir Hussein Mussavi, who has been out of power for nearly twenty years but is greatly respected due to his service during the war with Iraq, is consulted intimately about Iran's nuclear course. It appears that despite Western perceptions that the nuclear issue is decided by a narrow band of conservatives, Ayatollah Khamenei has broaden the parameters of the debate to include relevant elites from across the political spectrum in the nuclear deliberations. Thus, reformers out of power, moderate conservatives struggling against their reactionary brethren, as well as professionals from key bureaucracies are allowed to stress their points of view. Given the provocative nature of the nuclear program, Khamenei seems to be hoping that the burden of any ensuing international confrontation would be assumed by all political factions, as opposed to being the responsibility of only the conservatives. The systematic consolidation of power by the conservatives over the state does not necessarily mean that voices of restraint have been excised from the decision-making process.

In contrast to the hard-liners, the pragmatic elements within the Islamic Republic insist that Iran's integration into the international order and the global economy mandates accepting certain restrictions on its nuclear program. Although it is tempting to see this issue as divided between reactionaries and reformers, the coalition pressing for reticence features both pragmatists, such as Rafsanjani, who is currently the head of the Expediency Council, and Hasan Rowhani, former secretary for the Supreme Council on National Security— officials within the ministries and important elements of Iran's national security establishment who retain their status irrespective of who is president. The proponents of this strategy do not call for the dismantling of Iran's nuclear edifice but for the development of an advanced capacity within the flexible guidelines of the NPT. Given Iran's long-term commitment to the NPT and the prevailing international scrutiny, a provocative policy could invite multilateral sanctions and lead Iran's valuable commercial partners, such as the European Union, to embrace the U.S. policy of isolating and pressuring Iran. Thus, for this constituency, a hedging strategy can sustain Iran's nuclear program while maintaining its international ties.

Over the winter of 2005–2006, as Iran's reckless diplomacy generated a series of IAEA resolutions condemning its conduct and referring it to the UN Security Council, the members of this group called for restraint, and even for suspension of various nuclear activities. Rafsanjani took the lead in admonishing President Ahmadinejad: "We have reached a sensitive point. There is need for prudence on both sides."[27] The reformers went still further; in March 2006, Muhammad Reza Khatami, the head of the Islamic Participation Front, insisted, "We have written numerous letters to Leader Khamenei to explain that insisting on enriching uranium is not in the country's interest; that in this way we lose all the benefits gained over the past sixteen years; and that the only proper position is suspension of uranium-enriching activities and negotiations with the aim of fostering trust and having international oversight."[28] The more moderate elements see the nuclear program in a wider context of Iran's international relations. Given that Iran's pursuit of its nuclear ambitions damages other aspects of its foreign policy, this group favors compromise and even a potential suspension of the program.

Beyond the fears of sanctions and isolation, some proponents of nuclear restraint argue that such weapons do not necessarily serve Iran's strategic interests. Should Iran cross the nuclear threshold, the Gulf states and the newly independent Iraq are likely to gravitate further toward the American security umbrella. Indeed, under the auspices of the United States, a Persian Gulf security architecture may evolve with the purpose of containing and isolating the Islamic Republic. As Iran's former representative to the IAEA, Ali Akbar Salehi, emphasized in June 2004, "We cannot buy security by having nuclear weapons which only invite more threats against ourselves."[29]

Unlike their reactionary brethren, the more pragmatic elements appreciate that given Iran's "exceptional" nature and the eagerness of the

United States to publicize all of its infractions as a means of multi-lateralizing its coercive policy, a defiant posture may not serve it well. The influential moderate politician Mohsen Mirdamadi stipulated, "The reality is that our recent achievement in the area of nuclear technology has been part of our strength and created new opportunities for us in the international arena, but we should not turn this into a new threat. We should be careful not to bring the U.S. and Europe together."[30] To be sure, other states have surreptitiously developed nuclear weapons, but they did so with superpower acceptance—even complicity—and in an international environment that was not suspicious of their intent. Iran does not enjoy such advantages, since its revolutionary past and its continued engagement with terrorist organizations make many states wary of its motives. Tehran simply does not have the luxury granted to Israel or India. All this does not imply a propensity to renounce a weapons capability but a recognition of the need for restraint and the importance of the international community and its opinion.

Iran's pragmatists have increasingly been drawn to the North Korean model, as Pyongyang has adroitly managed to employ its nuclear defiance to extract concessions from the international community. Through a similar posture of restraint and defiance, threats, and blandishments, perhaps Tehran can also play the nuclear card to renegotiate a more rational relationship with its leading nemesis, the United States. The conservative publication *Farda*, with its ties to the hardline community, put forward such a proposition: "The credibility that these weapons have had and continue to have at the global level, their importance, is in the support they give to bargaining in international negotiations and advancement of the country's national interests." The influential conservative politician Muhammad Javad Larijani echoed this theme: "If our national interests dictate, we can go to the bowels of hell to negotiate with the devil."[31]

Hovering over this debate, once more, stands Ayatollah Khamenei. As mentioned, the Supreme Leader's instincts would be to support the reactionary elements in their call for defiance and pursuit of the nuclear option. But in his role as the guardian of the state, he must consider the nuclear program in the context of Iran's larger international relations. Thus far, he has opted for compromise and appeasement of all the factions involved in the debate. On the one hand, Khamenei has endorsed the acceleration of Iran's program and construction of an advanced nuclear infrastructure. Yet, he has also conceded the need for negotiations with the international community and has pressed the state toward a degree of restraint. All this may change, since Iran needs to make critical decisions regarding its nuclear program, with many of those decisions conditioned by the conduct of external actors, particularly the United States.

In assessing a state's nuclear path, it is important to note that its motivations cannot be exclusively examined within the context of its national interests and security considerations. Whatever strategic benefits such weapons offer a state, they are certainly a source of national prestige and parochial benefits to various bureaucracies and politicians. As such constituencies emerge, a state can cross the nuclear threshold even if the initial strategic factors that provoked the program are no longer salient. The emergence of bureaucracies and nationalistic pressures in Iran is generating its own proliferation momentum, empowering those seeking a nuclear breakout. As time passes, the pragmatic voices calling for hedging are likely to be marginalized and lose their influence within the regime.

THE POLITICS OF NUCLEAR WEAPONS

As Iran's nuclear program matures and becomes the subject of international scrutiny, another dynamic is entering the debate: public opinion. Far from being a source of restraint, the emerging public sentiment is that Iran, as a great civilization with a long history, has a right to acquire a nuclear capability. The recent disclosures of the sophisticated nature of Iran's nuclear program have been a source of pride for a citizenry accustomed to the revolution's failures and setbacks. Raf-

sanjani, one of the Islamic Republic's most astute politicians, acknowledged this trend when he said, "No official would dare allow
himself to defy the people on such an issue."[32] In March 2005, the Islamic
Republic even issued a postage stamp celebrating the achievements
of its nuclear energy program.[33] Washington's incendiary rhetoric and
its designation of Iran as part of an "axis of evil" that should not have
access to such technologies has only inflamed a highly nationalistic
population. In the popular discourse, the notions of sovereign rights
and national dignity are increasingly displacing calls for adherence to
treaty commitments.

Iran's experience during the past quarter-century with war, sanctions, and estrangement from the international community has fostered
a population that is somewhat unresponsive to external pressures.
Among the themes consistently propounded in the press is the notion
of American hypocrisy over the application of the NPT. The fact that
Israel has escaped criticism from Washington has been cleverly exploited by conservative politicians to arouse nationalistic backing for
Iran's acquisition of nuclear capabilities. Moreover, the attempt by
the United States to restrict membership in the exclusive nuclear
club has always irked the Iranian leaders and masses alike. America is
thus routinely condemned by Iranian writers, academics, and politicians as arrogant and self-serving. The leading conservative thinker,
Amir Mohebian, pointedly criticized the U.S. posture: "The Americans say in order to preserve the peace for their children, they should
have nuclear weapons and we should not." In a strange note of agreement, one of the foremost reformist activists, Mostafa Tajzadeh,
noted, "It's basically a matter of equilibrium: if I don't have a nuclear
bomb, I don't have security."[34]

Among the most vociferous critics of any accommodation on the
nuclear issue are student organizations. Iranian students are seen by
many analysts as a reliable barometer of public opinion, as they often
play a vanguard political role in significant movements in Iranian history. It is customary for Western audiences to identify Iranian students

with progressive causes, as they have been the most vocal advocates of greater democratization and reform of the Islamic Republic. On the nuclear issue, however, Iran's educated youth seem to view disarmament agreements as an abridgment of national rights and have warned their elders against capitulating to external pressures. Upon Iran's acceptance of the Additional Protocol, which called for more intrusive inspections of its nuclear plants in October 2003, Iran's universities were rocked with demonstrations against the agreement. In the prestigious Sharif Technical University, students passed a resolution equating the accords with "treason." In a meeting of university students from across the country in Bushehr (the site of Iran's nuclear reactor), an easily passed resolution proclaimed, "We, the Iranian students, consider access to nuclear energy as the legitimate right of the Iranian nation. We will never bow to oppression and hegemonic policies."[35] In 2004 yet another open letter signed by 1,700 students from across the country stated, "The nation will never accept any negligence or justifications from the officials with respect to the application of nuclear technology."[36] As public opinion becomes a factor in the nuclear deliberations, it is likely to further press the clerical elite in the direction of enhanced nuclear capabilities that can be transformed for military purposes.

Alongside this popular sentiment is the emergence of a bureaucratic and scientific establishment with its own parochial considerations. Under the auspices of the Revolutionary Guards, an entire array of organizations such as the Defense Industries Organization, university laboratories, and a plethora of companies (many of them owned by hard-line clerics) have provided the impetus for Iran's expanding and lucrative nuclear efforts. As with the students, Tehran's acceptance of the Additional Protocol in 2003 brought forth protest from these corners, with 250 of Iran's leading scientists signing an open letter, warning, "We the signers of this letter urge the government of the Islamic Republic to, under no circumstances, sign any letter which would create an impediment to our legitimate right to acquire knowledge and technology."[37] The continued Iranian negotiations with the

European states and the suspension of its program brought forth an-other rebuke by 1,375 professors who signed a letter calling for re-sumption of activities, which are, after all, legal under the provisions of the NPT.[38]

In an even more ominous manner, the Revolutionary Guard leader-ship has been dubious about the utility of treaties in terms of safe-guarding Iran's security interests. In a remarkable outburst, the commander of the Revolutionary Guards, Yahya Rahim Safavi, point-edly asked, "Can we withstand America's threats and domineering at-titude with a policy of détente? Will we be able to protect the Islamic Republic from international Zionism by signing conventions banning the proliferation of chemical and nuclear weapons?"[39] Although most members of the scientific community tend to at least limit their pub-lic declarations to calls for development of Iran's nuclear industry under the confines of the NPT, the more militant Revolutionary Guard leadership seems to be pressing for outright construction of the bomb. Disturbingly, the operational management of Iran's nuclear program rests in the hands of the hard-line elements who have scant respect for international treaties and obligations. The prestige and profits generated by this mission reinforce the strategic arguments for the prolongation of the nuclear program.

The surprising aspect of the public debate in Iran is the extent to which it mirrors the discussions that took place in China, India, and Israel before those states joined the nuclear club. National prestige, notions of sovereign independence, great-power hypocrisy, and the need for a viable deterrence posture against enemies, both imagined and real, dominate Iranian newspapers and official discourse. Al-though Iran initiated its program to address certain strategic challenges, as the program matures, nationalistic sentiments and patronage poli-tics are emerging as rationales for sustaining it. To be sure, the level of nationalistic pressure has not reached the heights achieved in India or Pakistan, but as time passes public opinion is likely to harden, belying the notion that prolonged negotiations and incremental pressure will somehow solve the problem. Even if the original strategic calculus that provoked the search for nuclear weapons alters, the program may actually continue as it becomes part of Iran's national identity.

A NUCLEAR FUTURE?

Today the Islamic Republic stands at a crossroads. For nearly three years, Iran was involved in delicate negotiations with Britain, France, and Germany regarding the direction of its nuclear program. Subsequently, it began contemplating a plan for outsourcing its nuclear enrichment activities to Russia. As Iran's nuclear program becomes the subject of deliberations at the UN Security Council, it is time for a more imaginative approach. Ultimately, the course of Iran's nuclear policy may be decided less by what the UN contemplates than by what the Americans do. The nature of Iran's relations with the United States and what type of security architecture emerges in the Persian Gulf are likely to determine Iran's decisions. It is neither inevitable nor absolute that Iran will become the next member of the nuclear club; its internal debates are real and its course of action still unsettled. The international community and the United States will have an immeasurable impact on Iran's nuclear future. A more inventive U.S. diplomacy can still prevent Iran from crossing the nuclear threshold and assembling a bomb.

As Iran grabs headlines and as its nuclear program becomes the subject of sensationalist accounts and exaggerated claims, it is important to appreciate that this is not the first time that the international community has faced a proliferation challenge. Since the inception of the atomic bomb, many states have looked at its awesome power as a solution to their security problems, yet their course of action was reversed. In the past two decades, states as varied as Brazil, Argentina, and Ukraine eventually retreated from the nuclear precipice. Although each state is different and must be viewed within the context of its national experiences, in all cases, diminishing external threats have been critical to their relinquishment of nuclear ambitions. In a similar vein, economic incentives such as favorable commercial ties and access to international lending organizations have been effective, because they provide palpable benefits to ruling elites. It is rare, however, for a state that views nuclear weapons as fundamental to its security interests to dispense with such weapons under relentless threats of military reprisal and economic strangulation. Decades of pressure and economic sanctions ultimately did not dissuade Pakistan from pursuing a nuclear option it felt was necessary for national survival. Similarly, it appears that China's tense relations with the United States ultimately pushed it toward an indigenous nuclear capability, irrespective of costs and burdens. In the end, it appears that a clever mixture of incentives and penalties can accomplish more in the realm of counterproliferation than can threats of military reprisal and economic coercion.

As Washington seeks to grapple with Iran's nuclear challenge, it must accept that its threats and its hostile rhetoric have limited effect in altering Iran's path. Indeed, a belligerent U.S. posture only assists those within the theocracy who argue that the American danger can only be negated through the possession of the "strategic weapon." Given the disutility of force and threats, a realistic engagement strategy may still alter Iran's nuclear course. President Ahmadinejad should not be the focus of U.S diplomacy, as his pathologies are immutable. However, should Washington and its allies craft a generous package of security assurances and measurable sanctions relief in exchange for Tehran's suspension of the critical components of its nuclear infrastructure, it may succeed in peeling away important clerical power brokers from the cause of nuclear arms.

Beyond crafting such a package, the additional key to resolving Iran's nuclear conundrum lies in international solidarity. It is unlikely that the Islamic Republic will be impressed with measures that do not enjoy multilateral consensus. It is thus critical for Washington to sustain the support of its European allies, and to the extent possible, keep China and Russia on board.

If Iran rejects this concerted diplomatic effort, then the United

States will have an easier time reaching a consensus through the United Nations to enact tough multilateral sanctions. Examining the past history of countries that have renounced nuclear weapons or potential weapons programs, the predominant theme is that these renunciations took place only after those countries experienced a lessening of external threats. A more constructive American diplomacy can still go a long way to assure the success of its nonproliferation pledges.

7

IRAN'S
NEW IRAQ

Iran's relations with no other country have been as complicated and tortuous as its ties with Iraq. It is often assumed that Iran and Iraq are natural antagonists, destined to have relations marked by friction and tension. Given the countries' prolonged war in the 1980s and their sustained attempts to assert influence in the Persian Gulf, such a narrative has a degree of historical justification. Still, today emphatic voices suggest that the post-Saddam Iraq with its empowered Shiite majority is likely to emerge as a close ally, if not an actual subsidiary, of the Islamic Republic. The question then becomes, which of these two accounts actually comes closest to reality?

The turbulent history between the two nations can alternatively support a variety of assessments and predictions. It is true that the two sides fought a vicious war that destroyed both countries' infrastructure and scarred a generation. And yet, how does one explain the long periods of cooperation between them in the years since Iraq assumed its formal independence in 1932? The answer lies in the domestic political complexion of the two parties. When both Iran and Iraq were governed by conservative monarchies, they managed to regulate their competition, contain their differences, and even cooperate on issues of common concern. However, the revolutionary, Ba'athist regime in Iraq, which took power in 1968, found the Pahlavi dynasty objectionable, just as Iran's theocrats would later find Saddam Hussein reprehensible. All this is not to suggest that the two sides are free of territorial disputes or regional ambitions that may provoke difficulties. But such tensions are harder to resolve by regimes that are ideological antagonists.

Much in the Middle East changed in the past few years as Saddam's tyranny was displaced by American military intervention. The political empowerment of the Shiite community in Iraq is likely to portend better relations with Iran, since many of Iraq's leading Shiite political actors have close and intimate ties with the Islamic Republic. Despite the alarmist discussions regarding Iran's determination to spread its revolution next door, for Tehran the critical issue remains preventing Sunni domination of Iraqi politics, as in the past such a monopoly of power by a distinct minority group had led it to embrace an aggressive pan-Arabist ideology as a means of justifying its political hegemony. The rulers of the Islamic Republic have no illusions that the Shiites in Iraq are likely to concede to their authority, but they are merely seeking a more amenable set of interlocutors next door. For the first time since the overthrow of the Hashemite monarchy in 1958, Iraq is no longer a revisionist state infused with discursive pan-Arabist pretensions. After all the diplomatic maneuvers and conflicts, it was the American invasion that finally opened the possibility of not just improved but friendly relations between two of the Middle East's bitterest enemies.

In yet another paradox of the Middle East, two other antagonists of the region, the United States and Iran, now find themselves uneasily on the same side of the Iraq debate. A cursory examination of the news coverage will often find U.S. officials complaining about Iran's conduct, its disturbing influence, and its unsavory activities. For their own reasons, both parties have come to view democratic pluralism as the most suitable path for the future of Iraq. The Bush administration's missionary zeal to promote representative governments across the Arab world actually stems from a judicious perception that in the end, democracies constitute the most peaceful form of government. In the meantime, an Iranian regime that seeks to diminish the power of its Sunni foes and keep Iraq weak and divided is also pressing for representative government that is destined to strengthen the provinces at the expense of central power, and the Shiites at the expense of the Sunnis. The success of democratic rule in Baghdad is thus one of the few things that both Washington and Tehran can agree on.

To properly appreciate the changing dynamics of Iran-Iraq relations, we must assess the critical turning points in this relationship since the inception of modern Iraq. Such an examination will reveal that more than territorial disputes or contending hegemonic aspirations, it was ideology that caused tension and ultimately war between these two states. While the monarchical governments managed to contain their disputes, the ideological regimes of Saddam Hussein and the Iranian mullahs ultimately waged a devastating war against each other. Today, for the first time, ideology does not seem a source of friction and tension between the two states, portending a more stable Persian Gulf.

IRAN AND THE OLD IRAQ

During the interwar years, a conservative elite, often composed of landowners and tribal sheikhs, dominated the landscape of Arab politics. The traditional Hashemite monarchy that reigned in Baghdad belonged to this class, as its fears of revolutionary radicalism and Soviet encroachment made it an ally of the West. The common foreign policy outlook, shared institutions, and ties to America's anti-Communist containment network led to an unprecedented degree of cooperation between Baghdad and Tehran, as both parties were committed to the preservation of the regional status quo.[1]

By the 1950s, the Middle East was a changed region. A new middle class had emerged with its own political and economic ambitions that could no longer be confined to the framework conceived by the conservative monarchies. An Arab Cold War had descended on the region, with the pro-Western monarchical regimes being challenged by radical republics professing neutralism abroad and socialism at home. No state embodied this struggle more than Egypt as its dynamic leader, Gamal Abdel Nasser, captured the imagination of the Arab political class. Although typically indifferent to inter-Arab intrigues, the Shah viewed the resistance against Nasserism as a momentous battle. The monarchies of Iran and Iraq once more found themselves on the same side, resisting the same foes and struggling under the same banner.

The 1958 coup in Iraq, leading to the bloody overthrow of the Hashemite monarchy, dramatically altered the once cordial relations between Iran and Iraq. The new radical officer corps led by Abdul-Karim Qasim loudly proclaimed its pan-Arab mission and proved openly disdainful of the monarchy next door as a relic of a reactionary era. Although in the past national interests had bound the two countries together, ideological discord was the new order of the day. Territorial disagreements, particularly over the disputed Shatt al-Arab waterway, seemed insoluble as the two countries viewed each other with suspicion and fear.

Iraq's impulsive ruler, Qasim, now claimed the Iranian province of Khuzestan with its Arab population as "Arabistan" and christened the Persian Gulf as the "Arabian Gulf." The intricate 1937 treaty detailing arrangements for the mutual use of the Shatt al-Arab waterway were also dismissed by Iraq's strident nationalists as an intolerable infringement of Arab rights. The new republican regime not only challenged the legitimacy of the Iranian government but also its territorial boundaries. The Iraqi government that sanctioned its power through claims of pan-Arabism and as the self-appointed defender of the larger Arab community viewed its Persian neighbor in distinct ethnic terms. For the new masters of Baghdad, Iran was a stagnant Persian monarchy sustained in its power by Western imperial preference, while for the Shah, the militant Iraqi government's self-professed identity with the radical Arab bloc, its pro-Soviet inclinations, and its determination to claim the Gulf for the Arab cause was bound to be a threat. The Hashemite monarchy may have had serious differences with Iran, but it did not contest the essential integrity of the Pahlavi regime.

The arrival of the Ba'athist regime through a bloody coup in 1968 further anguished the Iranian state. The Ba'athist ideology was even more strident in its claim of unifying the mythical Arab community and resisting pro-Western regimes. The Sunni-dominated government also effectively disenfranchised the Shiite and Kurdish majorities and looked abroad for its legitimacy. The Sunnis were dominating Iraq not for crass parochial purposes, the Ba'athists claimed, but for the larger cause of Arab solidarity. The vicissitudes of unstable internal order, the determination of an imperious Sunni populace, and the imperatives of Arab politics fostered an aggressive foreign policy. Baghdad now became the benefactor of a wide variety of leftist and pan-Arab opposition forces in the Gulf and openly appealed to the Arabs who lived in Iran's oil-rich southern provinces. With its ties to the Soviet Union and its revolutionary outlook, Iraq represented a continued and escalating threat to Iran.

The ascendance of a radical regime in Baghdad coincided with important changes in Iran's foreign policy orientation. Rising oil revenues and American benevolence allowed the Shah to nurture his aspiration of creating a powerful military to police the Gulf. An overextended America, struggling in its Vietnam quagmire, was happy to cede this role to the ambitious Persian monarch. After all, the Nixon Doctrine called for arming pliable proxies willing to shoulder the burdens of the Cold War. While the Shah may have been inclined to share the spoils of the Nixon Doctrine with the conservative monarchy of Saudi Arabia and accept a twin-pillar policy, no such deference was yielded to the Ba'athist regime. The Shah signaled his attitude in no uncertain terms, warning his local challengers that if they "do not respect Iran's legitimate rights in the Persian Gulf, they must expect Iran to show the same attitude toward them."[2]

For the Ba'athist state, with its claims as the guardian of Arabism, Iran's preeminence constituted a transgression against both its ideological commitments and regional aspirations. Baghdad denounced Iran's assertions as "illegal ambition in Iraq's territorial waters and the Arabian Gulf."[3] Iraq's propaganda once more focused on fomenting uprisings among the Arab-speaking population in Khuzestan. The new Iraqi regime even invoked the sacred cause of resisting Israel, claiming that Iran was working in conjunction with the Jewish state to provoke a crisis in the Gulf as a means of undermining Arab solidarity against Israel.[4] In the aftermath of Egypt's defeat at the hands of Israel during the 1967 war, Iraq sensed a unique opportunity to assume the mantle of Arab leadership and perceived its relations with Iran in a larger Arab context. Border clashes, deportation of Iraqis of Iranian origin, and a strident propaganda campaign now characterized relations between the two erstwhile allies.

Such conflict was not without its share of victims. By the early 1970s Baghdad was locked into one of its perennial conflicts with its restive Kurdish minority. The cynicism of Iran's policy was on ample display, as the Shah viewed the Kurdish struggle for autonomy as an effective means of pressuring Iraq into acquiescing to his territorial demands and his quest to assume greater control over the contested Shatt al-Arab waterway. The prevailing imbalance of power and the Iraqi regime's preoccupation with its internal conflicts forced it to acquiesce to the Algiers Accords in March 1975, granting Iran much of its demands. Having achieved his strategic aims, the Shah brutally cut off his assistance to the Kurds, sacrificing his ally of convenience. Not for the last time, Kurds would find themselves betrayed by an external power pledging friendship and solidarity.

By 1979, the mutual ascendance of Saddam Hussein in Iraq and Ayatollah Khomeini in Iran added further fuel to this combustible mix. In essence, both states were now led by dogmatic politicians who were prone to accept great risks in pursuit of their objectives. As both leaders sought to impose their ideological templates on the region, conflict between the two states became nearly inevitable.

SADDAM'S WAR

Too often in history, the rise of revolutionary regimes leads to wars and conflict.[5] Revolutionaries tend to perceive their ideals as universally applicable and the existing order as necessarily iniquitous. The demarcation between domestic politics and foreign affairs soon blurs, frequently evaporating all together. The cause of revolutionary affirmation mandates the export of the new order, demonstrating its vitality and vigor. More so than any of its predecessors, the Iranian revolution not only exhibited these sentiments, but its particular religious character made its forceful exportation all the more important. As we have seen, Khomeini waged his revolt not just to displace the Shah's monarchy but also to usher in a new epoch.

Such a pattern of revolutionary provocation was soon evident as the ayatollahs decried the Ba'athist regime, offering material and moral sanction to its many opponents. A strident secular state seeking to organize the region under the banner of pan-Arabism and allying itself with the atheist Soviet regime was a particular affront to Khomeini. In the initial heady days, when Iran's euphoric clerics had managed to overthrow a formidable monarchy, the revolution appeared awesome, ferocious, and relentless. In such an atmosphere, caution and restraint did not always guide Tehran's new rulers.[6]

For its part, the Ba'athist regime viewed its Islamist neighbor with an equal degree of contempt and concern. As the vanguard of a secular, modern Arab order, the resurgence of traditional institutions and religious politics was belittled by the Ba'athists as irrational retrogression. The Islamic Republic with its regional mandates and ideological claims was a unique threat to Saddam's rule.[7]

The tense relations between the two states was further strained as Iran's message of revolutionary defiance proved particularly attractive to at least a segment of Iraq's Shiite majority. Organized opposition forces such as the al-Dawa Party soon conducted violent campaigns against Ba'athist targets and officials, most likely with Iranian complicity. The minority Sunni regime, shielding its absolute power behind the veneer of pan-Arabism, must have felt particularly vulnerable to Khomeini's appeal to the hard-pressed Shiite populace. The Iraqi counterreaction featured all the brutality and excess exemplified by Saddam's tyranny, as the Shiite community was subject to relentless reprisals, and some of its most venerable clerics were summarily executed. However, such harsh repressive measures did not ease Saddam's mind, since he feared that the contagion of Khomeinism may yet destabilize his rule. Once more, ideological antagonisms intruded, intensifying suspicions and making violence an attractive option for the perennially impetuous Iraqi leader.

To attribute the emerging conflict between the two states to ideological incompatibility is to discount Saddam's overweening ambitions. By 1980, Egypt's acceptance of the Camp David Accords had effectively removed one of the principal obstacles to Iraq's leadership of the Arab world. Moreover, the revolutionary chaos in Iran and the decimation of its officer corps by the vengeful mullahs was leading Saddam to perceive that a decisive military strike would not only provoke the collapse of the theocratic regime but consolidate Iraq's leadership of the Arab realm. A combination of threats and opportunities was proving irresistible to a leader prone to taking great and dangerous risks.[8]

As border clashes between the two states intensified, Saddam openly castigated the "mummy Khomeini" and implored the Iranian masses to "find someone else other than the rotten Khomeini."[9] By the summer of 1980, Saddam took the inflammatory step of renouncing the 1975 Algiers Accords, which had provided a framework for operating the contested Shatt al-Arab waterway. The Iraqi dictator simply claimed that "since the rulers of Iran have violated this agreement from the beginning of their reign as the Shah before them, I announce before you that we consider the March 1975 agreement abrogated."[10] Finally, on

September 22, 1980, Saddam took the catastrophic decision to invade Iran, beginning one of the longest and most destructive wars in the modern history of the Middle East.

Even in the context of strained relations between the two states since 1958, Saddam's invasion of Iran was a stark departure from the previous pattern. To be sure, there had been sporadic border clashes and both parties had supported proxies against each other, but a full-scale military invasion cannot be seen as a mere continuation of the existing tensions. In essence, Saddam dramatically altered the nature of the conflict between the two states and escalated tensions to a new level. Indeed, had Saddam not reached the pinnacle of power, the controlled rage between the two states might well have persisted as it had for over two decades. But as a rash ruler with ambitions to establish his state as the leader of the Arab world and the hegemon of the Gulf, Saddam perceived a unique opportunity to rid himself of his theocratic nemesis next door. The defeat of Iran would not just evaporate a strategic challenge, but it would lead the grateful Gulf sheikdoms to accept Iraqi predominance and the larger Arab realm to acclaim the vanquisher of the Persian hordes. On the other side, Khomeini stood with his own determinations, which would lead to the continuation of the war despite its human and material costs. To the mix of ideological animosity and territorial dispute was now added the personality of two dogmatic leaders, indifferent to the suffering and welfare of their citizenry. The Iran-Iraq war was consequently destined to be one of the most prolonged and devastating conflicts in the annals of warfare.[11]

The Iran-Iraq war was unusual in many respects, as it was not merely an interstate conflict designed to achieve specific territorial or even political objectives. This was a war waged for the triumph of ideas, with Ba'athist secular pan-Arabism contesting Iran's Islamic fundamentalism. As such, for Tehran the war came to embody its revolutionary identity. The themes of solidarity and sacrifice, self-reliance and commitment not only allowed the regime to consolidate its power but make the defeat of Saddam the ultimate test of theocratic legitimacy. War and revolution had somehow fused in the clerical cosmology. To wage a determined war was to validate one's revolution-ary ardor and spiritual fidelity. The notion of compromise and armistice was alien to the Islamic Republic, as its commitment to the war tran-scended conventional calculations.[12]

Iraq would soon discover the problem with invading a revolutionary state infused with a messianic ideology: the imperatives of caution and pragmatism are lost on the militant elite. As an ideologically driven state, Iran never defined the war in terms of territory lost or gained but as a spiritual mission seeking moral redemption. For the clerical rulers, Iran had been attacked not because of its provocations or territorial disputes but because the Islamic Republic embodied a virtuous order. This was an infidel war against the Islamic revolution, the "Government of God," and the sublime faith of Shiism. "You are fighting to protect Islam, and he is fighting to destroy it," Khomeini told the Iranian people.[13] In a similar vein, Rafsanjani emphatically declared, "The fact that we are not making peace stems from the Koran and the honor of Islam."[14] The clerical leadership genuinely in-sisted that the war was a blessing, as it would either lead to a momen-tous victory for the forces of piety or to martyrdom, which was itself the ultimate form of salvation. Thus, the sacrifices of the war were exalted even if the ultimate outcome was not an Iranian triumph.

Throughout the duration of the conflict, religious discourse and symbols were used to present the war to the public. The duty of the righteous Muslim was to resist oppression and wage war against ene-mies seeking to tarnish Islam. The importance of patience and stead-fastness was also noted, however, as God would reward not just the zealous but those who persisted in their ardor despite setbacks and suffering.[15] Such claims may seem self-serving, designed to galvanize a populace called to endure significant difficulties for an undeter-mined period of time. For the clerical leadership this was not just a gesture of cynical manipulation of popular sentiments, however, but a genuine expression of their ideological framework of the war. Seldom in their many declarations and speeches does one find the ruling elite preoccupied with the limited territory in dispute or Saddam's violation of agreements governing relations between the two states. The sweeping, universalistic rhetoric revealed that for Tehran this was a more profound, even an existential, struggle between the forces of Islamic virtue and a profane Ba'athist ruler.

During Saddam's later conflicts with the United States, he would be castigated by American politicians as an aggressor, a genocidal maniac, even another Hitler. Yet the Islamic Republic's distinct ideological approach to the war eschewed such terms for the more emotive Koranic designation of Saddam as a heretic, an embodiment of evil plotting against the true essence of Islam. In a sense, the clerical rulers appropriated the rhetoric of the Muslim empires that had battled the armies of the Crusaders, where the issue was not mere aggression but a collision of two contending civilizations—in this case, the ethical Islamic Iran against Saddam's world of dissimulation, treachery, and cynicism.[16]

Given such perceptions, the Islamic Republic's military doctrine avoided issues of tactics and strategy in favor of revolutionary fervor. Ayatollah Khomeini captured this sentiment by stressing, "Victory is not achieved by swords; it can only be achieved by blood."[17] While traditional armies sought a coherent command structure and access to necessary armaments, Iran was to rely on its culture of martyrdom and sacrifice, on the theory that moral superiority and the power of faith were sufficient to overcome Iraq's devastating war machine, generously supplied by the Western powers seeking to contain Iran's ambitions.

Nor did Iran's war aims reflect the limits of its power. Tehran's objective remained the complete destruction of Saddam's regime and the elimination of the Sunni domination of Iraq's politics. The fact is that after 1982, when Iran evicted Iraqi forces from its territory, Baghdad was prepared to cease the war. However, Khomeini and his clerical brethren insisted on the continuation of the conflict until their maximalist objectives were achieved. The problem for Iran was that its military capabilities were not sufficient to realize its inflexible aims. The gap between determination and capacity ensured a stalemate, as neither side was powerful enough to impose a solution on the other, while Tehran was simply unwilling to reach a compromise solution to end the war.

After 1982, the war settled into a pattern of bloody deadlock, reminiscent of the carnage of the First World War, where the capture of inches of territory would consume countless lives. A dogmatic Iran would unleash sporadic, large-scale offensives using human waves that would inevitably be repulsed by Iraq's better-equipped army. Then an inevitable lull would ensue, only to be shattered by the grisly pattern of another failed operation. As the war persisted, both parties sought to alter tactics and cultivate new allies in order to somehow breach the stalemate. It was in this context that Iraq introduced chemical weapons to an already deadly battleground.[18]

Iraq's employment of chemical weapons against Iran began in 1983, and after their initial battlefield use, the list of targets was gradually expanded.[19] Nor did the Iraqi leadership deny its right to utilize such weapons to fend off Iranian attacks. By 1984, Iraqi military commanders were boasting of how they used "insecticide" to exterminate "the swarms of mosquitoes."[20] The former Iraqi foreign minister, Tariq Aziz, was uniquely honest when admitting the use of such weapons, albeit in retaliation for what he said was Iran's similar deployment of chemical weapons.[21] After eight UN investigations, sheaves of evidence from eyewitness accounts, and captured Iraqi documents, it can be declared conclusively that while Iraq did employ weapons of mass destruction, there is no indication of Iran's similar use, belying Aziz's spurious claims of just retaliation.[22]

In the end, the principal strategic utility of chemical weapons is to terrorize the combatants and demoralize the population. Saddam was successful in this regard, because Iraq's systematic use of chemical agents gradually undermined the confidence of Iran's zealous volunteers and the cohesion of its armed forces. Throughout the war, Iran's hard-won battlefield gains were often reversed by Baghdad's use of weapons of mass destruction. In a similar vein, the potential targeting of cities, which became much easier by the mid-1980s once Iraq developed long-range missiles, dramatically frightened Iran's civilian population, leading to mass exodus from cities and towns. The pressure exerted by an increasingly frightened population and the beleaguered armed forces proved a heavy burden for the clerical hard-liners seeking to perpetuate the war until victory.

In the meantime, the apparent internationalization of the conflict was yet another lever pressing the clerical leadership to end the war. The massive aid and intelligence information offered to Iraq by the Western powers was supplemented in the latter stages of the conflict by a robust U.S. naval presence protecting Gulf commerce from Iranian menace. Given that the Gulf sheikdoms' oil profits were allowing them to generously subsidize Iraq's war machine, Iran's inability to disrupt that trade offered Iraq another important advantage. As battlefield losses mounted, the international community simply would not allow Saddam to fall. It baffled Iran's leaders and citizens alike how the Western bloc, with its emphasis on human rights and democratic values, had come to embrace a tyrannical Sunni ruler.

By 1988, Iran's population was exhausted and war-weary. Eight years of sacrifice and hardship had not produced the much-pledged victory. The steady stream of volunteers who sustained Iran's war effort had been reduced to a trickle, compelling the regime to impose draconian conscription measures to meet its basic manpower needs. The huge offensive operations with their human wave assaults were no longer a possibility as draft evasion and the loss of revolutionary ardor compelled the army to reduce the scope of its activities. More pragmatic officials, such as Rafsanjani, now began to implore Khomeini that the time had come for ending the conflict. The war that had been so useful in terms of consolidating the revolution now began to threaten the theocratic edifice through popular disenchantment, demoralized youth, and grumblings within the armed forces.

The final event that pressed Iran's internal debate toward an armistice was the accidental shooting down of an Iranian airliner in July 1988 by a U.S. naval vessel, the USS *Vincennes*. Despite America's apology and an offer of compensation for the 290 passengers killed, Tehran assumed that this was a signal of a more vigorous American involvement on behalf of Iraq.[23] Iranian officials now feared that prolonging the war with Iraq would lead to direct U.S. military engagement to overthrow the Islamic Republic. In an unprecedented move, the commanders of Iran's regular armed forces and the Revolutionary Guards, who had been so at odds about how to wage the war, informed the central government that they lacked the capability to protect the state against both Iraq and America.[24] The military's judgment was endorsed by all the relevant institutions, including the firebrands in the parliament; the president of the republic, Ali Khamenei; and senior economic advisers. Such combined pressures finally compelled Khomeini to inform the nation of his decision to cease the conflict.[25] Crestfallen, he confronted his countrymen and proclaimed the end of the war:

> Today, this decision was more deadly than drinking hemlock. I submitted myself to God's will and drank this drink to His satisfaction. To me, it would have been more bearable to accept death and martyrdom. Today's decision is based only on the interest of the Islamic Republic.[26]

Despite its revolutionary determination, Iran fought the war with disadvantages it could not overcome. Given the absence of reliable and generous allies, an inability to gain steady sources of weapons, and international isolation, Tehran had to rely exclusively on its own resources to achieve the unrealistic goal of the destruction of Saddam's regime. Iraq may not have been able to defeat Iran, but proved sufficiently resilient to rebuff Iranian offensives. As the war dragged on, the gap between Iran's objectives and its capabilities continued to widen, imposing a dose of reality on a regime that took pride in defying conventional calculations.

The Iran-Iraq war ended nearly two decades ago, and in the intervening period Iranians have come to deal with the causes and legacy of the most prolonged conflict in their country's modern history. As with Americans wrestling with the Vietnam War, Iranians, after an initial determination to forget, are struggling with the wounds of a controversial conflict. In many ways, the war continues to define the parameters of Iran's political culture and international orientation. In the 2005 presidential election, Rafsanjani's role in the war became a subject of controversy as questions were asked as to why he and the leadership of the Islamic Republic at that time did not end the war in 1982 when an armistice was apparently available.[27] And, of course, Ahmadinejad, himself a war veteran, did much to emphasize his service on behalf of the nation and the lessons that it imprinted on his consciousness.

Today in Iran, one rarely finds a family that has not been affected by the war—the loss of a son, a disabled relative, the hardship that all had to suffer. Memoirs, books, scholarly conferences, and journalistic accounts deal with the war, its continuing legacy, and its visible scars. The war, as with much of history in Iran, is a living enterprise.[28] Increasingly, after much contemplation and discussion, a consensus is beginning to emerge both in public circles and among the governing elite that the cause of Iraq's persistent belligerence was the Sunni domination of its politics. The Sunni minority was always looking abroad for glory and pan-Arabist acclaim to sanction its hold on absolute power. For the clerical oligarchs a stable Iraq is one where the majority Shiite and Kurdish populations have a determining role in the governing deliberations. Given Iraq's demographic realities, the electoral process will ensure the rise of the Shiite community and effectively diminish the power and influence of the Sunni populace. In a strange paradox, the war has made the Iranian leaders forceful advocates of democratic pluralism next door.

Such emerging perceptions are consistent with the Islamic Republic's discourse and propaganda during the war. Throughout the conflict, Iran was careful to distinguish between Saddam and the Iraqi populace. In numerous speeches, Khomeini noted the dissimilarity between Saddam and his Sunni power base and the vast majority of the Iraqi population. The Sunni elite's embrace of Ba'athist ideology had essentially transformed them into heretics, Khomeini argued. Thus, the war was waged not against a people, but a system—the Sunni-dominated, secular Ba'athist order. In a clever move, the vast majority of the Iraqi populace was absolved of its complicity in the war as the Ba'athist Sunnis were depicted as agents of anti-Muslim transgression, with the Iraqi people also serving as one of their chief victims.[29]

Beyond Iraq, the war also shaped Tehran's views of the larger international community. The Western powers' indifference to Iraq's use of chemical weapons against Iran has led to a pervasive suspicion of the international order, particularly its American guardian. The notion that Iran's tangible security interests can best be achieved by relying on international conventions and treaties has a limited audience in a country that has suffered substantial casualties at the hands of Saddam's chemical warfare. It is here that the legacy of the war makes the development of a nuclear capability all the more attractive to the clerical rulers. Moreover, America's lack of concern about Iran's sufferings continues, as the indictments against Saddam brought after the U.S. invasion still do not include his war crimes against Iran. Such persistent insensitivity has caused an uproar in Iran, as Tehran continues to demand that the Iraqi dictator stand trial for his abuse of the Iraqi people and invasion of Kuwait, and for his indiscriminate use of weapons of mass destruction against Iranian soldiers and civilians. So long as the United States ignores these requests, the wall of mistrust between the two countries is likely to remain intact.

As Iran's rulers look next door, there is a new Iraq. The once docile and repressed Shiite forces have now been empowered, and the once imperious Sunni Arabs stand isolated and marginalized in a country in which they dominated politics for many decades. The future of Iraq remains uncertain, but one thing that appears definite is that the ideological antagonisms that once led to tension, conflict, and ultimately war between the two states have all but evaporated. For the mullahs,

America's invasion offers enormous challenges but also a remarkable set of opportunities.

IRAN AND THE NEW IRAQ

On July 7, 2005, a momentous event took place in Tehran. Saadun al-Dulaimi, Iraq's defense minister, arrived there and formally declared, "I have come to Iran to ask forgiveness for what Saddam Hussein has done."[30] The atmospherics of the trip reflected the changed relationship as Iranian and Iraqi officials easily intermingled, signing various cooperative and trade agreements and pledging a new dawn in their relations. In yet another paradox of the Middle East, it took a hawkish American government with its well-honed antagonism toward the Islamic Republic to finally alleviate one of Iran's most pressing strategic quandaries.

Since the beginning of Operation Iraqi Freedom in 2003, the Bush administration has periodically complained about Iran's mischievousness and intervention in Iraq's politics.[31] The question then becomes, what are Iran's priorities and objectives in Iraq? Does Iran seek to export its revolution next door and create another Islamic Republic? Is it in Iran's interest to intensify the prevailing insurgency and further entangle America in its bloody quagmire? Do Iran and the United States have common interests in the troubled state of Iraq?

As Iraq settles into its disturbing pattern of violence and disorder, the Islamic Republic has contending, and at times conflicting, objectives next door. The overarching priority for Tehran is to prevent Iraq from once more emerging as a military and ideological threat. As we have seen, a consensus has evolved among Iran's officials that the cause of Iraq's aggressive behavior was the Sunni domination of its politics. Thus, the empowerment of a more friendly Shiite regime is an essential objective of Iran's strategy. Given the fears of a spillover from a potential civil war and the fragmentation of the country, however, Iran's leaders also want to maintain Iraq's territorial integrity. Finally, there is the menacing U.S. military presence in Iraq. Contrary to the notion that Iran seeks to fuel the insurgency as a means of deterring the United States from attacking its suspected nuclear facilities, Tehran appreciates that a stable Iraq is the best means of ending the American occupation. These competing aims have yielded alternative tactics, as Iran has been active in subsidizing its Shiite allies, dispatching arms to friendly militias, and agitating against the American presence.[32]

Since the demise of Saddam, a curious conventional wisdom is emerging as many in the Washington establishment and the Sunni elite of the Middle East ominously warn of a rising "Shiite Crescent" and how a mini-Islamic Republic is being created in at least the southern part of Iraq. King Abdullah of Jordan has taken the lead in warning his Western counterparts of such dire developments, exclaiming, "If Iraq goes to the Islamic Republic, then we have to open ourselves to a whole set of new problems that will not be limited to our borders."[33] The monarch's alarmism was echoed by Saudi foreign minister Saud al-Faisal: "We fought a war together to keep Iran from occupying Iraq after Iraq was driven out of Kuwait. Now we are handing the whole country over to Iran without reason."[34] The region's beleaguered Sunni princes and presidents, nurturing their own conspiracy theories, sense Iranian machinations and intrigue behind all that is transpiring in war-torn Iraq. But the question remains: What type of relationship does Iran have with Iraq's Shiite community? After all, given that many Shiite leaders in today's Iraq spent decades in exile in Iran, is it unthinkable that a client Iranian state can be established in a critical segment of Iraq?

Although Iraq's Shiite political society is hardly homogeneous, the two parties that have emerged as the best organized and most competitive in the electoral process are the Supreme Council of the Islamic Revolution in Iraq (SCIRI) and the al-Dawa Party. Both parties have intimate relations with Tehran and allied themselves with the Islamic Republic during the Iran-Iraq war. SCIRI was essentially created by Iran, and its militia, the Badr Brigade, was trained and equipped by the Revolutionary Guards. For its part, al-Dawa is Iraq's longest-surviving Shiite political party, with a courageous record of resisting Saddam's repression. Under tremendous pressure, al-Dawa took refuge in Iran, but it also established a presence in Syria, Lebanon, and eventually Britain. Despite their long-lasting ties with the Islamic Republic, however, both parties appreciate that in order to remain influential actors in post-Saddam Iraq they must place some distance between themselves and Tehran. The members of SCIRI and al-Dawa insist that they have no interest in emulating Iran's theocratic model, and that Iraq's divisions and fragmentations mandate a different governing structure. As former prime minister Ibrahim al-Jafari, the head of the al-Dawa Party, insists, "Not all the Shiites are Islamists and not all Islamists believe in *velayat-e faqih*. Cloning any experience is inconsistent with the human rights of that country."[35] In a similar vein, Adel Abdul Mahdi, the leading figure within SCIRI, emphasized, "We don't want either a Shiite government or an Islamic government.[36] Their persistent electoral triumphs reflect not just superior organization but a successful assertion of their own identity. Still, al-Dawa and SCIRI retain close bonds with Iran, and have defended the Islamic Republic against American charges of interference and infiltration. In the end, although both parties have no inclination to act as Iran's surrogates, they are likely to provide Tehran with a sympathetic audience and an alliance that, like all such arrangements, will not be free of tension and difficulty.

Although less well publicized by Tehran, it appears that Iran has established tacit ties with the radical Shiite cleric Moqtada al-Sadr and has even supplied his Mahdi army. Unlike Iran's relations with SCIRI and al-Dawa, the Islamic Republic's ties to Sadr are more opportunistic, since they find his sporadic Arab nationalist rhetoric and erratic behavior problematic. Nonetheless, given his emerging power base, his strident opposition to the American occupation, and his well-organized militia group, Tehran has found it advantageous to maintain some links with Sadr. Among the characteristics of Iran's foreign policy is to leave as many options open as possible. At a time when Sadr is being granted an audience by the Arab leaders and dignitaries across the region, it would be astonishing if Iran did not seek some kind of relationship with the Shiite firebrand.

Finally, there is Iran's relationship with Iraq's most esteemed and influential Shiite cleric, Grand Ayatollah Ali al-Sistani. The Grand Ayatollah stands with traditional Shiite mullahs in rejecting Khomeini's notion that proper Islamic governance mandates direct clerical assumption of power. As we have seen, Khomeini's innovation contravened normative Shiite political traditions, making its export problematic, if not impossible. Thus far both parties have been courteous and deferential to each other, with Sistani refusing to criticize Iran and Tehran generous in crediting him for the Shiite populace's increasing empowerment. Rafsanjani made a point of emphasizing Sistani's role after the elections of the interim government, noting, "The fact that the people of Iraq have gone to the ballet box to decide their own fate is the result of efforts by the Iraqi clergy and sources of emulation, led by Ayatollah Ali al-Sistani."[37] For his part, Sistani maintains close ties to Iran's clerical community and routinely meets with visiting Iranian officials—a privilege not yet granted to U.S. representatives. Moreover, even though Sistani has not pressed for a theocracy, he still insists that religion must inform political and social arrangements. Once more Iran's reigning clerics have forged correct relations with the Grand Ayatollah and harbor no illusions that he would serve as an agent for imposition of their theocratic template on Iraq.

The professions of the region's Sunni elite notwithstanding, as the clerical regime plots its strategy toward Iraq it is not inordinately interested in exporting its failed governing model to an unwilling Shiite population. The opposition of the senior Iraqi clerical class and Shiite politicians has convinced Iranian officialdom that its policy next door should be guided by practical concerns as opposed to grand ideological missions. An influential Iranian politician, Muhammad Javad Larijani, plainly commented, "Iran's experience is not possible to be duplicated in Iraq."[38] Ali Akbar Velayati, now serving as a senior adviser to Khamenei, also agreed that the type of government that emerges in Iraq "is something for the Iraqi people to decide."[39] In a similar vein, Iran's leading newspaper, *Sharq,* stressed, "Even if Iraq's prime minister is an Islamic figure who lived in Iran for many years and fought against Saddam's regime shoulder to shoulder with the Iranian government, one cannot expect that he will implement the Iranian model of government in Iraq."[40] As such, Tehran's promotion of its Shiite allies is a way of ensuring that a future Iraqi government features voices who are willing to engage with Iran. The clerical rulers have no delusions about the Iraqi Shiite community subordinating its communal interests to Iran's prerogatives; they merely hope that promotion of Shiite parties will provide them with a suitable interlocutor. Iran's policy toward Iraq, as elsewhere in the Gulf, is predicated on carefully calibrated calculations of national interest, as opposed to a messianic mission of advancing the revolution.

Today the essential estrangement of the Iraqi Shiites from the larger Arab world, and the neighboring Sunni regimes' unease with their empowerment, makes the community more attractive to Iran. The ascendance of the Shiites may be acceptable to the Bush administration with its democratic imperatives, but the Sunni monarchs of Saudi Arabia and Jordan and the presidential dictatorships of Egypt and Syria are extremely anxious about the emergence of a new "Shiite Crescent." At a time when the leading pan-Arab newspapers routinely decry the invasion of Iraq as a U.S.–Iranian plot to undermine the cohesion of the Sunni bloc, the prospects of an elected Shiite government in Iraq being warmly embraced by the Arab world seems remote. Iraq's new Shiite parties, conservative or moderate, are drawn to Iran as they look for natural allies. It is unlikely that this will change because the political alignments of the Middle East are increasingly being defined by sectarian identities.

Although it is customary to speak of Iran's ties to the Shiites, the Islamic Republic has also sought to cultivate relations with the Kurdish parties, particularly Jalal Talabani's Patriotic Union of Kurdistan. As noted, the history of Iran's relations with the Kurdish population is contentious; the Shah mercilessly exploited the Kurds and then cast them aside when they proved inconvenient. Soon after assuming power, the Islamic Republic confronted Kurdish separatism, and one of its first challenges was the suppression of a determined Kurdish rebellion. However, during their long years of common struggle against Saddam, the two sides often cooperated with each other, and eventually came to establish relatively reasonable relations. For the past two decades, Iran not only sustained those ties but often housed substantial numbers of Kurdish refugees whenever they had to flee Saddam's war machine. Today, Iran's relations with Talabani are cordial and correct, as Tehran hopes that a degree of autonomy will persuade the Kurds to remain within a unitary Iraqi state.

The intriguing aspect of Iran's approach toward Iraq is the extent that it is conditioned by its wartime experiences as opposed to Islamic fervor. Iraq is a land of sectarian division, ethnic cleavages, and contending foreign policy orientations. As we have seen, the Sunni minority sought to sanction its authority under the Ba'athist regime by embracing a pan-Arabist enterprise and employing an aggressive transnational ideology as the foundation of its legitimacy. The Shiites and the Kurds also possess foreign policy goals, but these are more inclined toward improving relations with Iraq's non-Arab neighbors. In that sense there has always been a coincidence of interests among Iran's Persians and Iraq's Shiites and Kurds, as they have all harbored intense suspicions of the dominant Sunni class. As an important editorial in *Sharq* emphasized, "The great enmity between the two powers was not just the consequence of the eight-year war, but the nature of the ideology of the two in the course of the past quarter-century."[41] Indeed, that ideological antipathy has evaporated, as Iraq will no longer serve as an instrument of a Sunni elite with its revisionist schemes and preoccupations with inter-Arab intrigues.

Contrary to Washington's presumptions, the realization of Iran's objectives is not predicated on violence and the insurgency but on the unfolding democratic process. In a strange paradox, the Iranian clerical hard-liners, who have been so adamant about suppressing the reform movement, have emerged as forceful advocates of democratic pluralism in Iraq. Indeed, a democratic Iraq offers Iran political and strategic advantages. After much deliberation, Iran's theocrats have arrived at the conclusion that the best means of advancing their interests is to support an electoral process dedicated to constructing a state with strong provinces and a weak federal structure. Such an arrangement would empower the more congenial Shiite populace, contain the unruly ambitions of the Kurds, and marginalize Iran's Sunni foes.

Moreover, Iran's stratagem is not devoid of *realpolitik* considerations. A pluralistic Iraq is bound to be a fractious, divided state too preoccupied with its internal squabbles to contest Iran's aspirations in the Gulf. At a time when Iraq's constitutional arrangements are ceding essential authority to the provinces and favoring local militias over national armed forces, it is unlikely that Iraq will once more emerge as a powerful, centralized state seeking to dominate the Persian Gulf region, if not the entire Middle East. It would be much easier for Iran to exert influence over a decentralized state with many contending actors than over a strong, cohesive regime.

For Iran, however, Iraq remains a series of balancing acts. Tehran fears that the insurgency and even the democratic process itself may lead to the fragmentation of Iraq into three independent and unstable entities. Iran is an intact, ancient nation whose boundaries do not suffer from the artificiality of its Arab neighbors. Even so, Iran possesses a restless Kurdish population concentrated in the northeastern Azerbaijan province that may make common cause with a prospective Iraqi Kurdish state and agitate for autonomy. In its frequent contacts with the Iraqi Kurds, Iran has acknowledged their prerogatives and their sufferings under Saddam while nudging them toward continued membership in a confederated Iraqi state. Iran's speaker of the parliament, Gholam-Ali Haddad-Adel, stressed this point in February 2005: "Iran's permanent policy is to defend Iraq's territorial integrity."[42] Thus far, this delicate diplomacy seems to have succeeded, for despite their assertiveness the Kurds do not display a desire to leave Iraq altogether and set up a completely autonomous state. Since the U.S. invasion, Iran has persistently called on the Shiites and the Kurds to remain within a unitary state and establish elected institutions that can diminish the potency of the Sunni insurgency by granting that beleaguered populace an alternative channel for asserting its claims. Again, Iran's actual conduct contradicts the claims of those Arab dignitaries who charge that the Islamic Republic is seeking to fracture Iraq and establish a Shiite theocracy in the south. A more strategically minded Iran would prefer the Iraqi state to remain intact, although weakened and divided against itself. And the best manner of achieving this objective is to continue to press for democracy and pluralism.

Given Iran's interest in the stability and success of a Shiite-dominated Iraq, how does one account for the credible reports indicating that Tehran has been infiltrating men and supplies into Iraq? To be sure, since the removal of Saddam, the Islamic Republic has been busy establishing an infrastructure of influence next door that includes funding political parties and dispatching arms to Shiite militias. For the United States, with its perennial suspicions of Iran, such activism necessarily implies a propensity toward mischief and terror. Iran's presence in Iraq, however, can best be seen within the context of its tense relations with the United States, if not the larger international community. Such influence and presence provides Iran with important leverage in dealing with the Western powers. The fact that America and its allies may believe that Iran will retaliate in Iraq for any military strikes against its nuclear facilities implicitly strengthens Tehran's deterrence against such a move. At a time when Iran's nuclear ambitions are at issue, it is not in the theocracy's interest to unduly disabuse the United States of that impression.

Should the Islamic Republic's implied deterrence fail and the United States does strike its nuclear installations, then Iran's extensive presence in Iraq will give it a credible retaliatory capacity. Yahya Rahim Safavi, commander of the Revolutionary Guards, has plainly outlined Iran's options: "The Americans know well that their military centers in Afghanistan, the Gulf of Oman, the Persian Gulf, and Iraq will come under threat and they may be vulnerable because they are in Iran's neighborhood."[43] The fact remains that Iran's network in Iraq is not necessarily designed for attacks against America, though it does offer the theocracy a variety of choices should its relations with the United States significantly deteriorate.

Nor can one suggest that Iran is determined to fuel the insurgency as a means of compelling an American withdrawal, thus establishing its preeminence in the Gulf. Although the assertion of Iranian dominance in the Persian Gulf region is partly contingent on a withdrawal of the U.S. presence, to some extent pressures in the United States and Iraq are once again achieving Iran's objectives. The Bush administration's invasion of Iraq is a contentious political topic in the United States, with a majority of the American people regretting the decision to intervene. In the meantime, as the political process unfolds and Iraqis make their own deals and arrangements, it is likely that many in Iraq would see an American occupation as provocative and nationalistically objectionable. A proud state that has long viewed itself as a vanguard nation and the seat of Islamic civilization cannot long tolerate the infamy of being the only occupied Arab country. Iran does not have to inflict damage on the United States to provoke its withdrawal from Iraq, because the natural trajectory of events makes a reduced American presence in the Gulf nearly inevitable.

Iran's model of ensuring its influence in Iraq is also drawn from its experiences in Lebanon, another multiconfessional society with a Shiite population traditionally left out of the spoils of power. Iran's strategy in Lebanon was to dispatch economic and financial assistance to win Shiite hearts and minds while making certain that its Shiite allies had sufficient military hardware for a potential clash with their rivals. As such, Iran's presence was more subtle and indirect, and sought to avoid a confrontation with America. Not unlike its approach to Lebanon, Iran today is seeking to mobilize and organize the diverse Shiite forces in Iraq while not necessarily getting entangled in an altercation with the more powerful United States.

It is a truism of international relations that national interests and strategic imperatives define conflicts between nation-states. Too often the composition of domestic political order and ideological inclinations are cast aside for arguments rooted in power politics. The relations between Iran and Iraq contravene this established pattern of analysis. Both states have often clashed over their territorial demarcations, warily eyed the other's regional ambitions, and toyed with supporting local actors more amenable to their desires. Yet it would be a misreading of history to suggest that Iran and Iraq are destined to be antagonists and that their relations will inevitably be marked by tension and conflict. Prior to the 1958 Iraq revolution, the conservative monarchical regimes that governed the two states forged intimate ties. The changing ideological nature of the two regimes in the succeeding years did much to exacerbate their difficulties. The Shah's monarchy perceived revolutionary Iraq as a threat not because of its capabilities but because of its radical orientation. In a similar vein, Saddam's secular state saw Khomeini's Islamic fundamentalism as a challenge not because of the power of Iran's decimated armed forces but because of the lure of its ideals. In this context, all the unresolved territorial issues and disagreements took the shape of more menacing threats. These were no longer disputes that states could resolve, or at least manage, but were seen as indications of an aggressive posture. In due course the ambitions of Saddam and Khomeini, the two states' conflicting transnational aspirations, and their contending ideologies made a prolonged war inevitable.

As the Bush administration contemplated its invasion of Iraq in the aftermath of the September 11 tragedies, it is unlikely that it appreciated how its plans would enhance Iran's stature and security. The Islamic Republic now stands as one of the principal beneficiaries of America's regime-change policy. However, in assessing the ironies and paradoxes of the Middle East, one need not descend into a zero-sum game, whereby any measure that benefits Iran is necessarily viewed as endangering America's interests. Much of the tension and instability that has afflicted the critical Persian Gulf region in the past three decades has stemmed from animosity between Iran and Iraq. The contested borders, proxy wars, and finally a devastating eight-year conflict between the two powers not only destabilized the Middle East but threatened the global economy, with its reliance on the region's petroleum resources. The new Iraq emerging from the shadow of the American invasion will not just be a more humane society than the tyrannical Saddam Hussein regime, it will also be a more peaceful state willing to coexist easily with its Persian neighbor. And that development is not just good for Iran and Iraq, but also the United States.

8

ISRAEL AND
THE POLITICS OF
TERRORISM

On December 8, 2005, on one of his first visits abroad, President Ahmadinejad stunned much of the international community with this statement:

> Some European countries insist on saying that Hitler killed millions of innocent Jews in furnaces, and they insist on it to the extent that if anyone proves something contrary to that they condemn that person and throw him in jail. Although we don't accept this claim, if we suppose it is true, our question for the Europeans is: Is the killing of innocent Jews by Hitler the reason for their support to the occupiers of Jerusalem? If the Europeans are honest they should give some of their provinces in Europe—like in Germany, Austria, or other countries—to the Zionists and the Zionists can establish their state in Europe. You offer part of Europe and we will support it.[1]

Ahmadinejad's statement was quickly condemned by the United Nations, the European Union, and the United States. Iran's reactionary president had managed to unite the leading international actors in denunciation of his beleaguered nation. Despite the disavowals of Iran's diplomats, Ahmadinejad's anti-Israel statements have long been a mainstay of the theocratic regime's discourse. A strident opposition to Israel frequently edging toward anti-Semitism has often been invoked from a wide variety of platforms and forums of the Islamic Republic.

As we have seen, during the last two decades Iran has gradually displaced ideological imperatives with national-interest calculations as a guide to its international policy, but this trajectory has not affected its approach to Israel, which still reflects the lingering influence of its revolutionary Islamic heritage. For a generation of Iranian clerics, Israel is an illegitimate entity, usurping sacred Islamic lands in the name of a pernicious ideology: Zionism. Israel is also castigated as an agent of American imperialism, suppressing regional states at the behest of its superpower benefactor. From Tehran's perspective, opposition to the peace process serves two distinct goals. On the strategic front, any conduct that obstructs the extension of Israel's influence in the Middle East and polarizes its domestic politics is advantageous to Iran, which fears that the integration of Israel into the region will diminish its own power. On the political front, through an active support for the Palestinian rejectionist groups and Hezbollah, Iran can strengthen its Islamic credentials and highlight its determination to combat "Zionist encroachment." Unlike many other dimensions of its policy, Iran's incendiary opposition to Israel has been sustained because it satisfies both its strategic designs and its ideological mandates.

It is Iran's opposition to the State of Israel that has entangled it in the unsavory world of terrorism. The manner in which Iran expresses its opposition to Israel is to sustain a variety of terrorist organizations plotting against the Jewish state. The irony is that in the past decade, Iran's terrorism portfolio has gradually contracted, as Tehran no longer supports violent groups in the Persian Gulf or assassinates Iranian dissidents abroad. However, so long as Iran provides subsidies to groups such as Hezbollah and Palestinian Islamic Jihad it earns its place among the world's most ardent supporters of terrorism.

As with much in the Islamic Republic, however, debates and dissents are ongoing about the character of Iran's anti-Israeli policy. The hard-line elements who are devoted to the revolution's dogma insist on an absolutist opposition, while the more pragmatic factions stress the costs and burdens that such an uncompromising posture has yielded. The theocratic regime is again struggling with the legacy of its founder, and seeking an uneasy balance between its Islamist convictions and its national commitments.

THE MONARCHICAL PAST

Since the inception of the Islamic Republic, Iran's clerical politicians have persistently denounced Israel and question its legitimacy, if not its right to exist. All this may seem curious, because Iran has never fought a war with Israel and has no territorial disputes with the Jewish state. Indeed, throughout the monarchical years, Israel and Iran established constructive relations.

Although the birth of Israel was greeted by a series of Arab-Israeli wars, the predominantly Shiite and Persian state of Iran, with its own history of animosity toward the Sunni Arab powers, viewed the ascendance of a Jewish state as potentially beneficial. Not long after the establishment of the State of Israel, the Pahlavi dynasty cultivated close but informal ties with Jerusalem. A modernizing monarch with pro-American tendencies viewed such relations as natural, since Israel would be a potential repository of technology and a source of political support for a regime seeking better relations with Washington. Nonetheless, as the head of a Muslim nation, the Shah was mindful of his constituents' sensibilities and was careful to conceal his ties with Israel. Despite subsequent clerical imputations, the Shah continually pressed Israel toward accommodation of the Palestinians, and Iran often voted with the Arab bloc at the United Nations and various other international organizations.

For its part, a beleaguered Israel seeking to consolidate its power welcomed relations with Iran. During the 1950s, the Israeli prime minister David Ben-Gurion formulated his concept of the "outer ring," which would guide successive generations of Israeli politicians hoping to escape their regional isolation.[2] The concept holds that the best way to counteract Israel's tense and problematic relations with the "inner ring"—the predominantly hostile Arab states surrounding Israel—was for Jerusalem to foster better relations with the non-Arab states (such as Iran and Turkey) at the periphery of the Middle East. This policy might not necessarily relieve the pressure facing Israel, but it would ease its isolation and establish a precedent of forging proper ties with Muslim nations. Under the banner of the outer ring, Israel and Iran developed important and mutually satisfactory relations on issues ranging from economic dealings to security cooperation. Despite all the changes that have occurred during the intervening five decades, and Israel's peace treaties with the states of Jordan and Egypt, Ben-Gurion's concept still has a hold on the imagination of some Israeli leaders. Indeed, one reason why Israeli officials continued their arm sales to Iran during the post-revolutionary period was in the hope of maintaining at least some contact with Iran's military establishment.[3]

Despite a degree of popular indifference, the Shah's relations with Israel triggered opposition from two critical sectors, the clerical establishment and the secular intelligentsia. Even before the establishment of the state of Israel, the mullahs had warily eyed the Zionist influx into the Holy Land. The notion of "infidel" transgressions against Islamic lands and the unique status of Jerusalem to the Muslims ensured that the clerical estate looked with apprehension and alarm at the developments in Palestine. As early as the 1940s, the esteemed Ayatollah Muhammad Khorasani established active ties with the emerging Palestinian leadership that was spearheading the resistance to the Zionist enterprise. Ayatollah Abdolqasem Kashani, who would later emerge as a critical player in the 1953 oil nationalization crisis, spent the late 1940s organizing protest marches against the Jewish state. It was in the face of such sustained clerical opposition that the Shah downgraded his ties with Israel in its early days. Indeed, Iran was one of the few states that voted against the 1947 United Nations resolution partitioning Palestine.

A similar antagonism toward Israel would characterize Khomeini's evolving Islamist ideology. Under the pressures of the clerical hierarchy, Khomeini maintained a level of political silence until the late 1950s, when he finally established himself as one of the leaders of the clerical community. His political emergence was characterized by a determined opposition to Israel, which at times proved indistinguishable from antagonism to Jews in general. During the crisis of 1963, which constituted the first attempt by the religious associations and secular opposition to unify against the monarchy, Khomeini pressed the notion that the Shah was an agent of Zionism, attributing the monarchy's quest to marginalize the clerical establishment to Jewish machinations. Khomeini insisted that all Iranians "felt repugnance" about Tehran's ties with Israel.[4] In his many speeches, he routinely implored his fellow clerics to remain defiant and often mentioned the danger of "Israel and its agents."[5]

During his exile in Iraq, Khomeini continued to express his disdain for the Jewish state and the imaginary forces that sustained its power. In his book *Islamic Government,* which established the basis for theocratic rule, Khomeini indulged in his own bit of anti-Semitic rhetoric by claiming, "Since its inception, the Islamic movement has been afflicted by the Jews, for it was they who first established anti-Islamic propaganda."[6] The Jews were depicted as financial hoarders, distorters of the Koran, and imperialist agents. "We must protest and make people aware that the Jews and their foreign masters are opposed to the foundations of Islam," he implored.[7] As with President Ahmadinejad four decades later, Khomeini often failed to differentiate between Judaism and Zionism, and his denunciations of Jews resembled the crass anti-Semitism so prevalent in Arab literature and popular expressions.

Beyond his Islamist objections, as an adroit politician, Khomeini recognized that the younger generation of Iranians attuned to the sermons of the Third World had come to sympathize with the Palestinian cause. Indeed, the gradual transformation of the attitude of Iran's intelligentsia paved the way for an alliance with the clergy that proved so formidable during the revolution. The Iranian intellectual class was initially fascinated with Israel as a small minority struggled and succeeded against great odds. Israel appeared a country on the move, easily reconciling its religious traditions with democratic norms. It was a modernizing state, establishing a vibrant industrial economy in a region littered with stagnating Arab autocracies. Iranian intellectuals began to make pilgrimages to Israel and wrote approvingly of a pioneering spirit of a minority populace that was defying the regional trends of reaction and backwardness.

As with much in the Middle East, Israel's resounding defeat of the combined Arab armies in June 1967 changed many popular attitudes, and the Israeli occupation of the West Bank and Gaza proved particularly emotive to the secular opposition. Similarly, the national liberation struggles sweeping the Third World had a great impact on Iran's intellectual class, and they began to depict the Israeli occupation as another European colonial enterprise. Iran's famed intellectual Jalal Al-e Ahmad led the charge by insisting that the West had created Israel "so that the Arabs should forget the real troublemakers in their midst of Israeli troublemaking, the French and American capitalists."[8] Along these lines, Israel was now condemned as a "racist state," a source of capitalist exploitation, and a colonial beachhead in a critical region of the developing world.

During the 1960s, as Iran's younger generation began to agitate against an increasingly unaccountable monarchy, Israel, with its intimate ties to the Shah, proved a tantalizing target of denunciation. These charges were not entirely without merit; Israel had not only established collaborative ties with Iran's armed forces but its intelligence services were instrumental in training the Shah's notorious secret police, SAVAK. At a time when Israel was receiving approximately 75 percent of its energy requirements from Iran, the nexus between the Jewish state and the repressive monarchy had become all too obvious.

As the revolution gathered strength, hostility to Israel proved an effective means of unifying the differing strands of opposition. The Shah's dictatorial tendencies and Israel's harsh occupation policies appeared connected in the imagination of Iran's revolutionaries. However facile it may seem, many leading opposition figures began to paint a picture of the Shah and Israel as collaborators determined to suppress the hard-pressed populations of Iran and Palestine. As such, antagonism to the monarchy and opposition to Israel's occupation were no longer disparate struggles but part of the same seamless narrative.

The triumph of Khomeini and his clerical brethren was inevitably going to alter the dynamics of Iranian-Israeli relations. However, given the manifold problems that the Islamic Republic was confronting, the intensity of its animosity toward Israel came as a surprise to many observers. Contrary to many expectations, the force of revolutionary grievances and Khomeini's long-honed suspicions ensured that Iran's militancy would not be confined to mere rhetorical fulmination. The Shah's subtle and cautious strategic relationship with Israel was now displaced by an Islamist paradigm that viewed Israel as a source of Muslim repression. The struggle against the Jewish state was seen as an affirmation of revolutionary identity and Islamist idealism. It would be difficult for the regime to retreat from a stance that it had elevated to a position of moral obligation.

THE REVOLUTION COMES TO POWER

Iran's Islamic polity is a contradictory state that has perennially confounded both its allies and critics. Despite periodic lapses and conflicts with the international community, the trajectory of Iran's foreign policy has been a gradual assertion of national interest imperatives over ideological preferences. Whenever national interest mandates collided with revolutionary pretensions, the Islamic Republic retreated, becoming careful, even judicious. Israel stands as an exception to this norm simply because the typical clash between interests and dogma did not take place. The reality is that the Islamic Republic's ideologically strident position has often resulted in strategic benefit. Iran's ardent embrace of the Palestinian cause allowed an isolated Shiite regime to project its influence to the heart of the Arab world and mobilize regional opinion behind its claims. All this is not to suggest that Iran did not pay a price for its conduct, as part of the reason for the imposition of U.S. sanctions and international censure has been Tehran's dogmatic rejection of Israel. But to Iran's rulers the price paid seemed justified, given the ideological and strategic advantages that Iran derived from its uncompromising posture.[9]

As with much in the Islamic Republic, Iran's animosity toward Israel can be traced back to Khomeini's dictates.[10] In his eyes, the unforgivable sin was the original one, namely, the creation of a Jewish state that displaced Palestinian Muslims. In a sense, Iran's antagonism toward Israel exceeded even its opposition to the United States. After all, the United States may have been a pernicious imperial power, but it is America's conduct, not its right to exist, that is contested. Israel, on the other hand, is seen as an unlawful entity, irrespective of its actual policies and behavior. No peace compact or negotiated settlements with the aggrieved Palestinians could ameliorate that essential illegitimacy.[11]

This ideology was soon enunciated by Iran's empowered revolutionaries. Among Khomeini's first declarations was a call to Muslims to "prepare themselves for battle against Israel."[12] Rafsanjani went so far as to publish a book, *Esra'il va Qods-e Aziz,* claiming that resistance to the Jewish state was the sacred duty of "every Muslim and anyone who believes in God."[13] Thus when President Ahmadinejad calls for "Israel to be wiped off the map," as he did in a speech in October 2005, he is reflecting an entrenched ideological position embraced by many figures within Iran's Islamic polity. The international community and media may be hearing such denunciations for the first time, but for those who have paid close attention to the deliberations of the Islamic Republic, such intemperate rhetoric is not particularly new.

As with its depiction of Saddam during the Iran-Iraq war, Iran's view of Israel lapsed into a religiously defined image. This was a struggle between a pristine Islamic civilization and a blasphemous Zionist creed. In this conflict between good and evil, light and dark, it was a religious obligation to resist the profane Jewish entity.[14] The liberation of Jerusalem was not considered a sole Palestinian responsibility but an Islamic obligation to be undertaken by the entire Muslim world. Such a conflict would lead to the destruction of Israel and to a greater Islamic cohesion and solidarity. It was natural, even inevitable, for the new Islamic regime in Iran to lead this crusade.

In essence, Iran's position exceeded the calculations of both the Arab states and mainstream Palestinian organizations. For the past three decades, the Arab struggle has implicitly acknowledged the reality of Israel and has sought territorial concessions to establish a Palestinian homeland. At times terrorism and at times diplomacy were employed to redraw the boundaries, but all such schemes recognized the existence of Israel. The Iranian policy was not designed to readjust territorial demarcations but to evict the Jewish populace from the Middle East. The sacred land of Islam was not to be partitioned to accommodate Zionist aspirations but reclaimed for the Muslim world.

Given the provocative nature of Iran's stance, once in power Khomeini sought a subtle differentiation between Iranian Jews and the State of Israel. On the one hand, Khomeini's pan-Islamic ambitions and his perception that the vitality of the revolution was contingent on its export implied that he could not envision a Middle East that featured a thriving Jewish state. Yet he also began to somewhat temper his indiscriminate denunciation of Jews within Iran, and he even assured the local Jewish community that "Islam will treat Jews as it treats other groups of the nation. They should not be put under pressure."[15] Although since the overthrow of the Shah the legitimate fear of persecution and discrimination have led many Jews to leave

Iran, its Jewish community remains the largest in the Middle East outside Israel.

As the theocratic regime consolidated its power, it appeared at pains to differentiate its opposition to Zionism from its hostility to the larger Jewish community. The mullahs have often acknowledged the sufferings that the Jews experienced in Europe, attributing them to Christendom's inhumanity. The treatment of Jews in Europe was contrasted with the relative tolerance of Islamic civilization, where Jewish communities prospered for centuries. The creation of Israel was condemned as an attempt by Europe to assuage its conscience at the expense of the Palestinians. In his polemical and fundamentally flawed 1997 book on Israel, former foreign minister Ali Akbar Velayati insisted that the West sought to resolve its "Jewish problem" by foisting them on the Arabs.[16] Another former Iranian official, Sirius Nasseri, chimed in, stressing that the Palestinians paid the "price of European crimes in Auschwitz and Treblinka."[17] Again, President Ahmadinejad's comments regarding the need to relocate Israel to the European continent is not necessarily novel, but it is part of a larger discourse of the Islamic Republic.

As with many regimes in the Middle East, Iran has indulged in its share of Holocaust revisionism. The infamous *Protocols of the Elders of Zion* has been routinely published by state agencies, and prominent Holocaust deniers are at times offered a platform in Iran for spewing their odious views. The Supreme Leader Khamenei has even gone so far as claiming, "There are documents showing close collaboration of Zionists with Nazi Germany, and exaggerated numbers relating to the Jewish Holocaust were fabricated to solicit the sympathy of world public opinion, lay the ground for the occupation of Palestine, and justify the atrocities of the Zionists."[18] In essence, Khamenei views the Holocaust as a fabricated narrative to justify a Jewish homeland. Even in this context, Ahmadinejad's denunciation of the Holocaust as a "myth" stands in contravention of the Islamic Republic's previous rhetoric, which at least stipulated that a grave genocidal crime did take place in Europe, although the number of fatalities may have been exaggerated to validate the Zionists' strategic determinations.

A similarly incendiary and insensitive approach has characterized Tehran's attitude toward the ideology of Zionism. While Iran's clerical leaders may have sporadically displayed a benign attitude toward the local Jewish community, their condemnation of Zionism has been stark and categorical. To them, Zionism is a racist, exclusionary ideology that should be opposed by all who care about human rights. Iran's propaganda insists that Zionism was inflicted on the region by the force of arms, sustained by bloodshed, and perpetuated by the sinister designs of politicians inclined to achieve power by subjugating the indigenous population. The complex history of the Zionist movement and its claims and aspirations were typically caricatured, as fiery sermons, Jerusalem days, and conferences calling for the annihilation of Israel replaced a rational assessment.

The persistence of Iran's hostility to Israel cannot be attributed solely to its Islamist pretensions, however, as the strategic benefits that the theocracy derives from its policies serve to reinforce its anti-Zionist posture. At a time when Arab regimes have gradually conceded the legitimacy of Israel, and regional debates revolve around the dimensions of the Jewish state as opposed to its actual existence, there appeared a real opportunity for Iran to step into a vacuum, embracing an inflammatory approach to Israel that also enjoys support on the Arab street. By stressing its categorical opposition to Israel, Iran brandished its Islamist credentials, gaining widespread support in unexpected quarters. At a time when a number of influential Arab leaders have signed treaties with Israeli politicians, Iran appeared resolute, defiant, and powerful. To be sure, Iran has not had any direct military confrontation with Israel and has often suggested that, given the geographic necessity, the brunt of the conflict be borne by frontline states and the Palestinians themselves. As such, Iran's opposition to Israel has always had a degree of convenience, insisting on hostility without direct engagement in the conflict. The facts are that Iran's armed forces have never suffered the devastation at the hands of Israel that the Egyptian military did and Iranian cities have never been targeted by the Israeli air force as Jordanian cities were during successive Arab-Israeli wars. The theocracy essentially exploited the Palestinian struggle to assert its influence, garner popular approbation, and affirm its claims as a regional power.

It can be argued that without the Arab-Israeli conflict, Iran's essential insularity would have endured. The Islamic Republic's ardent embrace of the Palestinian cause has allowed it to transcend its isolation and inject its voice in the most important debates in Arab politics. It is unlikely that without mutual hostility to Israel, for example, Iran could have forged such intimate ties with the secular Syrian regime. Moreover, the Arab-Israeli tensions that often played out in the tragic country of Lebanon offered Iran an opportunity to enter the politics of the Levant. It was only after the Israeli invasion of Lebanon in 1982 that Iran began to energetically organize the long-quiescent Shiite population of southern Lebanon, eventually creating and nurturing the lethal Hezbollah organization. In essence, it was not so much the revolutionary sermons and Islamist calls but the reality of conflict between Israel and its neighbors that allowed an opportunistic Iran to assert its influence beyond its borders at a limited cost.

Given Iran's sustained antagonism toward Israel, how does one explain the secret arms deals between the two states that commenced in 1981, culminating in the notorious Iran-Contra scandal? As we saw in chapter 7, from Iran's perspective the outbreak of the war with Iraq altered its entire strategic and political calculations. Facing a formidable Iraqi army, generously supplied by both the Western powers and the Soviet Union, an isolated Iran required weapons from any source possible. The ideological imperative of resisting Israel and the practical requirements of the war now clashed, forcing Tehran to prioritize its hostilities. Given the imminent Iraqi danger, Iran was compelled to engage in transactions with the despised Israeli state that fundamentally violated its revolutionary doctrine.

In the meantime, Iraq's invasion in 1980 created considerable anxiety in Jerusalem. Despite the Islamic Republic's belligerent rhetoric, Israel still identified Saddam's regime, with its nuclear determinations and pan-Arabist ambitions, as its foremost challenge. Foreign minister Moshe Dayan even stressed that if U.S.–made weapons did not soon reach the Islamic Republic, Iran would collapse, leaving Israel to face a triumphant Saddam.[19] Thus began one of the most sordid, amoral episodes in the politics of the Middle East. Secret meetings in Europe, Israeli delegations to Tehran, and eventually large-scale shipments of arms became the order of the day. The intriguing aspect of the arms deals is that they continued even after Israel's invasion of Lebanon, when Iran was actively mobilizing the Shiite community against Israel. Paradoxically Israel was dispatching arms to Iran while Tehran and Jerusalem were engaged in a proxy war in southern Lebanon.

For some observers the arms transactions reflect the propensity of the two antagonists to transcend their animosities and displace ideology for practical considerations as a guide to their relations. This is a fundamental misunderstanding of the arms deals, as they were forged in compulsion and cynicism. The Islamic Republic's ideological animosity was in no way ameliorated, since Khomeini continued to denounce Israel, while Iran materially assisted a wide variety of anti-Israeli terrorist organizations. The Israeli position was best described by one of its officials, who conceded at the time, "One of the main reasons for cooperation between the two countries is the likely access of Iraq to the atomic bomb and its unconditional support for the PLO. Baghdad is our first enemy."[20] Although in subsequent years Israeli devotees of Ben-Gurion's "outer ring" concept have romanticized these arrangements as potentially foretelling a different relationship with Iran, such anticipations are misplaced and self-serving. To read too much into such furtive and sporadic deals, and view them as indications of a potential shift in Iran's ideological antipathy toward Israel, is a mistaken assessment of the events. Two antagonists fortuitously sharing the same immediate foe came together to deal with their more urgent threat while determined to confront each other at a later date.

Whatever Iran's disdain for Israel may be, it shares no borders with the Jewish state nor is it taken into the counsel of Arab states plotting their strategy. Thus, the only manner through which Iran can express its hostility toward Israel is terrorism. More than any other factor, it is Iran's militancy toward Israel that has done much to transform it into a pariah state relying on unsavory terrorist organizations that share its pathologies.

THE INSTRUMENTS OF TERROR

During the past three decades, Iran has forged intimate ties with leading Palestinian militant groups such as Hamas and Islamic Jihad, as well as Lebanon's Hezbollah, which it essentially created. Hamas, however, has its own sources of power and has been the beneficiary of much assistance from the Gulf sheikdoms as well as the Palestinian community itself. It is thus not an organization beholden to Iran, nor does it necessarily adhere to the dictates of the theocratic regime. In terms of Palestinian resistance, Iran has been much closer to Palestinian Islamic Jihad, a smaller but deadlier organization. Overshadowing all these groups are Iran's ties with Hezbollah, a Shiite force in Lebanon, much more in tune with the messages of Iran's clerical class. As the Islamic Republic plots its strategy, it must be aware that a potentially successful peace process and the changing dynamics of Lebanese politics may yet diminish its influence over its unruly clients. A more concentrated focus on Islamic Jihad and Hezbollah denotes the precariousness of relying on terrorist organizations as a means of projecting power.

Islamic Jihad evolved in the 1980s as a splinter group from the Muslim Brotherhood and the Palestine Liberation Organization. Many of its leaders and rank-and-file members were recruited in Israeli prisons and radicalized during the struggle against the occupation. From the start, Islamic Jihad emphasized violence as the only suitable means of fostering change, and pointedly dismissed negotiation and compromise. It hews to a stern fundamentalist vision portraying the conflict with the Jewish state as a battle between good and evil, between heresy and belief. The members of Islamic Jihad are dedicated to its absolutist belief system, indoctrinated in its strict discipline, and committed to its code of secrecy. Unlike Hamas, Islamic Jihad does not operate an extensive social welfare network, but views itself as a small vanguard force that will employ terror to destabilize and ultimately dislodge the Israeli state.[21]

Iran's Islamic revolution proved a source of inspiration to the Jihad activists; it demonstrated the power of religion and the ability of the devout to overcome superior force. Khomeini's own teachings and determined opposition to both the United States and Israel offered a powerful model of emulation. Among the Palestinian organizations, Iran soon emerged as a sustained benefactor of Islamic Jihad. Although a Sunni organization, the sectarian divide was papered over as Islamic concepts of jihad and martyrdom were invoked as unifying symbols between a Shiite state and a Sunni movement. Islamic Jihad allowed Iran to have an inroad into Palestinian politics and an ability to claim credit for Palestinian resistance that ultimately compelled Israel into negotiations. Muhammad Baqer Zolqadr, deputy minister of the interior and former second in command of the Revolutionary Guards, echoed this sentiment: "The Palestinian Intifada was born because of the Islamic Revolution and it is the consequence of the Iranian people's steadfastness vis-à-vis the superpowers."[22]

Today, the continued conflict between a hawkish Israeli government and a recalcitrant Palestinian leadership has enhanced the fortunes of radical groups pressing for violence and terror. The resounding electoral triumph of Hamas in the parliamentary elections of January 2006 denotes the cost of a stalemated peace process. In such a milieu, Islamic Jihad and Iran effectively exploit the Palestinian grievances to advance their claims. However, a reinvigorated peace process, offering Israelis viable security and the Palestinians their long-cherished dream of statehood, will inevitably diminish Islamic Jihad's power and Iran's influence. In the end, the Islamic Republic may yet have miscalculated with its failure to craft a constructive agenda and basing its policy exclusively on the changing fortunes of a small terrorist organization.

Just north of Israel, Lebanon has always been a hotbed of conflict between sectarian forces, culminating in a bitter civil war in the 1970s and 1980s. Following the Israeli invasion of 1982 to evict the Palestinians, who were using Lebanon as a sanctuary to launch terror attacks, Iran became more directly involved in Lebanese affairs. In conjunction with its Syrian ally, Iran began to mobilize the Shiite community, offering financial and military assistance to its militant allies. The Shiites constituted the largest communal group in Lebanon but were traditionally excluded from positions of political and economic power. Iran's Revolutionary Guards and diplomats energetically organized the various fledgling Shiite organizations and essentially created Hezbollah. Through provision of social services, an impressive fund-raising capability, and an increasingly sophisticated paramilitary apparatus, Hezbollah gradually spread its influence, subsuming many of the remaining Shiite associations and assuming a commanding position in Lebanon's politics.[23]

Hezbollah first came into the American consciousness when its suicide bombers attacked the U.S. Marine barracks in Beirut in 1983, killing 241 U.S. soldiers. At Iran's behest, Hezbollah went on a string of kidnappings and hostage takings, some captives eventually bartered away for U.S. arms during the Iran-Contra Affair. In the 1990s, Hezbollah's operatives were also implicated in the killing of Iranian dissidents in Europe and an attack against a Jewish community center in Argentina. A grim record of suicide bombings, assassinations, and kidnappings soon made Hezbollah a terrorist organization with an impressive global reach. Even before the rise of al-Qaeda, Hezbollah had assumed a prominent place in the world of fundamentalism, as it not only introduced new tactics to Islamist resistance such as suicide bombings but also ingeniously utilized religion to justify its use of indiscriminate violence.

Despite its multiplicity of attacks around the globe, Israel has been

Hezbollah's favorite target. Hezbollah's forces waged a long and costly guerrilla war against Israel, eventually contributing to its decision to withdraw from southern Lebanon in 2000. Israel's departure has not lessened Hezbollah's animosity; the Lebanese group trains Hamas activists and periodically shells Israeli settlements across the border. In the summer of 2006, Hezbollah took the provocative step of abducting and killing Israeli soldiers, provoking a massive Israeli counterattack. Nevertheless, the Hezbollah paradigm of confronting superior military power with suicide bombings and a low-intensity guerrilla campaign has now been embraced by the region's militants as their preferred model of waging war. The case of Iraq demonstrates that even its Sunni insurgents are willing to learn from their Shiite counterparts, as U.S. troops are now subject to the same deadly tactics that facilitated the eviction of Israel from its security perimeter in Lebanon.

Iran's motivations for supporting Hezbollah thus stem from an interlocking set of ideological and strategic calculations. As we have seen, the "revolution without borders" sought to refashion regional norms and spread its message throughout the Middle East. In practice, Iran's appeal proved limited to beleaguered Shiite minorities in states such as Saudi Arabia, Bahrain, and Lebanon. The fact that most of these Shiite communities eventually traded in Iranian support for accommodation with the ruling elite limited the Islamic Republic's reach to perennially fractious Lebanon. In a real sense, Hezbollah remains the only palpable success of Iran's largely self-defeating attempt to export its revolution. On the strategic front, Hezbollah allowed Iran to project its influence to the Arab world at minimal cost. However, the events of 2006 demonstrated that relying on a terrorist organization whose rash conduct can potentially spark a regional war can entangle the Islamic Republic in difficulties it may not have anticipated.

Hezbollah has always been burdened by its dual identity. It is at once a political party seeking integration in Lebanon's multi-confessional society, yet it is also an Islamist vanguard force dedicated to confronting Israel. For a long time, such duality seemed easily reconcilable, as Hezbollah's successful eviction of Israeli troops from southern Lebanon measurably enhanced its prestige and enabled it to assume a commanding position in Lebanese politics.[24] Iran could claim credit for a Hezbollah that was both a model for Islamists as well as a political force in the Levant. The rising stature of its protégé allowed Iran a voice in deliberations well beyond its actual military capabilities.

Yet even politically astute organizations are capable of grave misjudgments. In the heady days of the summer of 2006, when the Palestinian fires were burning, Hezbollah decided to join the fray. In this sense, the Shiite party misjudged both Israeli reticence and the temper of the Lebanese people. At a time when Lebanon had finally reclaimed its autonomy (with the departure of Syrian forces) and was focused on economic development, Hezbollah failed to appreciate that its relevance could not be predicated on its dedication to armed struggle against Israel. As Lebanon once more plunged into violence and disorder, Hezbollah's vaunted military capability was degraded and its judgment questioned by its once-ardent constituents. Hezbollah's patrons in Tehran, who were undoubtedly informed of its plans, must have experienced a degree of buyer's remorse. Their most esteemed protégé stands in an uncharacteristically beleaguered position, distrusted by contending sectarian groups in Lebanon as well as by many Arab leaders. It may be difficult for Hezbollah to remain a significant instrument of Iranian policy in this charged atmosphere.

The Islamic Republic may be an ardent supporter of terrorism, but it is also a cautious power. Despite its depiction of Israel as a threat to the cohesion of the Islamic bloc, Iran has avoided direct military confrontation with the Israeli military machine. In essence, Iran has always found itself in a peculiar position, as it seems caught between its incendiary rhetoric and an unwillingness to commit forces to the actual struggle against the Jewish state. Successive Iranian regimes have sought to escape this conundrum by subsidizing terrorist organizations that share its determination to obstruct diplomatic efforts to resolve the Arab-Israeli conflict. Yet it is apparent to many in the region that Iran's strident opposition to Israel has had a degree of convenience; the Islamic Republic has insisted on perpetuation of hostilities while avoiding direct engagement in the conflict.

In the 1990s, the contradictions in Iran's posture became more glaring, as a seemingly successful peace process launched by the Clinton administration confronted the theocratic regime with the difficult balancing act of sustaining its absolutist opposition to Israel while mending fences with leading regional powers inclined to accept a political settlement. Although in the past Iran's strategic requirements and ideological determinations easily coincided, the unfolding Oslo peace process forced Tehran toward an important modification of its anti-Israeli posture. As with many constructive developments that took place in the Islamic Republic during the late 1990s, the harbinger of that positive change was Muhammad Khatami.

FROM KHATAMI TO AHMADINEJAD

Khatami's presidency ushered in important changes in Iran's international orientation. The new president and his reformist allies recognized that Iran's divisive diplomacy and inflammatory rhetoric had led to a debilitating isolation damaging its international standing and economic requirements. In order to reclaim its place in the global society and revitalize its economy, Iran had to join the march of modernity and accommodate itself to some basic realities. As Iran was awaking from its Islamist torpor, it confronted a changing regional landscape. Throughout the 1990s, prominent Arab leaders—including such implacable foes of Israel as Yasser Arafat—journeyed to the White House to sign peace compacts with Israel. In 2002, even the Arab League, under the prodding of the Saudis, contemplated its own plans for ending the Arab-Israeli conflict. The era of anti-Zionist confrontations seemed finally to be coming to a close as the Palestinian recognition of Israel provided justification for the reigning Arab regimes to abandon a costly struggle that had resulted only in military defeat and political anguish. An Iran seeking integration in the regional political order and reconciliation with the leading Arab powers could not be seen as engaging in conduct detrimental to their interests.

Beyond such strategic calculations, the reformist leadership whose power was predicated on electoral consent recognized how Iran's stance against Israel had alienated its own citizens. In the 1960s Iranian youth with their Third Worldist pretensions and anticolonial shibboleths had found the Palestinian cause a worthy struggle, but their postrevolutionary offspring demonstrated scant interest in Palestine's liberation. Beset by persistent unemployment and a suffocating cultural milieu, Iran's youthful populace is well aware that the ideological hubris of their parents resulted only in economic stagnation and a tarnished international reputation. The reality of Iran today is that after decades of propagating anti-Israeli sermons, the theocratic oligarchs have failed to convince their constituents why a country that shares no borders with Israel and has no Palestinian refugee problem should continue with its dogmatic policy. The irony of the Islamic Republic is that its anti-Israeli antagonism is largely a privilege of its narrowly defined elite. Reformist politicians seeking not just to empower the citizenry but to craft a government responsible to the masses had to take account of these widespread popular sentiments.

The most thunderous denunciation of Iran's policy came from an unlikely source, a former minister of interior who emerged as one of the most admired reformist politicians, Abdollah Nuri. Given his popularity and stature, Nuri was one of the first victims of the conservative crackdown, when in 1999 he was convicted on spurious charges and imprisoned for five years. Nuri's trial was broadcast daily by the state media and proved to be riveting television, as Iranians across the country gathered around their sets to hear the unthinkable. In a pointed rebuke to the hard-liners, Nuri proclaimed, "What do Iranians gain from this attitude except being blamed for supporting terrorism?" The former interior minister stipulated, "The current conditions are not ideal, but we must come to terms with realities and avoid being a bowl warmer than the soup."[25] In light of Iran's self-defeating policy, Nuri invoked the heretical proposition that it was time not only to reassess but to discard Khomeini's views on Israel.

Nor was Nuri an isolated voice; increasingly, such sentiments were openly expressed in the reformist circles. An influential reformist daily, *Bonyan,* dared to cross the redlines of the Islamic Republic by pointing to the international opprobrium that had resulted from Iran's support for terrorist organizations. In an important 2002 editorial, *Bonyan* suggested that "Iran's interests have been jeopardized by this allegation on numerous occasions."[26] In a similar vein, Mohsen Mirdamadi, a leading liberal politician and the head of the reformist parliament's foreign affairs committee, stated:

> We have certain ideals about Palestine, but we also face certain limitations. Can we be more Palestinian than Palestinians? I don't believe that this should be the case. But if we insist on our posture, no one in the Islamic world is going to support us and we will be an isolated and forsaken country.[27]

Beyond such assertions, many reformers contested Iran's policy as impractical, given the gap between its declared objectives and actual commitment. The reformers mocked the hard-liners as indulging in belligerent declarations while confining themselves to provision of modest aid to radical Palestinian groups that had no chance of threatening Israel's actual existence. Such an illogical policy had no prospect of redeeming the pledge of "wiping Israel off the map," and its only success was in triggering economic sanctions on Iran's fledgling economy.

It was here that Khomeini's legacy created a reality that the Islamic Republic found difficult to escape. For the hard-liners committed to guarding the dogma of the state, opposition to Israel was an indication of ideological reliability and revolutionary valor. In a curious manner, the fact that Iran's policy had no chance of realizing its stated purpose of destroying Israel mattered little, since expressed hostility was seen as an indication of loyalty to the pillars of the revolution. Even the more moderate elements, struggling with so many aspects of the theocracy's self-defeating ideology, appeared restrained by this legacy and unwilling to pay the political price for a fundamental revision of a crucial aspect of Khomeini's vision. The fact was that for Khatami and the reformers, Iran's approach toward Israel was not the foremost area of concern, as domestic political reforms and more critical foreign policy issues such as potentially seeking a different relationship with America limited their incentive to struggle against a well-entrenched policy. This is not to suggest that no change occurred, however, as once more behind the scenes Khatami forged an important consensus for a more pragmatic approach to the Israeli-Palestinian conflict.

While on the surface Iran's animosities appeared intact, Khatami quickly changed the tone of the regime's rhetoric. As part of his "Dialogue of Civilizations" advocacy, the reformist president left the door ajar to participation by Jewish scholars. Departing from the norms of Iran's discourse, Khatami pointedly rejected anti-Semitism as a Western phenomenon without precedent in the Islamic civilization. "In the East we have had despotism and dictatorship, but never fascism and Nazism," he declared.[28] While Khomeini had often edged toward an anti-Semitic depiction of Jews, and his hard-line followers had insisted on castigating Arab politicians who entered peace treaties with Israel, Khatami offered a fundamentally different approach.

In his influential CNN interview of January 1998, Khatami unveiled Iran's more nuanced policy toward the Israeli-Palestinian dispute. Much of the coverage of Khatami's broadcast interview focused on his offering of an olive branch to the United States and his denunciation of the peace process as flawed and unjust. But Khatami also took the occasion to stress, "We don't intend to impose our views on others or stand in their way."[29] Foreign ministry spokesman Hamid Asefi reiterated this position, noting that Iran "will in no way interfere with the decisions of the Palestinian groups. We respect all decisions taken by the majority of the Palestinians."[30] In essence, the theocratic regime implied that it was prepared to acquiesce to a peace treaty acceptable to the Palestinian authorities and the leading Arab states.

This was a subtle yet perceptible change from Khomeini's unrelenting hostility to Israel.

The most important test of Iran's new policy came at the 2002 Arab League meeting that endorsed Saudi Crown Prince Abdullah's peace resolution calling for the collective Arab recognition of Israel should it pull out of the occupied territories. In the past, this would be an occasion for Iranian fulminations against Arab pusillanimity and commencement of conferences featuring militant Palestinian groups vilifying the proposal. However, this time, Khatami took the lead: "We will honor what the Palestinian people accept."[31] Foreign minister Kamal Kharrazi similarly characterized the communiqué of the Arab League meeting as the "most generous peace initiative by Arab states and, in its most optimistic sense, this plan is the repetition of the UN resolutions."[32] After decades of struggle against any measure calling for acknowledgment of Israel's rights, the Iranian regime appeared to grudgingly accept certain inevitable realities.

It is inconceivable that Khatami's regime could have taken such positions without the consent and approval of the Supreme Leader Ali Khamenei. Although it is difficult to decipher the opaque backroom politics of the theocratic regime, it is not unreasonable to suggest that Khatami once more managed to press a reluctant Supreme Leader to accept another important revision of the revolution's bombastic claims. Iran continued to offer material assistance to Palestinian militant groups and Hezbollah, but Tehran stipulated the conditions for a potential end of the conflict. Whatever its ideological dispositions, the clerical state recognized that its interests in the Middle East and its relations with key Arab states outweighed a lonely struggle against a peace process that was buttressed by a regional consensus. The critical question remained whether this hard-won position would survive the rise of a reactionary politician seeking to revive the "roots of the revolution."

Mahmoud Ahmadinejad came into office in 2005 determined to rekindle the revolutionary fires that seemed long extinguished. As part of an austere generation of war veterans that bemoaned society's indifference to Khomeini's legacy and the sacrifices of the revolution, Iran's new president persistently advocated turning back the clock. Ahmadinejad's vision for Iran constitutes an anachronistic mixture of statist economic policies, reimposition of Islamic cultural strictures, and reversal of the limited political freedoms that Iranians had come to enjoy during the reformist interlude. It would be on the international stage, however, that Ahmadinejad would garner the greatest attention—and cause considerable alarm and anxiety among both his countrymen and his larger global audience.

During one of the peculiar conclaves of radicals, reactionaries, and militants from across the Middle East that is all too familiar to observers of the Islamic Republic, Ahmadinejad issued his infamous call for the eradication of Israel. Far from being chastened by the international outcry, he followed up his outrageous remarks by denying the Holocaust as a "myth." For a politician who had advocated revitalizing the pan-Islamic dimension of Khomeini's revolution, the flagrant attack on Israel was a natural, even routine affair. After all, one of the core pillars of Khomeini's vision was the notion that Israel was an illegitimate entity and an imperial infringement on the Islamic realm.

Beyond the glare of publicity and international condemnations, however, what was missed about Ahmadinejad's speech was his attempt to reverse the "Khatami compromise": "Anybody who takes a step toward Israel will burn in the fire of the Islamic nation's fury," declared the new president.[33] In essence, Ahmadinejad was suggesting that the Islamic Republic would no longer be prepared to accept a peace treaty that was endorsed by the Palestinian officials and the Arab states. Indeed, Iran would not merely continue its assistance to radical Palestinian groups determined to scuttle any peace treaty but potentially would renew its earlier policy of seeking to subvert Arab regimes that normalized ties with the Jewish state. At a time when the Middle East peace process appeared in shatters, Ahmadinejad may have perceived a unique opportunity to exploit the Palestinian cause to assert his influence on the larger regional deliberations. But in Iran all politics are local. By embracing an inflammatory posture toward Israel, Ahmadinejad sought to press the theocratic regime, with its increasing penchant toward diplomacy rather than confrontation, toward a more defiant international outlook. He proved mistaken on both accounts.

The notion that Iran can project its influence in a significant manner in the Middle East on the platform of anti-Zionism and calls for extinction of Israel is illusory. Although Ahmadinejad's speech may have played well on the Arab street, it did not impress the incumbent regimes still inclined to deal with Israel in the framework of negotiations. Indeed, Ahmadinejad's statements caused considerable unease in Riyadh, Cairo, and other regional capitals, where the rulers once more feared the return of the 1980s when a mischievous Iran continually interfered in their domestic politics. Ironically, a speech designed to extend Iran's influence may have served the cause of its further isolation.

A more subtle backlash also occurred within the Islamic Republic itself, where the "Khatami compromise" appeared to survive its most determined challenge. The foreign ministry was the first to issue its rebuke of Ahmadinejad: "The Islamic Republic of Iran adheres to the UN Charter and has never used or threatened the use of force against any country."[34] The powerful head of the Supreme National Security Council, Ali Larijani, followed suit: "The situation of Iran with respect to Palestine is the same as the past. This is a decision of Palestinians about how to reclaim their rights."[35] Given Iran's power structure, such statements would not have been invoked without the approval of Khamenei and the regime's essential power brokers. Despite the usual Western recriminations against the so-called hapless Khatami, one of his more enduring accomplishments is a sturdy consensus for a more tempered approach to the Arab-Israeli conflict, which not even the rise of a new generation of reactionaries could disrupt.

After nearly three decades of constant change and reform, Iran's hostility toward Israel seems the most entrenched of its foreign policy determinations. The Islamic Republic's approach is still largely conditioned by an ideology that perceives Israel as a civilizational affront and a pernicious agent of American imperialism. However, the persistence of such animosity cannot be attributed exclusively to Iran's Islamist ideology. After all, throughout the 1980s Khomeini and his firebrands castigated Saudi monarchs in equally harsh terms, depicting the House of Saud as purveyors of "American Islam." In due course, as Iran's national interests collided with its ideological claims, it gradually abandoned its animus toward the Saudi regime and embarked on a prolonged détente that has benefited both states. The problem with Iran's incendiary approach toward Israel is that its defiance has served both its ideological mandates and its strategic calculations. As such, there has never been a sufficient incentive for the clerical oligarchs to abandon a policy whose costs in terms of U.S. sanctions and criticism seemed bearable.

The one occasion on which Iran adjusted its dogmatic policy toward the Jewish state was during the Khatami presidency, when a unique confluence of internal and regional developments pressed the theocracy toward a reconsideration of its policy. A reformist government intent on regaining Iran's international stature and integrating the Islamic Republic into the global economy seemed determined to blunt the ideological edges of the regime. In the meantime, as the Arab-Israeli peace process was moving forward, Iran's defiance isolated it from the mainstream of regional politics. Tehran may have reflexively opposed an American-sponsored peace plan, but once important actors like Saudi Arabia embraced the cause of a negotiated settlement and crafted a regional consensus behind such proposals, Iran was willing to accept the inevitability of peace.

In the heady days of the reformist tenure, it appeared that Iran might finally end its prolonged engagement with terrorism. The Islamic Republic had abandoned its terrorist allies operating in the Persian Gulf, and had shut down assassination squads targeting the exile community. The Arab-Israeli arena was one of the last frontiers where Iran still employed terrorism to advance its political objectives. However, even a Khatami government that did much to lessen Iran's attachment to terrorism ultimately failed to dispense with the radical groups plotting against Israel.

Today, given the consolidation of conservative power within Iran and the collapse of diplomatic efforts to ensure a viable Israeli-Palestinian peace, Iran's policy is unlikely to change in a measurable manner. All this is not to suggest that Iran's militancy is constant; for despite its belligerent rhetoric, the Islamic Republic's stance toward Israel has changed and the "Khatami compromise" remains alive despite attempts by the new government to revert to a more militant stance. In the end, the best manner of extracting Iran from the Arab-Israeli arena is for the United States and the key Arab states to launch a concerted diplomatic effort to resolve the remaining differences between Israel and the Palestinian Authority. Given Hamas's predominance, this may seem far fetched. However, the Middle East is often a land of surprises. Should the burdens of governance temper the Palestinian leadership's militancy, then there may yet exist the possibility for a negotiated solution. Such a development would not just diminish Iran's radicalism, but would remove a corrosive dispute that has done much to undermine the stability of the Middle East.

CONCLUSION:
GETTING IRAN RIGHT

Iran today is a country in transition. As a theocratic state struggling to conceive a governing order that accommodates both its religious convictions and its republican claims, it is often caricatured as a rigid regime governed by retrogressive mullahs in the name of an ossified ideology. An essentially pragmatic power that nonetheless bases some of its foreign policies on radical revolutionary values, it is routinely castigated as a state determined to upend the regional order. Too often when American policymakers look at Iran they see shadows of the democratic transitions that swept Eastern Europe in the aftermath of the Cold War, or of Latin American authoritarian regimes capitulating to popular pressures. Given the complexities of Iran, it is best to set aside all the comparative models and understand the Islamic Republic on its own distinct terms.

On the eve of its momentous revolution, Iran's triumphant clerics perceived it all to be so easy, as their new order would somehow transcend its contradictions, harmonizing Islamist injunctions and democratic aspirations. During the first decade of the revolution, Aya-tollah Khomeini's stature and undisputed authority overshadowed the paradoxes of the state. Through the force of Khomeini's transcendant charisma, the fractious factions within Iran's body politic were com-pelled to negotiate their differences and temper their ideological claims. In the meantime, elections primarily served as public appro-bations of Khomeini's policies and sanctioned his choices and repre-sentatives. But a series of events in the late 1980s irrevocably shattered this pattern of governance. The end of the prolonged war with Iraq, followed a year later by Khomeini's death, coupled with the emer-gence of a younger generation, ended the consensus underpinning the theocratic regime. Once-concealed competitive impulses and ide-ological divisions became apparent, and the consensus was eventually subverted by a restive public.

The post-Khomeini regime quickly fractured as competing factions of clerics and politicians became enmeshed in an internecine debate over the essence and direction of the theocracy. Some dedicated dis-ciples of Khomeini sought to sustain the existing order and continued to insist that religious discipline and revolutionary values were the most important guideposts for social organization. Two decades of self-defeating policies and the emergent postrevolutionary majority had altered the national landscape, however, producing a reform movement that called for a state whose legitimacy was predicated on popular sanction. In the middle were the pragmatists, less focused on revolutionary pedigree or democratic pluralism, who stressed the need for an economically efficient order that at least met the material needs of Iran's restive middle class and burgeoning youth movement. The intriguing aspect of the Islamic Republic is that elections and plebiscites don't seem to dislodge any of these factions from the na-tional scene; they persist, continually battling each other for influence and making perennial comebacks.

The durability of the Islamic Republic and the resilience of its fac-tions have invited yet another misplaced American initiative, a State Department plan to spend $85 million to promote democracy in Iran.

The Bush administration is seemingly taking a page from Eastern Europe, where the United States used radio broadcasts and direct assistance to opposition groups to help undermine authoritarian governments. However, the conditions in Iran bear little resemblance to those that accompanied the downfall of dictatorial regimes in Europe. The Iranian theocracy is not as brittle as its Eastern European counterparts, nor is the idea of broadcasts of any value in a society already drenched in information and debate. Indeed, the Bush administration's rhetoric—and now financial support—makes life more difficult for the democratic advocates it is intended to buttress, since they are now vulnerable to being castigated as agents of the "Great Satan."

In the meantime, Iran's international orientation was undergoing its own evolution, discarding its radical patrimony for the sake of national interest. After decades of failing to refashion regional norms, the clerical rulers finally confined their Islamist imagination within Iran's borders. Despite continued revolutionary pronouncements, Iran has evolved from a revisionist state seeking to export its governing template to a rational state that bases its foreign policy on pragmatic calculations. This transformation is neither complete nor absolute: Iran's approach to the Israeli-Palestinian conflict is still derived from a self-defeating calculus comprised in equal parts of domestic political considerations and ideological imperatives. As such, the theocracy is capable of a bewildering range of policies, from practical dealings with Russia to relentless opposition to the peace process.

As a state that is neither revolutionary nor fully pragmatic, Iran poses a challenge that has confounded two generations of American policymakers. Contrary to the presumption in Washington that the Islamic Republic is a fragile state about to collapse if America exerted determined pressure, the theocratic regime with all its unresolved contradictions and power struggles is likely to endure. The reality of Iran today is that its internal struggle is not a simple conflict between the mullahs and the people. The flexibility and decentralization of Iran's Islamic order ensures that it will perpetuate its ruling elite and retain its ardent supporters. The theocracy's complex institutional arrangements, whereby elected branches of government beholden to the public are frequently at odds with nonelected bodies, belies the notion of clear demarcation between the regime and the public. Thus the starting point of any judicious policy assessment is to set aside the chimera of regime change that still tempts many in Washington.

Since the inception of the Islamic Republic, the United States has pursued a policy of containment in various forms, essentially relying on political coercion and economic pressure to press Iran in the right direction. The failure of this policy is routinely documented by the U.S. State Department, which insists on issuing reports denouncing Iran as the most active state sponsor of terrorism and warning that its nuclear program is rapidly advancing toward weapons capability. The American diplomats fail to appreciate how, after twenty-seven years of sanctions and containment, Iran's misbehavior has not changed in any measurable manner. Even more curious, the failed policy of containment enjoys a widespread bipartisan consensus, as governments as different as the Clinton and Bush administrations have largely adhered to its parameters. Although at times the Bush White House has indulged in calls for regime change, its essential policy still reflects the containment consensus. In Washington policy circles evidently nothing succeeds like failure.

The other facet of U.S. policy is its emphasis on "linkage." Successive American administrations have maintained that before full-scale normalization of relations can take place, an entire range of Iranian policies would have to alter. Consequently, even if Iran were to suspend critical components of its nuclear infrastructure, it could not anticipate measurable relief from sanctions or a resumption of diplomatic ties with America. In essence, all aspects of Iran's objectionable practices are linked together: Tehran must cease its opposition to the peace process, renounce terrorism, and abandon its nuclear program before enjoying the benefits of routine ties with the United States. Instead of relying on a comprehensive diplomatic process that would address both American and Iranian concerns, Washington has insisted on its preconditions. The problem with the policy of linkage is that it has produced paralysis—a paralysis that in the end may yield a nuclear Iran still sustaining its ties to terrorist organizations. For progress to be made, the United States must not just revise its policy of containment but discard its practice of linkage.

In essence, this is a battle of two domestic political systems. Given the provocative nature of Iran's policies and its many areas of objectionable conduct, successive U.S. administrations have feared offering concessions to Iran unless they can be assured that the totality of Iran's foreign policy alters. At the same time, after nearly three decades of hostility and suspicion, Iran's oligarchs have limited trust in America and remain unconvinced, after all the rhetoric from American leaders, that the United States has abandoned its essential goal of regime change. It is the dissonance of these two political orders and the lack of imagination and courage by politicians on both sides that has led to the persistence of this most peculiar of stalemates.

In May 2006, Secretary of State Condoleezza Rice took a significant step in Washington's dealings with Iran, announcing American readiness to participate with Iran in multilateral talks focused exclusively on the nuclear issue. The problem with this diplomatic gesture is that it miscasts the dispute between the United States and Iran as a mere disarmament disagreement. Iran's quest for nuclear arms stems primarily from its tense relationship with the United States. Any diplomacy with a chance of meaningful success has to be broad enough to take into consideration both American and Iranian grievances. So long as political and strategic discord between the two states remains unresolved, it is unlikely that a durable nuclear accord can be negotiated.

In dealing with Iran, it is time for not just a policy shift but a paradigm change. In crafting its strategy toward Iran, the United States might draw lessons from the history of its relations with the People's Republic of China, another ideological regime oscillating between moderation and militancy. The history of U.S.–Chinese relations is similarly laden with emotional baggage, as China fought a war against America in Korea, did much to sustain the Vietnamese resistance, and spent decades demonizing the United States and its political class. Yet somehow compelling common interests have allowed the two parties to transcend their historical animosities and forge constructive relations. Today, the United States and China continue to have significant differences and equally important shared objectives. As such, Washington and Beijing cooperate with each other on certain issues while actively disagreeing on a range of others. America's opposition to China's Taiwan policy does not preclude dealing with Beijing on the issue of North Korea and the stabilization of Northeast Asia. Moreover, since Richard Nixon's breakthrough diplomacy, successive U.S. administrations have appreciated that trade and commerce, designed to integrate China into the global economy, is an effective means of circumscribing the regime's revisionist impulses. When it comes to China, America has wisely abandoned both its policy of containment and its presumptions of linkage—the United States and Iran can move toward a similar model of competing and cooperating at the same time.

The best manner of arriving at such a mature relationship is to commence direct negotiations with the Islamic Republic on the issues of critical importance—Iran's nuclear program, its sponsorship of terrorism, and the future of Iraq. As Iran edges closer to a nuclear capability, the unresolved nature of this issue threatens to press the theocracy toward crossing the threshold, and potentially even assembling a bomb. Iran's involvement with terrorism has been most manifest in the Arab-Israeli arena, and credible accounts, such as the *9/11 Commission Report*, suggest that elements within the theocracy are harboring al-Qaeda suspects. Moreover, as the U.S. presence in Iraq recedes, it behooves Washington to contemplate a strategy of bringing in regional powers to the task of reconstructing and rehabilitating Iraq.

The practical operational aspect of such diplomacy should envision three separate negotiating tracks, whereby each of these issues is considered by both sides. However, dispensing with linkage, progress on any one track should not be necessarily contingent on the others. For instance, if the United States and Iran are making important strides on the nuclear issue, negotiations should not be discontinued because of lack of progress on terrorism or Iraq. Having stipulated the essential autonomy of each individual track, it is important to stress that in actual practice progress on any one of these issues is bound to have positive reverberations for the others. An Iran that finds its security situation improved and is benefiting from lucrative commercial deals with American firms is bound to be a country more open to tempering its radical tendencies regarding terrorism.

Given the imminence of the nuclear danger and the need to fashion a political strategy for Iraq, these two issues ought to assume priority in any set of negotiations. Iran's nuclear ambition stems from a desire to craft a viable deterrence capability against a range of evolving threats, particularly from the United States. Instead of relying on threats of sanctions, a more effective way to convince Iran to suspend the critical components of its nuclear infrastructure is to find ways to diminish its strategic anxieties. Should Washington dispense with its hostilities, assure Iran that its interests will be taken into account as it plots the future of the Persian Gulf, and relax its economic prohibitions, then the case of nuclear proponents within the clerical state would be significantly weakened. After years of inconclusive negotiations with the European powers, international rebukes, and sporadic military intimidation, it is time to appreciate that threats only harden the stance of the theocratic regime and enhance the strategic utility of the bomb.

On a separate track, negotiations should focus on Iraq and the best means of coordinating U.S. and Iranian policies there. Since toppling Saddam Hussein's regime, Washington has worked hard to limit Iran's influence in Iraq, repeatedly warning Tehran to steer clear. Although Iran has been busy buttressing the fortunes of its Shiite allies and arming their militias, beneath the veneer of recriminations and accusations the two powers actually have many interests in common. Tehran, like Washington, is keenly interested in avoiding a civil war and sustaining Iraq as a unitary state. Moreover, the clerical regime appreciates that the best means of realizing its objectives in Iraq is through the electoral process, which is bound to empower the Shiite community. A functioning and legitimate Iraq state would be equipped to neutralize the insurgency, sap the Ba'athists of their remaining power, and incorporate moderate Sunnis into an inclusive governing order. It is no accident that Iran's mischievous mullahs have emerged as forceful advocates of democratic pluralism in Iraq, seeking to temper the simmering sectarian violence that threatens the country's political cohesion.

The starting point for any negotiations should be recognition that Iran will wield enormous influence over the future of Iraq, and the challenge for Washington is to work with Tehran to channel that influence in a constructive direction. As it seeks to craft a common agenda based on common interests, Washington ought to learn from the successful model it used to bring order to Afghanistan after displacing the Taliban. There, the United States established an international network that brought in all the regional powers with a stake in that country's reconstruction. Through such a framework for Iraq, the United States and Iran can engage in productive negotiations and succeed in harmonizing their policies. Iran, for instance, can backstop U.S. efforts at economic reconstruction through its ties to the Iraqi merchant community, particularly in the south, and its own official aid to Baghdad. Moreover, the United States may have boots on the ground, but America's coercive potential would benefit from being buttressed by Iran's "soft power." Iran's seminaries, clerics, businessmen, and politicians hold powerful sway over elites in Baghdad as well as elsewhere in Iraq. Tehran is in the best position to temper the Shiite community's secessionist tendencies and rein in recalcitrant actors such as Moqtada al-Sadr. So long as the United States views Iran as a competitor and its influence as fundamentally pernicious, it will be impossible to arrive at such an arrangement. Conversely, should Washington and Tehran join forces rather than compete for power, the two parties can go a long way toward preventing the fragmentation of Iraq and the destabilization of the critical Gulf region.

By far the most entrenched of Iran's positions is its opposition to the peace process, an opposition that is often expressed through terrorism. Iran's antagonism toward Israel is rooted in its revolutionary heritage and buttressed by the strategic benefits that such a policy has garnered. Tehran for a long time perceived the advantages that it gains from such a posture as worth the price in terms of U.S. sanctions and criticism. To change Iran's policy, Washington must alter that calculus. Should Iran enter a constructive relationship with the United States, then, for the first time, its bellicosity toward Israel will lead to a potential loss of tangible benefits. Indeed, the history of the Islamic Republic denotes that the theocratic regime is prepared to dispense with terrorism once offered sufficient incentives.

A cursory look at Iran's international relations reveals that its militancy is not constant; its pragmatic curtailment of terrorism in the Persian Gulf and Europe demonstrates that diplomatic pressure and economic incentives can encourage moderation from the Islamic Republic. The lessons of the experiences of the European and Gulf states are indeed instructive. Long-standing practices of the Islamic Republic were the assassination of dissidents living in Europe and support for opposition forces in the Gulf sheikdoms. These reached their apex in 1992, when Iranian agents assassinated Kurdish leaders in the Mykonos Restaurant in Berlin. The 1997 conviction of Iranian officials in a Berlin court led the European Union to promptly withdraw its envoys from Tehran, and Germany imposed trade restrictions on Iran. Given the value of European commercial trade and diplomatic ties, Iran abandoned the practice of targeting exiles abroad, and closed one of the darker chapters in its terrorism portfolio. Similarly, a precondition for Saudi Arabia and the Gulf states normalizing relations with Iran was its cessation of support for opposition groups within those countries. Once more, given the strategic and economic value of resumed relations, Iran ceased its interference in the internal affairs of the Gulf states. Both episodes reveal Iran's susceptibility to targeted diplomatic pressure and economic incentives: states possessing such levers are in a position to influence Iran's behavior.

As the United States and Iran attempt to resolve their differences on the issues of nuclear arms and Iraq, a certain negotiating momentum is bound to move Iran away from its opposition to the peace process and its reliance on terrorism. The essence of this diplomacy is to focus on areas of possible agreement, with the two powers gradually transcending their animosities and entering a new stage of relations. Once Washington and Tehran reach that plateau, then it may be possible to arrive at an understanding on the thorny issue of terrorism. Although it is far-fetched to suggest that Iran can be a valuable player in the war on terrorism, a more comprehensive diplomacy can still go a long way toward ensuring that it does not remain the benefactor of such a wide range of terrorist organizations.

The essence of this new approach is an appreciation that for the foreseeable future the Islamic Republic will remain a problem to be managed. This approach is neither one of containment nor an alliance but a policy of selective partnership on an evolving range of issues. By integrating Iran into the global economy and the regional security dialogue, the United States can foster links that allow cooperation on issues of common concern. America has a stake in the outcome of Iran's internal struggles, but merely asserting its doctrine of containment and periodically calling for regime change is unlikely to bring about a democratic transition. Conversely, by assimilating Iran into the prevailing order, Washington can do much to undermine the hard-liners who require American belligerence and international isolation to consolidate their power. In the long run, a subtle policy of selective engagement would not only create incentives for Iran to play a responsible role in the region, but also slowly compel its leadership to transcend the ideological traps that have alienated it from large sections of its population.

In the post–September 11 era, the United States will face not a single global challenge but a series of local contenders for power. Iran is such a contender: a medium-sized power seeking to influence the political trends in its region. The best manner of dealing with such a state is through employment of the full range of diplomatic, political, and economic tools. The United States would be wise to abandon the rhetoric of the early Reagan years and the policies of the Cold War era. In the end, America's determination to stabilize the Middle East requires a more imaginative approach for the Islamic Republic of Iran.

NOTES

INTRODUCTION: GETTING IRAN WRONG

1. www.whitehouse.gov.

2. Islamic Republic News Agency (hereafter IRNA), February 1, 2006.

3. Hamid Algar, *The Constitution of the Islamic Republic of Iran* (Berkeley, Calif.: Mizan Press, 1980).

1. KHOMEINI'S LEGACY

1. Baqer Moin, *Khomeini: The Life of the Ayatollah* (New York: St. Martin's Press, 1999), 199–223; Daniel Brumberg, *Reinventing Khomeini: The Struggle for Reform in Iran* (Chicago: University of Chicago Press, 2001), 98–120; Hamid Dabashi, *Theology of Discontent: The Ideological Foundations of the Islamic Revolution in Iran* (New York: New York University Press, 1993), 409–85.

2. For Khomeini's important work, see Ruhollah Khomeini, *Hukumat-e Islami* (Tehran: 1980); *Islam and Revolution: The Writings and Declarations of Imam Khomeini,* trans. Hamid Algar (Berkeley, Calif.: Mizan Press, 1981); *Kashf al-Asrar* (Tehran: 1942); *Nashq-e Rowhaniyyat dar Islam* (Qom: 1962).

3. A. Davani, *Ayatollah Borujerdi* (Tehran: 1993); M. Falsafi, *Khaterat va mubarazat-e Hojjat al-Islam Falsafi* (Tehran: 1997), 99–120; M. Rezavi, *Hashemi va*

enqelab (Tehran: 1997), 94–100; Vanessa Martin, *Creating an Islamic State: Khomeini and the Making of a New Iran* (London: I. B. Tauris, 2000), 48–69.

4. Roy Mottahedeh, *The Mantle of the Prophet: Religion and Politics in Iran* (New York: Simon and Schuster, 1985); Shahrough Akhavi, *Religion and Politics in Contemporary Iran: Clergy-State Relations in the Pahlavi Period* (Albany: State University of New York Press, 1980), 91–117; Hamid Dabashi, "Shiite Islam: The Theology of Discontent," *Contemporary Sociology* (March 1986); David Menshari, "Shiite Leadership in the Shadow of Conflicting Ideologies," *Iranian Studies* (1980); James Bill, "Power and Religion in Contemporary Iran," *Middle East Journal* (Winter 1982).

5. M. Rajabi, *Zendegi-ye Siyasi-ye Imam Khomeini* (Tehran: 1991), 220–25.

6. Jalal al-Din Madani, *Tarikh-e Siyasi-ye Mo'asser-e Iran* (Qom: 1982), vol. 1.

7. Ruhollah Khomeini, *Sahifeh-ye Nur* (Tehran: 1982), 198.

8. Alexander Knysh, "Ifran Revisited: Khomeini and the Legacy of Islamic Mystical Philosophy," *Middle East Journal* (Fall 1992); Hamid Algar, "Religious Forces in Twentieth Century Iran," in *The Cambridge History of Iran*, vol. 7, ed. Peter Avery, Gavin Hambly, Charles Melville (Cambridge: Cambridge University Press, 1991), 750–52.

9. Michael Fischer, *Iran: From Religious Dispute to Revolution* (Cambridge: Harvard University Press, 1980), 61–104; Said Arjomand, "Shiite Islam and the Revolution in Iran," *Government and Opposition* (July 1982); see also "The Ulama's Traditional Opposition to Parliamentarianism, 1907–1909," *Middle Eastern Studies* (April 1981).

10. Jalal Al-e Ahmad, *Gharbzadegi* (Lexington, Ky.: Mazda Publishers, 1982); Mehrzad Boroujerdi, *Iranian Intellectuals and the West: The Tormented Triumph of Nativism* (Syracuse, N.Y.: Syracuse University Press, 1996), 52–65; Ali Mirsepassi, *Intellectual Discourse and the Politics of Modernization: Negotiating Modernity in Iran* (Cambridge: Cambridge University Press, 2000), 96–127; Sepehr Zabih, *The Left in Contemporary Iran: Ideology, Organization and the Soviet Connection* (London: Croom Helm, 1986), 113–57; Afsaneh Najmabadi, "Iran's Turn to Islam: From Modernism to a Moral Order," *Middle East Journal* (Spring 1987); Maziar Behrooz, *Rebels with a Cause* (London: I. B. Tauris, 1999), 3–47; Ervand Abrahamian, *Radical Islam: The Iranian Mujahedin* (New Haven, Conn.: Yale University Press, 1989), 81–105.

11. Moin, *Khomeini: The Life of the Ayatollah*, 66.

12. Ali Shariati, *Islamshenasi*, collected works, nos. 16–18 (Tehran: 1981); see also Shariati's *Jahat giri-ye tabaqati-ye Islam* (Tehran: 1980) and *Khudsazi-ye Enqelabi* (Tehran: 1977). For important works on Shariati, see Ali Rahnema, *An Islamic Utopian: A Political Biography of Ali Shariati* (London: I. B. Tauris, 1998); Hamid Dabashi, "Ali Shariati's Islam: Revolutionary Uses of Faith in Post-Traditional Society," *Islamic Quarterly* 27 (1983); Mansoor Moaddel, *Class, Politics and Ideology in the Iranian Revolution* (New York: Columbia University Press, 1993), 130–54.

13. Ruhollah Khomeini, *Velayat-e Faqih* (Tehran: 1978), 28.

14. Khomeini, *Sahifeh-ye Nur* (Tehran: 1982), 517.

15. Ibid., 120.

16. Khomeini, Hamid Algar, trans., *Islam and Revolution,* 180–81.

17. For the 1963 crisis, see Ervand Abrahamian, *Iran between the Two Revolutions* (Princeton, N.J.: Princeton University Press, 1982), 473–95; Hamid Algar, "Imam Khomeini, 1902–1962," in *Islam, Politics and Social Movements,* ed. Edmund Burk and Ira Lapidus (Berkeley: University of California Press, 1988), 263–88; see also Algar, "The Oppositional Role of the Ulama in Twentieth Century Iran," in *Scholars, Saints and Sufis: Muslim Religious Institutions in the Middle East since 1500,* ed. Nikki R. Keddie (Berkeley: University of California Press, 1972), 231–55; Ehsan Tabari, "The Role of Clergy in Modern Iranian Politics," in *Religion and Politics in Iran: Shi'ism from Quietism to Revolution,* ed. Nikki R. Keddie (New Haven, Conn.: Yale University Press, 1983), 47–72.

18. Moin, *Khomeini: The Life of Ayatollah,* 122–26.

19. Ruhollah Khomeini, *Sukhanraniha-ye Imam Khomeini dar Shish Mahe-ye Avval* (Tehran: 1980).

20. Rouhollah Ramazani, "Khumayni's Islam in Iran's Foreign Policy," in *Islam in Foreign Policy,* ed. Adeed Dawisha (Cambridge: Cambridge University Press, 1983), 9–32.

21. Ruhollah Khomeini, *Kashf-e Asrar* (Tehran: 1943), 45.

22. Ibid., 67.

23. *Keyhan,* March 21, 1980.

24. Ibid.

25. *Keyhan,* March 24, 1980.

26. Shaul Bakhash, *The Reign of the Ayatollahs* (New York: Basic Books, 1990), 52–71; Abrahamian, *Iran between the Two Revolutions.*

27. Asghar Schirazi, *The Constitution of Iran: Politics and the State in the Islamic Republic,* trans. John O'Kane (London: I. B. Tauris, 1998), 22–33; *The Constitution of the Islamic Republic of Iran,* trans. Hamid Algar (Berkeley, Calif.: Mizan Press, 1980).

28. *Ettela'at,* May 24, 1979.

29. For new studies on the hostage crisis, see David Harris, *The Crisis: The President, the Prophet and the Shah—1979 and the Coming of Militant Islam* (New York: Little, Brown, 2004); David Farber, *Taken Hostage: The Hostage Crisis and America's First Encounter with Radical Islam* (Princeton, N.J.: Princeton University Press, 2004); Kenneth Pollack, *The Persian Puzzle: The Conflict Between Iran and America* (New York: Random House, 2004), 141–81. For Iran's perspective, see Massoumeh Ebtekar, *Takeover in Tehran: The Inside Story of the 1979 Embassy Capture* (Burnaby, B.C: Talenbooks, 2000).

30. *Keyhan,* December 5, 1979.

31. Tehran Domestic Broadcast Services, November 5, 1979.

32. *Ettela'at,* November 8, 1979.

33. Ali Hussein Montazeri, *Khaterat* (Los Angeles: 2000), 201–9; Ali Khamenei, *Didgaha* (Qom: 1983), 143–69.

34. *New York Times,* November 21, 1981; "An Interview with Muhammad Musavi-Khoeniha," www.emrouz.com, October 31, 2005.

35. Hashemi Rafsanjani, *Khutbaha-ye Jum'eh* (Tehran: 1982), 167.

36. Tehran Persian Broadcast, September 22, 1980.

37. Quoted in Said Amir Arjomand, *The Turban for the Crown: The Islamic Revolution in Iran* (New York: Oxford University Press, 1988), 146.

38. Quoted in Daniel Brumberg, *Reinventing Khomeini,* 115.

2. CONSERVATIVES, PRAGMATISTS, AND REFORMERS

1. For a particularly incisive view of Khamenei, see Christopher de Bellaigue, "The Loneliness of the Supreme Leader," *New York Review of Books,* January 16, 2003; Dilip Hiro, *The Iranian Labyrinth: Journeys Through Theocratic Iran and Its Furies* (New York: Nation Books, 2005), 85–113.

2. For a detailed study of this relationship, see Saskia Gieling, "The Marja'iyaya in Iran and the Nomination of Khamenei in December 1994," *Middle Eastern Studies* (October 1997); Mehrad Haghayeghi, "Politics and Ideology in the Islamic Republic of Iran," *Middle Eastern Studies* (January 1993), 36–40.

3. For an incisive study on the emergence of the Revolutionary Guards in Iran, see Ali Gheissari and Vali Nasr, "The Conservative Consolidation in Iran," *Survival* (Summer 2005).

4. For a profile of Ahmadinejad, see Christopher de Bellaigue, "New Man in Iran," *New York Review of Books,* August 11, 2005.

5. International Crisis Group, "Iran: What Does Ahmadi-Nejad's Victory Mean?" (August 2005).

6. BBC Monitoring Service, April 21, 2001.

7. IRNA, September 2, 2002.

8. BBC Monitoring Service, October 25, 2002.

9. Associated Press, June 21, 2001.

10. *Khotut* (1994), 316.

11. *Sobh* (February–March, 1996).

12. For valuable studies on this period, see Bahman Baktiari, *Parliamentary Politics in Revolutionary Iran: The Institutionalization of Factional Politics* (Gainesville: University Press of Florida, 1996); Ali Ansari, *Iran, Islam and Democracy: Politics of Managing Change* (London: Royal Institute of International Affairs, 2000), 52–110; Anoushiravan Ehteshami, *After Khomeini: The Iranian Second Republic* (London: Routledge, 1995); David Menashri, *Post-Revolutionary Politics in Iran: Religion, Society, and Power* (London: Frank Cass, 2001), 13–78; Assef Bayat, *Street Politics: Poor People's Movement in Iran* (New York: Columbia University Press, 1993); Mansoor

Moaddel, *Class and Ideology in the Iranian Revolution* (New York: Columbia University Press, 1993), 199–255.

13. *Hamshahri,* February 27, 1996.

14. *Iran News,* February 9, 1993.

15. *Middle East Economic Digest,* June 14, 1991.

16. *Ettela'at,* November 6, 1991.

17. For good overviews of Iran's democratic struggles, see Ali Gheissari and Vali Nasr, "Iran's Democracy Debate," *Middle East Policy* (Summer 2004); Richard Bulliet, "Twenty Years of Islamic Politics," *Middle East Journal* (Spring 1999).

18. IRNA, April 21, 1997.

19. IRNA, July 21, 2005.

20. Mehran Kamrava, "The Civil Society Discourse in Iran," *British Journal of Middle Eastern Studies* (November 2001); Farhang Rajaee, "A Thermidor of 'Islamic Yuppies'? Conflict and Compromise in Iran's Politics," *Middle East Journal* (Spring 1999).

21. Daniel Brumberg, "Is Iran Democratizing?" *Journal of Democracy* (October 2000); see also his "Dissonant Politics in Iran and Indonesia," *Political Science Quarterly* (Fall 2001).

22. Robin Wright, *The Last Great Revolution: Turmoil and Transformation in Iran* (New York: Random House, 2001), 40.

23. Abdol-Karim Soroush, *Reason, Freedom, and Democracy in Islam* (New York: Oxford University Press, 2000), 88–131.

24. Abdol-Karim Soroush, *Modara va Modiriat* (Tehran: 1997), 350–65.

25. See Mohsen Kadivar, *Nazari-ye-ha-ye dowlat dar fiqh-e Shi'eh* (Tehran: 1999) and *Hokumat-e Valiye* (Tehran: 2000).

26. *Daily Star,* July 4, 2003; see also Geneive Abdo, "Rethinking the Islamic Republic: A Conversation with Ayatollah Hussein Ali Montazeri," *Middle East Journal* (Winter 2001).

27. *Nowruz,* July 10, 2002.

28. Olivier Roy, "The Crisis of Religious Legitimacy in Iran," *Middle East Journal* (Spring 1999).

29. *Salam,* March 17, 1992.

30. *Salam,* February 8, 1996.

31. For incisive journalistic accounts of this period, see Wright, *The Last Great Revolution,* 188–289; Elaine Sciolino, *Persian Mirrors: The Elusive Face of Iran* (New York: Free Press, 2000); Geneive Abdo and Jonathan Lyons, *Answering Only to God: Faith and Freedom in Twenty-first-Century Iran* (New York: Henry Holt, 2003), 131–258.

32. Shireen Hunter, "Is Iranian Perestroika Possible without Fundamental Change?" *Washington Quarterly* (Autumn 1998); Ali Gheissari and Vali Nasr, "Iran's Democracy Debate," *Middle East Policy* (Summer 2004).

33. *Resalat,* February 8, 1998.

34. *Jame'eh,* June 3, 1998.

35. Agence France-Presse (hereafter AFP), June 4, 2003.

36. IRNA, August 10, 2002.

37. *New York Times,* October 11, 2003.

38. *Los Angeles Times,* July 20, 2002.

39. *E'temad,* August 18, 2005.

3. IRAN'S PLACE IN THE GREATER MIDDLE EAST

1. Hamid Algar, *Islam and Revolution: The Writings and Declarations of Imam Khomeini* (Berkeley, Calif.: Mizan Press, 1981); Ali Akbar Velayati, *Iran va Mas'eleh-ye Felestin* (Tehran: 1997), 3–10.

2. Cited in Rouhollah Ramazani, *Revolutionary Iran: Challenge and Response in the Middle East* (Baltimore: John Hopkins University Press, 1986), 29.

3. Christin Marschall, *Iran's Persian Gulf Policy: From Khomeini to Khatami* (London: Curzon, 2003), 62–100; Nader Entessar, "Superpowers and Persian Gulf Security: The Iranian Perspective," *Third World Quarterly* (October 1988); Roy Mottahedeh, "Shiite Political Thought and Destiny of the Iranian Revolution," in *Iran and the Gulf: A Search for Stability,* ed. Jamal Al-Suwaidi (Abu Dhabi, U.A.E.: The Emirates Center for Strategic Studies and Research, 1996), 70–81.

4. Cited in J. Goldberg, "Saudi Arabia and the Iranian Revolution: The Religious Dimension," in *The Iranian Revolution and the Muslim World,* ed. David Menashri (Boulder, Colo.: Westview Press, 1990), 158.

5. David Menashri, "Khomeini's Vision: Nationalism or World Order?" and Farhad Kazemi and Jo-Anne Hart, "The Shi'ite Praxis: Democratic Politics and Foreign Policy in Iran," both in *The Iranian Revolution and the Muslim World;* Graham Fuller, *The Center of the Universe: Geopolitics of Iran* (Boulder, Colo.: Westview Press, 1991), 8–34; Marvin Zonis and Daniel Brumberg, *Khomeini: The Islamic Republic of Iran and the Arab World* (Cambridge, Mass.: Center for Middle Eastern Studies, Harvard University, 1987), 31–37.

6. Marschall, *Iran's Persian Gulf Policy,* 146–79; John Calabrese, *Revolutionary Horizons: Regional Foreign Policy in Post-Khomeini Iran* (New York: St. Martin's Press, 1994), 45–73.

7. Ali Akbar Velayati, "The Persian Gulf: Problems of Security," *Iranian Journal of International Affairs* (Spring 1991); Muhammad Javad Larijani, "Iran's Foreign Policy: Principles and Objectives," *Iranian Journal of International Affairs* (Winter 1996).

8. This point has been particularly emphasized by Louis Freeh. See Louis Freeh, *My FBI: Bringing Down the Mafia, Investigating Bill Clinton, and Fighting the War on Terror* (New York: St. Martin's Press, 2005). For an alternative view on the complexity of Khobar being an operation conducted by al-Qaeda and its affiliates as opposed to Iran, see Yitzak Nakash, *Reaching for Power: The Shi'a in the Modern Arab World* (Princeton, N.J.: Princeton University Press, 2006), 131; Olivier Roy, *Global-*

ized Islam: The Search for a New Ummah (New York: Columbia University Press, 2004), 52.

9. *Christian Science Monitor,* February 25, 2000.

10. R. K. Ramazani, "The Emerging Arab-Indian Rapprochement: Toward an Integrated US Policy in the Middle East?", *Middle East Policy* (June 1998); Mohsen Milani, "Iran's Gulf Policy: From Idealism to Confrontation to Pragmatism and Moderation," in *Iran and the Gulf: The Search for Stability,* ed. Jamal a-Suwaidi (Abu Dhabi, U.A.E.: Emirates Center for Strategic Studies and Research, 1996).

11. IRNA, August 23, 2005.

12. *Sharq,* July 26, 2005.

13. Shireen Hunter, "Iran and Syria: From Hostility to Limited Alliance," in *Iran and the Arab World,* ed. Hooshang Amirahmadi and Nader Entessar (New York: Palgrave Macmillan, 1990).

14. Shahrough Akhavi, "The Impact of Iranian Revolution on Egypt," in *The Iranian Revolution: Its Global Impact,* ed. John Esposito (Miami: University Press of Florida, 1990); Nader Entessar, "The Lion and the Sphinx: Iranian-Egyptian Relations in Perspective," in *Iran and the Arab World.*

15. R. K. Ramazani, *Revolutionary Iran: Challenge and Response in the Middle East* (Baltimore: Johns Hopkins University Press, 1986), 162–72.

16. Richard Mitchell, *The Society of the Muslim Brothers* (Oxford: Oxford University Press, 1993), 1–12.

17. Fawaz Gerges, *The Far Enemy: Why Jihad Went Global* (Cambridge: Cambridge University Press, 2005), 119–15; Gilles Kepel, *The War for Muslim Minds: Islam and the West* (Cambridge, Mass.: Belknap Press of Harvard University Press, 2004), 70–81.

18. *Jomhuri-ye Islami,* November 21, 2005.

19. Shireen Hunter, *Iran and the World: Continuity in a Revolutionary Decade* (Bloomington: Indiana University Press, 1990), 79–98; Graham Fuller, *The Center of the Universe: The Geopolitics of Iran* (Boulder, Colo.: Westview Press 1991), 168–88.

20. Robert Freedman, "Russian Policy Toward the Middle East: The Yeltsin Legacy and the Putin Challenge," *Middle East Journal* (Winter 2001); Hooman Peimani, *Regional Security and the Future of Central Asia: The Competition of Iran, Turkey and Russia* (Westport, Conn.: Praeger, 1998), 41–129.

21. Hanna Yousif Freij, "State Interests vs. the Umma: Iranian Policy in Central Asia," *Middle East Journal* (Winter 1996); Shireen Hunter, "Iran's Pragmatic Regional Policy, *Journal of International Affairs* (Spring 2003).

22. A. William Samii, "Iran and Chechnya: Realpolitik at Work," *Middle East Policy* (March 2001); Svante Cornell, "Iran and the Caucasus," *Middle East Policy* (January 1998).

23. Adam Tarock, "The Politics of the Pipeline: The Iran and Afghanistan Conflict," *Third World Quarterly* (August 1999); Valerie Piacentini, "The Afghan Puzzle,"

Iranian Journal of International Affairs (Summer 1996). Olivier Roy, "The New Political Elite of Afghanistan," in *The Politics of Social Transformation in Afghanistan, Iran and Pakistan,* ed. Myron Weiner and Ali Banuazizi (Syracuse, N.Y.: Syracuse University Press, 1994), 72–101.

24. Barnett Rubin, "The Fragmentation of Afghanistan," *Foreign Affairs* (Winter 1989–1990); see also "Post–Cold War State Disintegration: The Failure of International Conflict Resolution in Afghanistan," *Journal of International Affairs* (Winter 1993).

25. Hunter, *Iran and the World,* 130–38; Fuller, *Center of the Universe,* 230–31.

4. TURNING POINTS IN U.S.–IRANIAN RELATIONS

1. *Sharq,* August 22, 2005; *E'temad,* August 23, 2005.

2. Nikki R. Keddie, *The Roots of the Revolution: An Interpretative History of Modern Iran* (New Haven, Conn.: Yale University Press, 1981), 119–32; Kenneth Pollack, *The Persian Puzzle: The Conflict Between Iran and America* (New York: Random House, 2004), 48–50.

3. Benjamin Shwadran, *The Middle East, Oil, and the Great Powers* (New York: Council for Middle Eastern Affairs Press, 1959), 159.

4. William Roger Louis, "Britain and the Overthrow of the Mossadeq Government," in *Mohammad Mossadeq and the 1953 Coup in Iran,* ed. Mark Gasiorowski and Malcolm Byrne (Syracuse, N.Y.: Syracuse University Press, 2004), 126–78; William Roger Louis, *The British Empire in the Middle East: Arab Nationalism, the United States and Postwar Imperialism, 1945–1961* (Oxford: Oxford University Press, 1984), 632, 690, 651; John Darwin, *Britain and Decolonization: The Retreat from Empire in the Postwar World* (London: St. Martin's Press, 1988), 51–103.

5. Irvine Anderson, "The American Oil Industry and the Fifty-Fifty Agreement of 1950," in *Mussadiq, Iranian Nationalism and Oil,* ed. James Bill and William Roger Louis (Austin: University of Texas Press, 1988).

6. Jalil Bozorgmehr, ed., *Ta'qirat-e Mossadeq dar zendan* (Tehran: 1980), 114–17; Ervand Abrahamian, *Iran Between Two Revolutions* (Princeton, N.J.: Princeton University Press, 1982), 250–52; Richard Cottam, *Nationalism in Iran* (Pittsburgh, Penn.: University of Pittsburgh Press, 1979), 264–68; Cuyler Young, "The Social Support of Current Iranian Policy," *Middle East Journal* (Spring 1952), 125–43.

7. Homa Katouzian, *Mussadiq and the Struggle for Power in Iran* (London: I. B. Tauris, 1999), 78–113; see also "Problems of Democracy and the Public Sphere in Modern Iran," *Comparative Studies of South Asia, Africa and the Middle East* (1988): 31–37.

8. Farhad Diba, *Muhammad Mussadiq: A Political Biography* (London: Croom Helm, 1986); Katouzian, *Mussadiq and the Struggle for Power in Iran,* 1–78; James Bill, *The Eagle and the Lion: The Tragedy of American-Iranian Relations* (New Haven, Conn.: Yale University Press, 1989), 53–57; Dilip Hiro, *The Iranian Labyrinth: Journeys through Theocratic Iran and Its Furies* (New York: Nation Books, 2005), 64–70.

9. Dean Acheson, *Present at the Creation: My Years in the State Department* (New York: Norton, 1969), 509–11; Mary Ann Heiss, *Empire and Nationhood: The United States, Grest Britain and Iranian Oil, 1950–1954* (New York: Columbia University Press, 1997), 35–98; George McGhee, "Recollections of Dr. Mussadiq," in *Mussadiq, Iranian Nationalism and Oil*, 296–307; Mark Gasiorowski, *U.S. Foreign Policy and the Shah: Building a Client State in Iran* (Ithaca, N.Y.: Cornell University Press, 1991), 67–72; Melvyn Leffler, *A Preponderance of Power: National Security, the Truman Administration and the Cold War* (Stanford, Calif.: Stanford University Press, 1992), 446–95.

10. Kamran Dadkhah, "Iran's Economic Policy during the Mossadeq Era," *Journal of Iranian Research and Analysis* (November 2000); Homa Katouzian, "Oil Boycott and the Political Economy: Mussadiq and the Strategy of Non-Oil Economics," in *Mussadiq, Iranian Nationalism and Oil*, 203–28.

11. Shahrough Akhavi, "The Role of the Clergy in Iranian Politics, 1949–1954," in *Mussadiq, Iranian Nationalism and Oil*, 91–118; see also Akhavi, *Religion and Politics in Contemporary Iran: Clergy-State Relations in the Pahlavi Period* (Albany: State University of New York Press, 1980), 60–72.

12. Y. Alexander and A. Nanes, ed., *The United States and Iran: Documentary History* (Frederick, Md.: Alethia Books, 1980), 232–35.

13. Zachary Karabell, *Architects of Intervention: The United States, the Third World and the Cold War, 1946–1962* (Baton Rouge: Louisiana State University Press, 1999), 50–62; Walter Lafeber, *America, Russia and the Cold War, 1945–1984* (New York: Knopf, 1985), 125–46.; Ray Takeyh, *The Origins of the Eisenhower Doctrine: The U.S., Britain and Nasser's Egypt, 1953–1957* (New York: St. Martin's Press, 2000), 1–26.

14. Barry Rubin, *Paved with Good Intentions: The American Experience and Iran* (Oxford: Oxford University Press, 1980), 77–90; Bill, *The Eagle and the Lion*, 85–86.

15. Maziar Behrooz, "Tudeh Factionalism and the 1953 Coup in Iran," *International Journal of Middle East Studies* (August 2001): 363–82; see also Behrooz's *Rebels with a Cause* (London: I. B. Tauris, 2000), 3–16, and "The 1953 Coup in Iran and the Legacy of the Tudeh," in *Mohammad Mosaddeq and the 1953 Coup in Iran*, 192–96; Sepehr Zabih, *The Communist Movement in Iran* (Berkeley: University of California Press, 1966), chap. 5; Yann Richard, "Ayatollah Kashani: Precursor of the Islamic Republic?" in *Religion and Politics in Iran: Shi'ism from Quietism to Revolution*, ed. Nikki R. Keddie (New Haven, Conn.: Yale University Press, 1983), 101–24.

16. For the most comprehensive and insightful account of the coup, see Stephen Kinzer, *All the Shah's Men: An American Coup and the Roots of Middle East Terror* (Hoboken, N.J.: John Wiley & Sons, 2003); see also Kermit Roosevelt, *Countercoup: The Struggle for the Control of Iran* (New York: McGraw-Hill, 1979); S. Dorril, *MI6: Fifty Years of Special Operations* (London: Fourth Estate, 2000), 558–600; Mark Gasiorowski, "The 1953 Coup d'Etat in Iran," *International Journal of Middle Eastern*

Studies (August 1987): 261–86, and Bill, *The Eagle and the Lion,* 86–94; Marvin Zonis, *Majestic Failure: The Fall of the Shah* (Chicago: University of Chicago Press, 1991), 100–104.

17. Mark Bowden, "Mahmoud the Bashful," *Atlantic Monthly,* October 2005.

18. Massoumeh Ebtekar, *Takeover in Tehran: The Inside Story of the 1979 U.S. Embassy Capture* (Burnaby, B.C.: Talonbooks, 2000), 39–79; Ali Ansari, *Modern Iran Since 1921* (Harlow, Eng.: Longman, 2003), 226–29.

19. David Harris, *The Crisis: The President, the Prophet and the Shah—1979 and the Coming of Militant Islam* (Boston: Little, Brown, 2004), 197–277.

20. Bill, *The Eagle and the Lion,* 86; Christos Ioannides, "The Hostages of Iran: Discussion with the Militants," *Washington Quarterly* Issue 3 (1980); David Patrick Houghton, *U.S. Foreign Policy and the Iran Hostage Crisis* (Cambridge: Cambridge University Press, 2001), 65–70; Ebtekar, *Takeover in Tehran,* 44–45.

21. Mehdi Bazargan, *Mosalman-e: Ejtema i va Jahani* (Tehran: 1965); *Az Khodaparasti ta Khodaparast* (Houston: 1974); and *Enqelab-e Iran dar do Harakat* (Tehran: 1984). For important accounts of Bazargan, see H. E. Chehabi, *Iranian Politics and Religious Modernism: The Liberation Movement of Iran under Shah and Khomeini* (Ithaca, N.Y.: Cornell University Press, 1990); and "State and Society in Islamic Liberalism," *State, Culture and Society* (Spring 1985): 85–98.

22. Zbigniew Brzezinski, *Power and Principle: Memoirs of the National Security Advisor, 1977–1981* (New York: Farrar, Straus and Giroux, 1985), 475–76.

23. David Farber, *Taken Hostage: The Iran Hostage Crisis and America's First Encounter with Radical Islam* (Princeton, N.J.: Princeton University Press, 2005), 142.

24. Houghton, *U.S. Foreign Policy and the Iran Hostage Crisis,* 80–95; Warren Christopher, ed., *American Hostages in Iran: The Conduct of a Crisis* (New Haven, Conn.: Yale University Press, 1985), 72–144; Jimmy Carter, *Keeping Faith: Memoirs of a President* (Fayetteville: University of Arkansas Press, 1995), 462–90; Rubin, *Paved with Good Intentions,* 311–13.

25. Warren Christopher, *Chances of a Lifetime* (New York: Scribner, 2001), 97–98; Cyrus Vance, *Hard Choices: Four Critical Years in Managing America's Foreign Policy* (New York: Simon and Schuster, 1983), 376–83; Harold Saunders, "The Crisis Begins," in Christopher, ed., *American Hostages in Iran.*

26. Farber, *Taken Hostage,* 151–55.

27. Roy Mottahedeh, "Iran's Foreign Devils," *Foreign Policy* (Spring 1980): 19–35.

28. Paul Ryan, *The American Rescue Mission: Why It Failed* (Annapolis, Md.: Naval Institute Press, 1985); Pollack, *The Persian Puzzle,* 167–70; Zbigniew Brzezinski, "The Failed Mission: The Inside Account of the Attempt to Free the Hostages in Iran," *New York Times,* April 18, 1982; see also Brzezinski, *Power and Principle,* 487–500; Rubin, *Paved with Good Intentions,* 301–4.

29. Shaul Bakhash, *The Reign of Ayatollahs* (New York: Basic Books, 1984), 201.

30. Pollack, *The Persian Puzzle*, 170–80; Harris, *The Crisis*, 363–425; Farber, *Taken Hostage*, 180–90.

31. Joost R. Hiltermann, "Outsiders as Enablers: Consequences and Lessons from International Silence on Iraq's Use of Chemical Weapons During the Iran-Iraq War," in *Iran, Iraq and the Legacies of War*, ed. Lawrence Potter and Gary Sick (New York: Palgrave Macmillan, 2004).

32. Robin Wright, *In the Name of God: The Khomeini Decade* (New York: Simon and Schuster, 1989), 130–41.

33. James Bill, "The U.S. Overtures to Iran, 1985–1986: An Analysis," and Eric Hooglund, "The Policy of the Reagan Administration Toward Iran," both in *Neither East nor West: Iran, the Soviet Union, and the United States*, ed. Nikki R. Keddie and Mark Gasiorowski (New Haven, Conn.: Yale University Press, 1990).

34. For various perspectives, see Robert McFarlane and Zofia Smardz, *Special Trust* (New York: Cadell and Davis, 1994); George Schultz, *Turmoil and Triumph: My Years as Secretary of State* (New York: Scribner, 1993); Robert Gates, *From the Shadows: The Ultimate Insider's Story of Five Presidents and How They Won the Cold War* (New York: Simon and Schuster, 1996); Peter Kornbluh and Malcolm Byrne, *The Iran-Contra Scandal: The Declassified History* (New York: New Press, 1993); U.S. Congress, House, Select Committee to Investigate Covert Arms Transactions with Iran, and Senate, Select Committee on Secret Military Assistance to Iran and Nicaraguan Opposition, *Report of the Congressional Views* (Washington, D.C.: GPO, 1987).

35. Samuel Segev, *The Iranian Triangle: The Untold Story of Israel's Role in the Iran-Contra Affair* (New York: Free Press, 1988).

36. For an incisive examination of Israeli-Iranian relations, see Trita Parsi, "Israeli-Iranian Relations Assessed: Strategic Competition from Power Cycle Perspective," *Iranian Studies* (June 2005).

37. Bill, *The Eagle and the Lion*, 312; Pollack, *The Persian Puzzle*, 213.

38. R. K. Ramazani, "Iran and the United States: Islamic Realism?" in *The Middle East from Iran-Contra Affair to the Intifada*, ed. Robert Freedman (Syracuse, N.Y.: Syracuse University Press, 1991), 167–83.

39. Ibid., 169.

40. Ibid.

41. Statement by H. E. Seyyed Muhammad Khatami, president of the Islamic Republic of Iran, Eighth Session of the Islamic Summit Conference, 2.

42. *Christian Science Monitor*, February 25, 2000.

43. Muhammad Khatami, *Az Donya-ye Shahr* (Tehran: 1997), 14–15.

44. *Middle East Insight* (November–December 1997): 32.

45. Jahangir Amuzegar, "Khatami's Legacy: Dashed Hopes," *Middle East Journal* (Winter 2006): 67–70.

46. Muhammad Khatami, *Hope and Challenge* (Binghamton: Institute of Global Cultural Studies, Binghamton University, State University of New York Press, 1997), 19.

47. Interview with Khatami, CNN, January 8, 1998.

48. IRNA, December 9, 1997.

49. IRNA, January 28, 2002.

50. *Resalat,* June 22, 2002.

51. *New York Times,* May 27, 1993; see also Anthony Lake, "Confronting Backlash States," *Foreign Affairs* (March–April 2004).

52. *New York Times,* July 5, 1994.

53. F. Gregory Gause III, "The Illogic of Dual Containment," *Foreign Affairs* (March–April 1994).

54. U.S. Department of State, press statement, June 17, 1998; *New York Times,* December 16, 1997.

55. Reuters, February 29, 2000.

56. Pollack, *The Persian Puzzle,* xxv.

57. Ibid., 340.

58. Ibid., xxvi.

59. *Mideast Mirror,* May 20, 2000.

5. UNDER THE SHADOW OF SEPTEMBER 11

1. Quoted in Kenneth Pollack and Ray Takeyh, "Taking on Tehran," *Foreign Affairs* (March–April 2005): 22.

2. AFP, April 14, 2003.

3. *New York Times,* November 9, 2001.

4. Reuters, December 2, 2001.

5. *Dawn,* May 25, 2002.

6. IRNA, April 25, 2002.

7. IRNA, January 24, 2002.

8. *Entekhab,* April 14, 2002.

9. *Al-Sharq al-Awsat,* October 29, 2001.

10. AFP, October 10, 2001.

11. Quoted in Ervand Abrahamian, "Empire Strikes Back: Iran in U.S. Sites," in *Inventing the Axis of Evil* (New York: New Press, 2004), 96.

12. Condoleezza Rice, "Campaign 2000: Promoting the National Interest," *Foreign Affairs* (January–February 2000).

13. *New York Times,* February 1, 2003.

14. White House Press Office, "The National Security Strategy of the United States" (Washington, D.C.: GPO, 2002).

15. *Washington Post,* December 10, 2005.

16. For contending views on Bush's national security doctrine, see John Gaddis, "Bush's Security Strategy," *Foreign Policy* (November–December 2002); Robert Jervis, "Understanding the Bush Doctrine," *Political Science Quarterly* (Fall 2003); James Chace, "Imperial America and the Common Interests," *World Policy Journal* (Spring 2002); Charles Krauthammer, "The Unipolar Moment Revisited," *The National Interest* (Winter 2002–2003).

17. William Kristol, "The End of the Beginning," *Weekly Standard*, May 12, 2003.

18. Gerard Baker, "After Iraq, Where Will Bush Go Next?" *Financial Times*, April 14, 2003.

19. Jamie Glazov, "Iran, a Coming Revolution?" *Front Page Magazine*, September 18, 2002.

20. Bernard Lewis, "Time for Toppling," *Wall Street Journal*, September 27, 2002.

21. Associated Press, February 16, 2002.

22. U.S. Department of State, press release, August 2, 2002.

23. *New York Times*, February 8, 2002.

24. IRNA, March 2, 2002.

25. IRNA, June 5, 2005.

26. *Sharq*, June 6, 2005.

27. *New York Times*, June 26, 2005.

6. ALONG THE NUCLEAR PRECIPICE

1. www.whitehouse.gov/press/release, January 31, 2006.

2. For important studies on Iran's nuclear designs, see Shahram Chubin, *Whither Iran?: Reform, Domestic Politics and National Security* (Oxford: Oxford University Press, 2002); Geoffrey Kemp, *Iran's Bomb: American and Iranian Perspectives* (Washington, D.C.: Nixon Center, 2004); International Crisis Group, "Dealing with Iran's Nuclear Program," October 2003; Kenneth Pollack and Ray Takeyh, "Taking On Tehran," *Foreign Affairs* (March–April 2005).

3. *Wall Street Journal*, June 25, 2004.

4. Abbas Milani, Michael McFaul, and Larry Diamond, *Beyond Incrementalism: A New Strategy of Dealing with Iran* (Stanford, Calif.: Hoover Institution, 2005), 6.

5. IRNA, May 25, 2004.

6. AFP, May 25, 2004.

7. Cited in Shahram Chubin, "Iran's Strategic Environment and Nuclear Weapons," in *Iran's Nuclear Weapons Options: Issues and Analysis*, ed. Geoffrey Kemp (Washington, D.C.: Nixon Center, 2001).

8. Cited in Chubin, *Whither Iran?*, 73.

9. *Ya Lesarat*, October 22, 2003.

10. Cited in Wyn Bowen and Joanna Kidd, "The Iranian Nuclear Challenge," *International Affairs* 80 (March 2004): 264.

11. IRNA, September 13, 2004.

12. IRNA, May 17, 1998.

13. *New York Times,* June 7, 1998.

14. *Jomhuri-ye Islami,* November 3, 2004

15. *Aftab-e Yazd,* June 21, 2004.

16. Reuters, April 19, 2003.

17. *Iran News,* February 9, 2004.

18. *Jomhuri-ye Islami,* April 3, 2005.

19. *Resalat,* May 30, 2004.

20. IRNA, September 17, 2005.

21. *Jomhuri-ye Islami,* May 26, 2004.

22. *Farhang-e Ashti,* February 28, 2006.

23. *Keyhan,* February 12, 2006.

24. IRNA, September 22, 2004.

25. *Sharq,* October 25, 2005.

26. *Aftab-e Yazd,* October 16, 2005.

27. IRNA, January 11, 2006.

28. *La Repubblica,* March 4, 2006.

29. AFP, June 9, 2004.

30. *Sharq,* October 9, 2003.

31. *Sharq,* January 19, 2004.

32. IRNA, October 28, 2003.

33. Dow Jones International, March 14, 2005.

34. *Washington Post,* March 11, 2003.

35. IRNA, October 28, 2003.

36. BBC, November 8, 2004.

37. IRNA, October 30, 2003.

38. *Resalat,* October 6, 2004.

39. *Jame'eh,* April 27, 1998,

7. IRAN'S NEW IRAQ

1. Shahram Chubin and Sepehr Zabih, *The Foreign Relations of Iran: A Developing State in a Zone of Great-Power Conflict* (Berkeley: University of California Press, 1974), 163–212; Shaul Bakhash, "The Troubled Relationship: Iran and Iraq, 1930–1980," in *Iran, Iraq and the Legacy of War,* ed. Lawrence Potter and Gary Sick (New York: Palgrave Macmillan, 2004), 11–29; Efraim Karsh, "Geopolitical Determinism: The Origins of the Iran-Iraq War," *Middle East Journal* (Spring 1990).

2. Rouhollah Ramazani, *Iran's Foreign Policy, 1941–1973: A Study of Foreign Policy in Modernizing Nations* (Charlottesville: University Press of Virginia, 1975), 411.

3. *Keyhan,* January 14, 1969.

4. Ramazani, *Iran's Foreign Policy,* 418.

5. Stephen Walt, *Revolution and War* (Ithaca, N.Y.: Cornell University Press, 1996), chap. 6; Farhang Rajaee, "Iranian Ideology and Worldview: The Cultural Export of Revolution," in *The Iranian Revolution: Its Global Impact,* ed. John Esposito (Miami: Florida International University Press, 1990), 63–83.

6. Efraim Karsh, "From Ideological Zeal to Geopolitical Realism: The Islamic Republic and the Gulf," in *The Iran-Iraq War: Impact and Implications,* ed. Efraim Karsh (New York: St. Martin's Press, 1989), 13–26; Ehmund Ghareeb, "The Roots of Crisis: Iraq and Iran," in *The Persian Gulf War: Lessons for Strategy, Low and Diplomacy,* ed. Christopher Joyner (Westport, Conn.: Greenwood Press, 1990), 21–39.

7. Shahram Chubin and Charles Tripp, *Iran and Iraq at War* (Boulder, Colo.: Westview Press, 1991), 53–68; F. Gregory Gause, "Iraq's Decisions to Go to War, 1980 and 1990," *Middle East Journal* (Winter 2002): 63–69; Eric Davis, *Memories of State: Politics, History and Collective Identity in Modern Iraq* (Berkeley: University of California Press, 2005), 176–200.

8. R. K. Ramazani, *Revolutionary Iran: Challenge and Response in the Middle East* (Baltimore: John Hopkins University Press, 1986), 57–67; W. Thom Workman, *The Social Origins of the Iran-Iraq War* (Boulder, Colo.: Lynne Rienner Publishers, 1994), chap. 4; Majid Khadduri, *The Gulf War: The Origins and Implications of the Iran-Iraq War* (New York: Oxford University Press, 1988); Stephen Pelletiere, *The Iran-Iraq War: Chaos in a Vacuum* (New York: Praeger, 1992).

9. Gause, "Iraq's Decisions to Go to War," 67.

10. Ramazani, *Revolutionary Iran,* 61.

11. For important accounts of Saddam see Marion Farouk-Sluglett and Peter Sluglett, *Iraq Since 1958: From Revolution to Dictatorship* (London: I. B. Tauris, 1990), 255–69; Phebe Marr, *The Modern History of Iraq* (Boulder, Colo.: Westview Press, 1985); Charles Tripp, *A History of Iraq* (Cambridge: Cambridge University Press, 2000), 193–275; Kanan Makiya, *Republic of Fear: The Politics of Modern Iraq* (Berkeley: University of California Press, 1989).

12. Dilip Hiro, *The Longest War: The Iran-Iraq Military Conflict* (New York: Routledge, 1991); see also *The Iranian Labyrinth: Journeys through Theocratic Iran and Its Furies* (New York: Routledge, 2005), 241–95.

13. Chubin and Tripp, *Iran and Iraq at War,* 38.

14. IRNA, December 4, 1983.

15. Hashemi Rafsanjani, *Dar maktabi-jum'a: Majmu'eh-ye khotbaha-ye namaz-e jum'ah-ye Tehran* (Tehran: 1987), 80; Ali Khameini, *Dar Maktab-e Jum'ah. Majmu'eh-ye khotbaha-ye namaz-e jum'ah-ye Tehran* (Tehran: 1989), 366.

16. Saskia Gieling, *Religion and War in Revolutionary Iran* (London: I. B. Tauris, 1999), 40–107.

17. IRNA, November 10, 1987.

18. Ramazani, *Revolutionary Iran,* 70–86.

19. S. Taheri Shemirani, "The War of the Cities," in *The Iran-Iraq War: The Politics of Aggression,* ed. Farhang Rajaee (Gainesville: University Press of Flordia, 1993), 32–41.

20. *Time,* March 19, 1984; Human Rights Watch, *Iraq's Crime of Genocide: The Anfal Campaign against the Kurds* (New Haven: Yale University Press, 1995), chaps. 1 and 2.

21. *New York Times,* July 2, 1988.

22. Joost Hiltermann, "Outsiders as Enablers: Consequences and Lessons from International Silence on Iraq's Use of Chemical Weapons during the Iran-Iraq War," in *Iran, Iraq, and the Legacies of War,* 151–67.

23. Anthony Cordesman and Abraham Wagner, *The Iran-Iraq War: The Lessons of Modern War,* Vol. 2 (Boulder, Colo.: Westview Press, 1990), 318–20; Shaul Bakhash, *The Reign of the Ayatollahs: Iran and the Islamic Revolution* (New York: Basic Books, 1990), 273, Kenneth Pollack, *The Persian Puzzle: The Conflict Between Iran and America* (New York: Random House, 2004), 229–31.

24. Bakhash, *Reign of the Ayatollahs,* 274; Robin Wright, *In the Name of God: The Khomeini Decade* (New York: Simon and Schuster, 1989), 188.

25. Shahram Chubin, "The Last Phase of the Iran-Iraq War: From Stalemate to Ceasefire," *Third World Quarterly* (April 1989).

26. Pollack, *The Persian Puzzle,* 232.

27. "Why Did the War Continue?" *Sharq,* April 24, 2005; "The Continuation of War After Liberation of Khoramshar: An Interview with Former Foreign Minister Akbar Velayati," Baztab.com, April 14, 2005.

28. Farideh Farhi, "The Antinomies of Iran's War Generation," in *Iran, Iraq, and the Legacies of War,* 101–21.

29. Ruhollah Khomeini, *Sahifeh-ye nur: Majmu'eh-ye hazrat-e Imam Khomeini* (Tehran: 1991), 543.

30. Al-Jazeera, July 7, 2005; *Keyhan,* July 7, 2005.

31. *New York Times,* December 15, 2005.

32. International Crisis Group, "Iran in Iraq: How Much Influence?" (March 21, 2005); Kayhan Barzegar, "Understanding the Roots of Iranian Foreign Policy in the New Iraq," *Middle East Policy* (Summer 2005); Anoushiravan Ehteshami, "Iran's International Posture after the Fall of Baghdad," *Middle East Journal* (Spring 2004) and "Iran-Iraq Relations After Saddam," *The Washington Quarterly* (Autumn 2003).

33. International Crisis Group, "Iran in Iraq: How Much Influence?", 1.

34. Prince Saud al-Faisal, "The Fight against Extremism and the Search for Peace," speech presented at the Council on Foreign Relations, September 7, 2005.

35. *Al-Sharq al-Awsat,* February 28, 2005.

36. *Washington Post,* February 16, 2005.

37. IRNA, February 3, 2005.

38. Ray Takeyh, "Iranian Options: Pragmatic Mullahs and American Interests," *The National Interest* (Fall 2003): 53.

39. Dubai Al-Arabiya Television, February 6, 2005.

40. *Sharq,* July 18, 2005.

41. *Sharq,* July 8, 2005; *Shoma,* July 23, 2005.

42. IRNA, February 7, 2005.

43. *Fars News,* October 14, 2004.

8. ISRAEL AND THE POLITICS OF TERRORISM

1. IRNA, December 8, 2005.

2. Michael Bar-Zohar, *Ben-Gurion: A Biography* (New York: Delacorte Press, 1978), 200–45; Michael Brecher, *The Foreign Policy System of Israel: Setting, Images, Process* (New Haven, Conn.: Yale University Press, 1972).

3. Trita Parsi, "Israel-Iranian Relations Assessed: Strategic Competition from the Power Cycle Perspective," *Iranian Studies* (June 2005); Sohrab Sobhani, *The Pragmatic Entente: Israeli-Iranian Relations, 1948–1988* (New York: Praeger Press, 1989).

4. Baqer Moin, *Khomeini: Life of the Ayatollah* (New York: St. Martin's Press, 1999), 99.

5. Ibid.

6. Ruhollah Khomeini, *Al-Hukuma al-Islamiyya* (1970).

7. Hamid Algar, *Islam and Revolution: The Writings and Declarations of Imam Khomeini* (Berkeley, Calif.: Mizan Press, 1981), 127.

8. David Menashri, *Post-Revolutionary Politics in Iran: Religion, Society and Power* (London: Frank Cass, 2001), 270.

9. Shireen Hunter, *Iran and the World: Continuity in a Revolutionary Decade* (Bloomington: Indiana University Press, 1990), 98–131; Graham Fuller, *The Center of the Universe: The Geopolitics of Iran* (Boulder, Colo.: Westview Press, 1991), 119–36.

10. A representative sample of Khomeini's views on Israel and Jews can be found in *Felestin va Sahionism* (Tehran: 1984); *Azadi-ye Aqalliyatha-ye Mazhabi* (Tehran: 1984–85); *Felestin Az Didegah-e Imam Khomeini* (Tehran: 1998).

11. Emmanuel Sivan, "The Mythologies of Religious Radicalism: Judaism and Islam," *Terrorism and Political Violence* (Autumn 1991); Raphael Israeli, *Fundamentalist Islam and Israel: Essays in Interpretation* (Lanham, Md.: University Press of America, 1993).

12. *Jomhuri-ye Islami,* September 25, 1979.

13. Hashemi Rafsanjani, *Esra'il va Qods-e Aziz* (Qom: 1984), 45.

14. Yvonne Haddad, "Islamist and the 'Problem of Israel': The 1967 Awakening," *Middle East Journal* (Spring 1992).

15. Moin, *Khomeini: Life of the Ayatollah*, 265.

16. Ali Akbar Velayati, *Iran va Mas'aleh-ye Felestin* (Tehran: 1997), 183–84.

17. Menashri, *Post-Revolutionary Politics in Iran*, 272.

18. IRNA, April 21, 2001.

19. Behrouz Souresrafil, *Khomeini and Israel* (London: C.C. Press, 1989), 60.

20. *Christian Science Monitor*, August 6, 1981.

21. Ziad Abu-Amr, *Islamic Fundamentalism in the West Bank and Gaza: Muslim Brotherhood and Islamic Jihad* (Bloomington: Indiana University Press, 1994), 90–128; Gawdat Bahgat, "Iran, the United States, and the War on Terrorism," *Studies in Conflict and Terrorism* (March–April 2003).

22. IRNA, April 20, 2004.

23. Shimon Shapira, "The Origins of Hizballah," *Jerusalem Quarterly* (Spring 1988); Martin Kramer, "The Moral Logic of Hizballah," in *Origins of Terrorism: Psychologies, Ideologies, Theories, States of Mind*, ed. Walter Reich (Cambridge: Cambridge University Press, 1990). Also Martin Kramer, "Hizbullah: The Calculus of Jihad," in *Fundamentalism and the State*, ed. Martin Marty and R. Scott Appleby (Chicago: University of Chicago Press, 1993); Meir Hatina, *Islam and Salvation in Palestine* (Tel Aviv: Moishe Dayan Center for Middle Eastern and African Studies, 2001), 107–17; Daniel Byman, *Deadly Connections: States and the Sponsor of Terrorism* (Cambridge: Cambridge University Press, 2005), 79–117; R. K. Ramazani, *Revolutionary Iran: Challenge and Response in the Middle East* (Baltimore: Johns Hopkins University Press, 1986), 175–94.

24. International Crisis Group, "Hezbollah: Rebels without a Cause?" July 30, 2003; Amal Saad-Ghorayeb, *Hizbu'llah, Politics and Religion* (Sterling, Va.: Pluto Press, 2002), 20–68; Steven Simon and Jonathan Stevenson, "Declawing the 'Party of God': Toward Normalizing in Lebanon," *World Policy Journal* (Summer 2001); Richard Augustus Norton, "Hizbullah and the Israeli Withdrawal from Southern Lebanon," *Journal of Palestinian Studies* (Autumn 2000).

25. Abdollah Nuri, *Showkaran-e Eslah* (Tehran: 1999), 140–50.

26. *Bonyan*, March 6, 2002.

27. *Aftab-e Yazd*, May 9, 2002.

28. IRNA, September 21, 1998.

29. IRNA, January 8, 1998.

30. AFP, October, 17, 2002.

31. IRNA, March 13, 2002.

32. AFP, March 19, 2002.

33. *E'temad*, October 28, 2005.

34. IRNA, October 29, 2005.

35. *Sharq*, October 29, 2005.

ACKNOWLEDGMENTS

I began this project once I joined the Council on Foreign Relations, which has proven the most hospitable place to work. The Council's president, Richard Haass, has been an enormous source of support and constructive suggestions for how to improve this book. James Lindsay, in his role as the director of Studies, similarly proved generous with his time, and at critical junctures pressed me to further assess my assumptions. The insights and keen editorial eyes of both Richard and Jim made an important contribution to the completion of this project.

A number of colleagues and friends read through this manuscript with care and offered important comments and ideas. I feel a special debt of gratitude to Ervand Abrahamian, Daniel Brumberg, Daniel Byman, Farideh Farhi, Ali Gheissari, Nikki R. Keddie, Nikolas Gvosdev, Vali Nasr, Andrew Parasiliti, Kenneth Pollack, Rick Russell, and Hadi Semati. Throughout her year at the Council, Sanam Vakil gently challenged my views and pushed me to delve deeper into the conundrum of

Iran. The insight and wisdom of such valued colleagues helped immeasurably in honing my arguments and developing a more incisive narrative.

My literary agent, Larry Weissman, proved a patient source of support and assistance, with an enthusiasm and persistence on behalf of this project that went far beyond the call of duty. I have come away from this project intuitively trusting the judgment of my editor, Paul Golob. On many occasions Paul pressed me to reorganize the chapters and rewrite sections of this book. After ample complaining I realized that his ideas were uniformly correct and his perceptions uncannily on the mark.

Through the process of writing this book, I took much time away from my family during successive transitions. My wife, Suzanne, juggled the many aspects of our lives with her typical care and humor. Her devotion and love have sustained me through many frustrating evenings locked in my study. I started working on this book when my son, Alex, was born. It is to him that I dedicated this book, for he has proved a remarkable source of joy and delight for me.